A YELLOW HOUSE IN THE MOUNTAINS

A YELLOW HOUSE IN THE MOUNTAINS

A Story of Love and Refinement

Glenn L. Hileman II

979-8-9888228-0-6 Paperback
979-8-9888228-1-3 Hardcover
979-8-9888228-2-0 eBook
979-8-9888228-3-7 audiobook

Library of Congress Control Number: TXu 2-387-095

Any references to historical events, real people, or real places are used fictitiously. Names, characters, and places are products of the author's imagination.

Book design by Glen Edelstein, Hudson Valley Book Design

Printed by IngramSpark, Inc., in the United States of America.

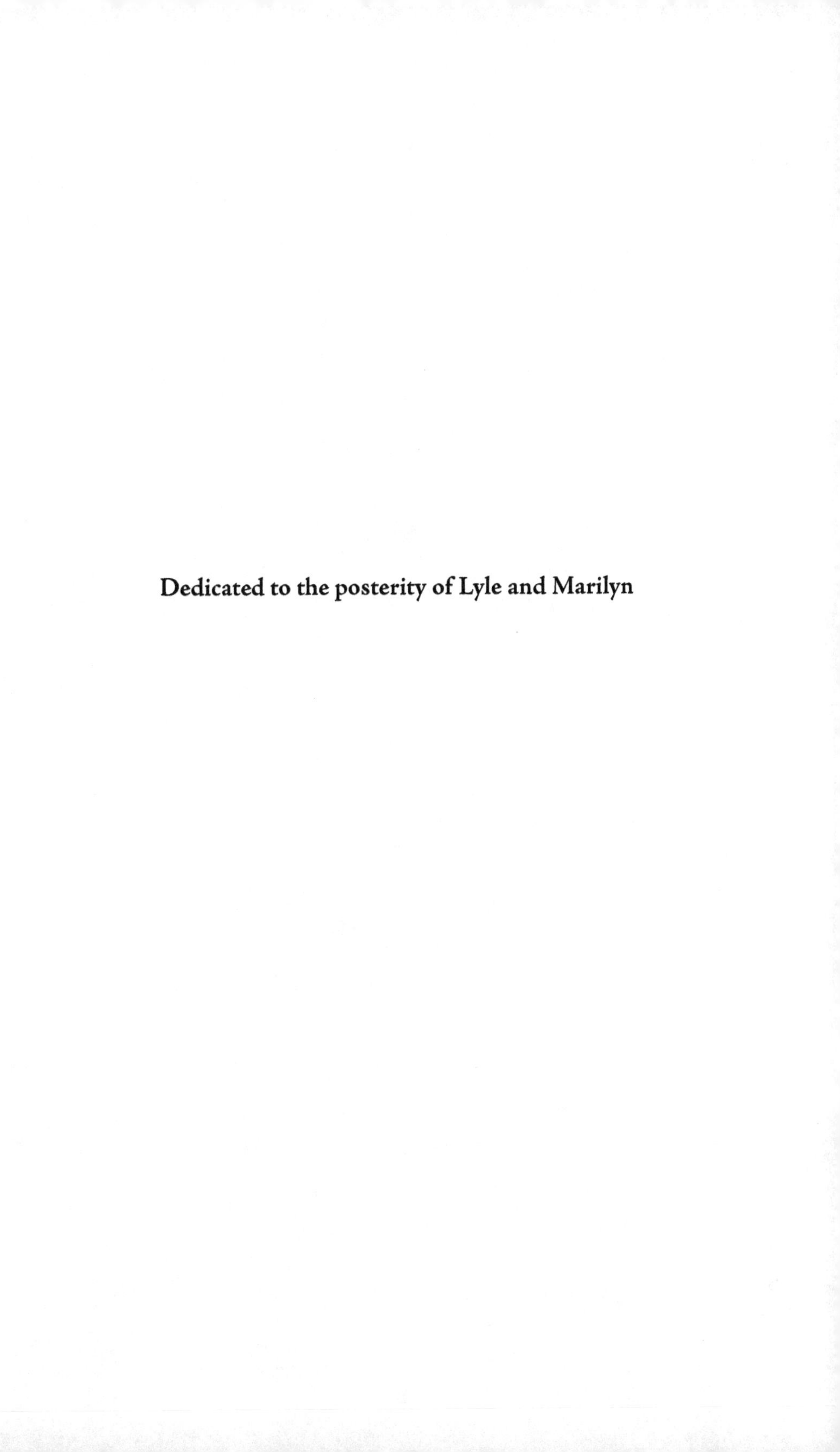

Dedicated to the posterity of Lyle and Marilyn

PREFACE

AN EXTRAORDINARY LIFE is worthy of emulation. But what of those who are far more ordinary? What can two ordinary, unremarkable people accomplish when they commit themselves to each other? What traits should one develop to find joy in living? Do dreams come true? If so, how? Can love last forever? When adversity arrives at one's doorstep, how can we cope? More importantly, what lessons are learned in the experiences that follow?

"I cannot tell a lie" is a quote often associated with the first President of the United States, George Washington. While not presidential, a similar quote associated with my mother reflected her ambition to never let details get in the way of a good story. She said, "I never lie, but I do embellish sometimes."

In Philippians 4:8, the Apostle Paul admonishes, "…if there is anything virtuous, lovely, or of good report, or praiseworthy, we seek after these things." My brother, Lyle S. Hileman, coined the following about our father Lyle Wayne Hileman: "

If there is anything virtuous, lovely, or of good report, or praiseworthy…he either married it, made it, designed it, built it, or belonged to it."

My parents were an unlikely match. When they met, they were both new to Wheat Ridge, Colorado. Navigating the teenage years is a challenge in itself, but their generation carried the additional burdens resulting from The Great Depression and World War II. Their story is one of faith, love and hope. They embraced the consequences of their actions and shared a belief that there is purpose in our mortal existence.

Their goals were ambitious and must have seemed out of reach, but they understood that with work and perseverance, their dreams could be achieved.

I hope my mother will smile upon the embellishing I may be guilty of in telling their story. I believe my father will take pleasure in allowing others to learn from his refinements and accomplishments in life. Together, Lyle and Marylin established a legacy that their posterity hopes to honor.

The events described in this story are true. Some events will seem unbelievable. Others, miraculous. Those who knew Lyle and Marylin can attest that they lived by faith, and with confidence that their love would extend beyond this life and into eternity. Their experiences provide a roadmap for navigating the challenges life throws at us all. By reflecting on their decisions and the following consequences, we better understand how values impact happiness.

Their love of God and family drove my parents' decisions and shaped their legacy. Marylin's brother, Mike Novakovich, coined a phrase that I think perfectly sets the stage for their story:

"Things always work out in the end. If things haven't worked out, it is not the end!"

CHAPTER ONE

LYLE'S EARS WERE huge and they protruded straight out of his head. He was so self-conscious of his ears that as a young boy, he wore a stocking cap to bed each night. He hoped that over time his ears would lay closer to his head. It didn't work.

He was the youngest child of Glenn and Lillian Hileman. His two brothers, Dick and Dale, were eight and ten when Lyle was born in 1934. He often wondered if he had been an "accident" but hesitated to ask his parents why they had waited so long after his brothers to have him. His brothers loved to tease him and while it annoyed Lyle, he admired his brothers and looked up to them.

Life for Lyle was often lonely. Dale enlisted in the military and Dick was an active teenager by the time Lyle began school. Lakewood, Colorado was an isolated, rural farming community, and the location of the family's farm. The Hileman family arrived in Colorado while the nation was recovering from The Great Depression. Shortly after their arrival, Lyle's father, Glenn, began searching for permanent housing.

"Lillian, I've found it!" Glenn said.

"A house?" she questioned.

"Well, kind of. Let me show you."

The couple drove west of Denver to the open fields of Lakewood.

"It's more than twenty acres," Glenn stated. "Look at the fields. Do you see the lake behind the cottonwoods?"

"I see it. It's beautiful. But Glenn, where's the house?"

Quickly walking a few feet up the hill near the road, Glenn reached for his wife's hand and pulled her to the highest point where there were 360-degree views. He waited as his wife looked on the mountains to the west. Turning, she could see the Denver city skyline. Glenn extended his arm, pointing, to direct Lillian's eyes toward the fields below.

"It's over there."

"That's a barn!" she exclaimed.

"Yes," Glenn responded. "And a good one. It will do until I can build a permanent home."

The family purchased the property in 1936 and the barn would become the home of Glenn, Lillian, and their three children. Farming was Glenn's primary focus, but true to his word, he immediately began drafting plans for a house. In addition to corn, lettuce and potatoes, the family raised turkeys, chickens, and pigs. While Lillian wasn't thrilled to be living in a barn, she did love the setting. As for Lyle, it was perfect.

Life on the farm provided an idealistic upbringing for young Lyle. Like many during the period, his family was poor. They lived in the barn with the animals, and yet, they were happy. In 1940, Glenn completed work on the promised new house. To the family, it felt like a mansion, but in reality, it was modest. It did, however, have a kitchen, two bedrooms, and even an indoor bathroom.

With the work on the home complete, the family worked hard raising crops and livestock. Farming required early morning chores and everyone was expected to help. After a long day working the farm, they would be exhausted but always had time in the evenings to gather in the family room to listen to the big Philco radio. Their favorite broadcast was The Lone Ranger. Their imaginations were consumed, as they visualized the scenery and action as voiced on this new medium. Lyle was captivated by *The Lone Ranger* and two other favorite broadcasts, The *Squeaking Door* and *Inner Sanctum*. They frightened him and provided his brother, Dick, countless opportunities to terrorize him. With Lyle lost in the story, Dick would employ various tactics to elicit his desired reaction. Flickering lights, screams, and banging pots and pans were always sure to make Lyle jump. Lyle complained to his mother but never received the sympathy he felt he deserved. The frequent pranks only served to expand Lyle's sense of adventure. His childhood on the farm fostered responsibility and independence, and he grew up quickly. It was expected.

Even as a young boy, Lyle contributed to the family's livelihood and his daily chores primarily involved the chicken coops. He never minded the task of gathering eggs from the hens, but he hated cleaning the coops. With multiple coops and dozens of chickens, there was an abundance of poop, which was considered a valuable fertilizer for the fields. Day after day, he would join his brother with a shovel and wheelbarrow as they worked their way through each coop. A large pile of waste was stored where their father could mix it with dirt and mulch before to spreading it over the crops.

While the work was difficult, Lyle still found pleasure in it as he was constantly joined by his best friend—the family dog, Duke. Duke was always the first to welcome Lyle home from school and accompanied him throughout each afternoon. Feeding the chickens was always an adventure with Duke by his side. The dog would never catch the chickens but loved chasing them around the farm. Lyle enjoyed watching Duke run in circles trying to get his nose on a bird.

Lyle's insecurities were magnified when he entered kindergarten and became the target of bullying.

"You look like a taxicab backing up with the doors open," one classmate shouted.

The laughter from the other children was more than Lyle could bear. Many school days ended with lonely walks home, while choking back tears. He knew he looked different than the other boys at school and longed to fit in.

When Lyle turned eight, his parents planned a special birthday dinner. Lyle had chosen his favorite dishes of cream corn casserole, mashed potatoes with gravy, and fried chicken. But as the meal was placed on the table, eating was of little interest to him. He was distracted by one present, much larger than the other packages. Lillian announced that no presents would be opened until after supper. Glenn was as anxious as Lyle; he had a special surprise for his son and seeing the suspense in Lyle's expression made him chuckle. Quickly consuming his plate of food, Lyle jumped from his chair and dashed to the gifts.

"Not yet," Glenn said.

Lillian refocused her son on their plans. "Lyle, come back to the table. You can open your gifts *after* we sing and cut the cake."

"C'mon Mom, light the candles," Lyle pleaded.

The candles were lit and the family sang a birthday song. The cake was cut, and for a brief moment, Lyle forgot about the presents while he took his cake and prepared it to his curious liking. He grabbed a bowl, placed the cake in it, and then proceeded to fill the bowl with milk. This was a trick he'd learned from his older brother. The beautifully prepared cake would absorb the milk and quickly turn into a soupy mix. Lillian didn't like it. The sound of her boys slurping their cake from a bowl was too much for her, but she smiled as she saw the contentment on their faces. After only a few minutes, the noise ended and the cake had been consumed.

"All right," Lillian said. "You can open your presents, but you have to open my gifts first." "Which ones are yours?"

"The three smaller ones. The bigger one is from your dad, and I don't approve."

Her comments added to the anticipation and Lyle quickly tore through the smaller packages revealing a pair of overalls, socks, and a wool shirt. Feigning enthusiasm for his mother's sake, Lyle eagerly moved on to the last present.

"Okay, Lyle. Open it up!" Glenn said, unable to contain his excitement.

As the paper flew into the air, Lillian wondered if this was a good idea. *I hope we don't regret this.*

Quickly, the wrapping was removed, exposing a long, rectangular box. For a moment Lyle struggled to open the package, but when he did, he burst with excitement. Before any words of counsel could be given, Lyle lifted the .22 long rifle and raised it to his cheek, taking careful aim at an imaginary target.

"Whoa! Hold on there Lyle," Glenn said.

Lillian added, "It's your gun, but there are rules."

After a review of gun safety and operating procedures, Glenn took his son into the fields where he and his boys enjoyed an evening of target practice. It was a birthday never to be forgotten, and Lyle's love for his father swelled. He turned to his father and exclaimed, "Dad, this is the best day ever."

Glenn's face beamed. A smile lifted his facial expression, exposing the deep wrinkles above his brow. Words weren't needed as he placed his arm around his son and took in a deep breath of the evening air. *This is a great day.*

CHAPTER TWO

In the fall of 1942, Lyle entered the third grade and was required to walk more than one mile to school. He enjoyed the walk and regularly turned the trip into an adventure. On most days, he was welcomed home by Duke, but on this day, his dog was nowhere to be found.

"Mom, have you seen Duke?" Lyle asked.

"Not for a few hours. Check the fields."

Lillian's reply only added to Lyle's concern.

He began searching and covered most of their property without success. Hopping over the ditch into a neighboring field, Lyle heard Duke's distress call.

"Duke!" Lyle yelled.

The barking increased until Lyle found his dog

"Oh no. Duke, Duke!"

The dog had been caught in a neighbor's trap and his leg was badly mangled. Lyle quickly went to work to release Duke's leg. Gathering Duke in his arms, he ran home. Lillian and Lyle did what they could to clean and dress the wound. By the time Glenn returned home later that evening, it was clear the dog was suffering and the injury was severe and infected.

"We need to put him down, Lyle," Glenn explained.

"Dad, no. I know he'll get better."

His older brother understood Lyle's heartbreak but also knew the family dog wouldn't survive the trauma.

"I'll do it, Lyle," Dick said

Dick then reached down and gathered Duke in his arms. Glenn handed Dick Lyle's twenty-two caliber rifle.

"I'm going with you," Lyle insisted. "I want to be with Duke."

Glenn was filled with emotion as he could hear the pain in his son's voice. "Are you sure that's a good idea, Lyle?"

"I have to!"

Dick and Lyle walked to the far end of their field.

Dick looked at his brother, now in tears. "He's hurting, Lyle. I think you should go home."

"No. He needs me."

Lyle bent down, laying close to his friend, and whispered into Duke's ear. He then gently stroked his head before standing up. The tears communicated to Dick the pain this loss would entail for his brother.

"Lyle, turn around," Dick demanded.

Without hesitating, Lyle turned his back to Duke. In the distance, he could see the house, but the shape was distorted through his tears. His gaze was interrupted by the sound of the rifle. Startled, Lyle jumped. Dick had fired the shot, ending Duke's suffering.

"I loved that dog. I really loved him." Lyle's knees buckled as he fell to the ground sobbing.

"Me too," Dick responded.

The boys dug a proper grave and buried their family pet.

Before leaving for home, Dick placed his arm around his younger brother. "Tomorrow, we'll get some wood and make a nice headstone."

Lyle liked the idea and asked, "Can I pick what it says?"

Dick nodded.

"It should say 'Always loved. Forever remembered.'"

Pausing for a brief moment, Dick replied, "Perfect."

CHAPTER THREE

Lyle's parents were aware he lacked confidence. Over the years, Dick's teasing had subsided, and he became the defender of his younger brother. There wasn't much he could do about Lyle's protruding ears, but he regularly included Lyle in pick-up games of baseball and football. By the time Lyle entered fifth grade, it was common for him to be playing ball with the older boys.

"Hey, Dick, how old is your brother?" a friend inquired.

Dick proudly responded, "He's only ten, but he's quick."

Lyle overheard his brother and for the first time he could remember, he felt a sense of satisfaction. Lyle's expertise in sports was the springboard for his acceptance among the boys his age and some older.

During the summer of 1945, the Hileman family gathered for a reunion at their farm in Lakewood, Colorado. While the adults enjoyed the conversation, the children were playing games on a patch of turf near the barn. Lyle's face was covered in sweat as he outmaneuvered side to side past the other boys in a game of Capture the Flag. He was noticeably faster than his cousins and couldn't be caught.

In frustration, one boy yelled out, "Hey Dumbo, no fair flying with those big ears."

Dick jumped into action. He grabbed the kid by the neck, wrestling him to the ground. With his body straddling the boy, his fist clenched and raised in preparation for a blow, he looked the kid straight in the eyes. "Take it back."

The others came to understand that teasing Lyle around his brother came with a risk. At school, kids recognized Lyle's older brother was a star athlete on the high school football team and that there would be consequences for bullying.

Even though Lyle was smaller than the others, he was lean and muscular. It wasn't unusual for Lyle to be the first one chosen when team sides were picked. But as he got older, he became more concerned about his height. When he entered middle school, Lyle's classmates were growing like weeds. Unfortunately, he hadn't had a growth spurt yet and wondered if he'd ever get tall. Lyle kept a record on the door molding of his bedroom. He had intentionally waited for the start of each month before having his mother hold a ruler across the top of his head, marking the progress. Month after month, the progress was negligible. "Mom, when am I going to start growing?" Lyle asked. "Dale and Dick are tall."

"Look, you've already grown nearly two inches this year," Lillian consoled.

"Two inches? I need to grow another five just to be average."

"Oh Lyle, relax. You're nearly as tall as me," Lillian said.

Lillian was only four foot, ten inches. Her encouragement only added to Lyle's frustration.

In November of 1947, Glenn and Lillian explored new opportunities. Glenn had become well-known for his ability to fix just about anything. The demands on his time increased as a housing boom was underway. Just five miles north of Lakewood was the fast-growing community of Wheat Ridge. With all the new homes being built, Glenn saw an opportunity to leverage his mechanical skills to provide builders and homeowners with heating and cooling services. Lillian knew the financial gains would be significant, but also recognized that with Glenn working full time to build his business, managing the farm would be impossible. They also knew a move would be hard on their Lyle, now thirteen.

"Dad, I don't want to move," Lyle protested. "We can't leave. We buried Duke here."

"Lyle, it's too late for that discussion. We've sold the farm."

Lyle loved his life on the farm in Lakewood. He'd grown up watching the areas around him change with roads, homes, and businesses but their twenty-acre homestead was a wonderland to him. Lyle's other worry was losing the friendships he'd formed after many years of trying to fit in. Ultimately, he understood his parents' decision, but leaving the only home he'd ever known would be devastating. Making new friends might be even harder.

As a compromise, Glenn agreed to drive Lyle to his school for the rest of his eighth-grade school year. Lyle missed the family farm in Lakewood. He missed the animals and even the chores. Most of all, he missed the wide-open spaces. Their new home was nice but was one of many that had been built on a long straight road. The houses looked identical and had small front yards with a bit larger areas in the back. The drive to school each day required passing 6th Avenue and Kipling, the site of their former home. Lyle's silence was an ongoing reminder for Glenn that the move wasn't without pain.

But moving wasn't all bad. The house was new and included numerous features the old house failed to deliver. Lyle had his own room and this house had a second bathroom. Lillian had a new kitchen with the latest appliances. The highlight for Glenn was the stand-alone garage that was large enough for all his tools. Between the tools and wood supply, there was no room to park the family car in the garage. To Glenn, it was a modest sacrifice in exchange for a space to create and pass along his love of woodwork to his youngest son.

In the new neighborhood, there were lots of kids Lyle's age. His ears kept pace with his growth, but none of his new friends ever mentioned them, let alone teased him. For Glenn and Lillian, the new business would occupy most of their focus. Dick and Dale enlisted in the navy after high school and Lyle was becoming more and more independent. However, dealing with a teenager was a skill set for which Glenn lacked enthusiasm. He had managed to raise his older boys, but with so much additional responsibility now, he lacked the patience. Mischievous would be one way to describe Lyle, but others, less tactful, would describe him as a troublemaker. An abundance of energy often led to disruptions in school. Trips to the principal's office or an occasional swat of the teachers ruler were the prices Lyle willing paid to entertain classmates. Glenn was exhausted from rearing kids and from the stress of operating his new business. The responsibility of disciplining Lyle would fall to his wife. She'd have to find the energy to "fix" Lyle. Glenn focused on keeping Lyle busy with chores and projects. It was a perfect arrangement.

Lyle was creative and talented. He spent hours in the garage turning wood into fun and useful things. His father was truly a gifted carpenter and Lyle would watch for hours as new and useful items were constructed. Time learning new skills in the garage was more the kind of education to which Lyle aspired.

In 1947, the return of the Soap Box Derby was the buzz of young boys across the nation. The amateur race began in Dayton, Ohio in 1934, with young boys adding axels and wheels to soap crates. The vehicles relied on gravity for motion and racing the handmade cars grew in popularity through 1941. Because of World War II, the race took a five-year hiatus but returned with great anticipation. Glenn suggested they purchase the necessary materials and work together on the creation of the car. Lyle would then compete. He quickly learned that working with his dad required discipline and focus. Work on design and aerodynamics provided Glenn with a chance to share drafting skills with his son. However, building the car's body and assembling the vehicle would fall primarily to Lyle.

"Son, I've done all I can. The rest is up to you," Glenn instructed.

Lyle was thrilled with the car and proud of their accomplishment. "I'll have it done tomorrow."

Glenn's face showed skepticism but he didn't say anything further. The next night, Lyle informed his dad the car was complete. The car body was made from wood and shaped to be aerodynamic. It was five feet in length and built in a fashion similar to a canoe. An opening on the top allowed the driver to enter and sit between the levers that controlled steering. When complete, the body of the car was attached to two axles that spun four metal wheels that were coated in rubber. The weight and dimensions had to follow strict guidelines. However, the driver had the liberty to add personal touches with paint or other decals.

"It looks great, Dad," Lyle said. "Come take a look."

Glenn circled the car, kneeling and running his hand across the various surfaces, taking in the finished specimen. Lyle waited anxiously for his assessment.

"It looks good, son, but to be great, you've still got a lot of work to do."

"What else is there?"

"Lyle, your paint hasn't been sanded and it will need at least three coats. Did you spin the axles with graphite?"

"I think it's good enough," Lyle argued.

Glenn paused for a moment as he walked around the car. His hand slowly followed the contours of the body. After examining the entire car, he stopped and looked straight into his son's eyes. "Listen, good enough won't win you any races and you know what I always say: If it's worth doing, it's worth doing right!"

Lyle began to speak but was interrupted by his father.

"You need to pay attention to the details. I guarantee there will be others that do."

Lyle wasn't thrilled about spending a few more days sanding and painting but considered the truth in his father's direction. He would keep at it until it was perfect.

As the Denver Regional racers assembled, Glenn and Lillian were amazed at the size of the crowd, more than three hundred. Even more surprising was the appearance of the other cars. As they walked around the field, they saw more than one hundred cars on display. None of the entries came close to the quality of Lyle's work. It was special. During the racing, Lyle came in third place in the first heat and by day's end, finished in second place overall. After the medals were awarded, they announced the judges had also selected Best of Show. Lyle hadn't realized the cars were judged on appearance and was stunned when his name was called. As he approached the judges, they held a big blue ribbon.

A judge extended his hand to congratulate Lyle and then handed him the ribbon. "Nice paint job kid."

The following year, Glenn and Lillian encouraged their son to compete again, but by this time Lyle had made new friends, and making the school football team was his focus. "I've decided to play football and training camp starts in July."

"But you've got races again in August," Glenn said. "I assumed you were going to try and win it all this year."

Lyle thought quickly about the potential recognition that might come, but concluded, "No. I'm done racing. Besides, the coaches think I can start as the running back."

His parents were disappointed as they felt the prior year's racing had bolstered his confidence; however, they weren't going to force him to participate. It would be his choice.

One of Glenn's co-workers mentioned his son was interested in competing in the derby but they didn't have the workspace or tools needed. He knew of the success Glenn and Lyle had enjoyed and asked if he could use their tools and garage. Given the fact that Lyle had moved on to football, Glenn offered their car to the family.

Later that night, the Hileman family gathered around the table to enjoy Lyle's favorite dish, creamed corn casserole. Lillian insisted dinner included conversation and no one was allowed to leave the table until everyone was finished. She loved this brief time with her husband and son and realized there wouldn't be many more before she and Glenn would be empty nesters.

"So, Glenn, how was work today?" Lillian inquired.

"Nothing too exciting, but I did tell Jonathan he could have the soap box car. His son wants to race."

"You can't give away my car," Lyle protested.

"Your car?" Glenn countered. "And where did the money for the materials come from?"

"But that's our car. I worked hard on it," Lyle shouted.

"Listen, it's taking up space and collecting dust. I've already told them to pick it up tomorrow night. It's done."

Lyle left the table abruptly and ran to his room. He lay on his bed stewing. *I can't believe he gave away our car. It will kill me to see that car go to some kid who won't appreciate it.* The longer Lyle pondered the situation, the angrier he became. Thoughts raced through his mind on how to best remedy the situation. He formulated a plan and waited until after he heard his parents shut the door to their room.

Quietly, he walked from his room, through the kitchen, and out the back door. The garage was dark but the night sky was bright enough that he could see the car near the front. He removed the plastic tarp that covered it. Dust filled the air as he threw the covering to the side. He slowly pushed his car towards the back of the garage and into the backyard. He then returned to the garage to grab some tools. Using a socket and wrench, Lyle began working to remove the wheels from the car. Once all four wheels were free, he carried them to the garage and hid them in a corner, carefully stacking wood to conceal their location. He then grabbed a can of gasoline and a matchbook. Back at his car, he poured the contents from the gas can over the wooden car. He then took a step back and reflected on the great memories he treasured building and racing this masterpiece. *This was our car. I'd rather see it burn than give it away.* In a matter of seconds, Lyle acted on his final decision, a point of no return. He struck the match, paused as the flame fully ignited, and threw it towards the car. He hadn't anticipated the magnitude of the explosion, nor the heat that erupted from the fire. Scared, he ducked away fearing the heat.

The sound of the fuel igniting brought both Glenn and Lillian to immediately rise to rigid, upright positions.

"What was that?" Lillian screamed.

The bright glow from the flames exposed the answer. Glenn flew from the bed and raced through the back door to find Lyle, standing straight, arms folded across his chest, near the hot-burning heap.

"What have you done?" Glenn shouted.

"I burned it! There was no way I was letting you give it away. That car was perfect and now I'll always remember it that way."

Glenn was stunned. *Why would he do this? It made no sense. This isn't right!* There was no saving the car from the flames, so Glenn stood next to his son watching the flames rise high into the dark sky. Glenn recognized a teaching moment emerge. "Lyle, you know that car could have brought another kid a lot of joy."

Lyle responded angrily, "Yeah, and made me miserable every time I saw it. You know that kid wouldn't take care of it like I did. I couldn't stand watching it get beat up."

"But Lyle, now that family has to spend the money and take the time to build a car. It was a kind gesture to offer it to them," Glenn said.

Lyle interrupted, "Dad, I loved that car but I loved the time we spent building it even more. The cost is nothing compared to the fun we had making it. I did them a favor."

Glenn had intended to teach his son a lesson in charity but instead, Lyle had opened his eyes. Still contemplating the matter, he moved towards his son.

Lyle, still defiant, retorted, "You had no right to give it away."

"You may be right, Lyle, but my decision was reversible. Yours is final. You're grounded."

CHAPTER FOUR

LYLE WAS LIKE many teens in his town. With few activities to occupy their time and even fewer jobs available, they would pass the time by going to school and fighting for status amongst their peers. Lyle and his friends considered themselves "The Cool Kids" and tried to project an image of toughness. Now in the ninth grade, they were all athletic and loved sports. They also liked to push the limits of the rules and sought adventure wherever they could. One day, on the school grounds, a boy from the band was riding a bicycle, approaching Lyle and his gang. He was carrying his guitar, not an easy task on a bike. As he neared Lyle, he could never have anticipated what would happen next. Lyle lunged toward the bike and shoved the boy as hard as he could. The guitar and bike went flying as the boy fell to the ground. Suggesting this teenager was a boy was a bit misleading. Tuffy Holland was six foot, two inches tall, and though barely fifteen, he weighed over 250 pounds.

"Hileman, I don't want to fight you, but I guess I'll have to."

Mission accomplished. News of the fight spread like wildfire throughout the school. It was to be at four o'clock behind the drugstore. If any of the teens had been more entrepreneurial, they could have made a fortune selling tickets. It was the biggest story of the day and while Lyle at five foot, six inches was much smaller, some boys were convinced he'd make short work of Tuffy.

At the appointed time, Lyle emerged from the crowd and approached Tuffy. Lyle was joined by his gang of thugs, all wearing denim jeans and white tee shirts. A pack of cigarettes was typically rolled into the sleeve for effect but always removed before heading for home. Lyle occasionally would smoke, mostly to enhance his appearance of being a bad boy. As the two boys approached each other, Lyle showed his athleticism and boxing prowess by dancing circles around Tuffy.

Bigger, but much slower, Tuffy was a bit confused watching this punk dart in and out, occasionally landing a punch. With Lyle's diminished stature, he would struggle to make contact anywhere near the chin and most of the blows were to Tuffy's belly and chest. Only minutes into the fight, it appeared Lyle had significantly more energy for the fight, but that would change quickly. Upon Lyle's next punch, Tuffy used his massive frame to grab Lyle in a bear hug. With Lyle now under his control, Tuffy used his size and strength to his advantage. In what seemed like a single motion, Tuffy lifted Lyle, turned him upside down, and then dropped him on his head. The blow knocked Lyle senseless and he struggled to get to his knees. Upon trying to stand, he lost consciousness and the fight was over.

It would take Lyle a few days to live down the embarrassment from defeat but the strike to his head knocked some sense into his brain. He needed Tuffy in the gang!

"Tuffy," Lyle shouted as he spotted him near the baseball field. His wide grin and twinkling eye communicated to Tuffy the intent of his inquiry was non-threatening. "I've been thinking. We need someone like you in our gang."

"What do you mean, someone like me? Like what?"

Lyle, concerned he may have offended his hopeful ally, explained further. "Tuffy, you're the strongest guy I've ever met. With you on our side, no one will ever mess with us."

"What do I get out of it?" Tuffy asked.

"I don't know what you get out of it, but I can tell you what you'll get out of. You won't be stuck with the losers in band. Plus, you'll have lots of new friends."

Lyle's response was persuasive. Tuffy knew playing an instrument in the school band failed to garner the attention of the girls. He could never figure out why all the cutest girls at school thought the boys in the gang were so desirable. He also understood that gaining the respect of Hileman and his thugs would prevent additional incidents like what he experienced only days earlier. Another benefit occurred to him. In ninth grade, he was at the top of the junior high pecking order but after the summer, he would fall to the bottom of the heap, being a lowly tenth grader at Wheat Ridge High School. Being associated with a group of tough guys might help in the transition.

"So just what do I need to do to join the gang?" Tuffy prodded.

"I thought you'd never ask," Lyle replied with a grin.

It was approaching nine -o'clock and the boys in the gang all knew they'd be expected home soon as it was a school night, but their adventure wasn't yet complete. Five of the six guys had completed the task but now it was Lyle's turn, as the leader and final participant.

"Okay, Hileman," shouted Steve, the artistic one in the group. "I'm ready for you."

Lyle removed his white tee shirt and sat in the prescribed chair as he nervously watched his friend carefully draw the previously agreed-upon emblem of the gang on his right arm, just below his shoulder. It was a popular tattoo amongst Marines during WWII and they'd seen it at the movie house. With pen in hand, Steve carefully drew a skull and then a knife that penetrated the top and exited at the bottom. It was magnificent. Once perfected, the only remaining step was the actual application of ink. Steve had an older brother who had taught him how to create a tattoo. While this night was his first attempt as an aspiring tattoo artist, the previous boys survived and the results looked pretty good. Lyle had seen the other boys cringe in pain, but none of them vocalized their suffering.

The first prick of the needled elicited a scream from Lyle. "For crying out loud, what was that?"

The others began laughing uncontrollably. Seeing the "tough guy" whining about the first prick of the needle amused them.

"Suck it up, Hileman," Lyle overheard.

It would be thirty minutes later before the self-inflicted torture would end. The ordeal was more stressful than Lyle had imagined, but now complete, each of the boys felt a keen sense of belonging. They carefully covered their new sign of unity with large bandages and tape before heading home.

The next morning, Lyle entered the kitchen after getting ready for school.

"What in the world have you done?" Lillian asked.

While getting dressed, Lyle thought he'd successfully covered the signs of the prior night's frivolity.

He now realized the shirt failed to conceal the large bandage underneath. "Oh, it's nothing, Mom."

"Did you get a tattoo? Your father's going to kill you," Lillian shouted.

Lyle knew he was in trouble. His mom left the kitchen in disgust.

She returned only a minute later holding a bottle of iodine and cotton balls. "Take off the shirt."

"Why. What are you going to do?" Lyle asked.

"First, I'm going to make sure it's not infected. Then, I want to see what you thought was so important as to scar yourself. I'm hoping it's a heart with *MOM* written through it."

Lyle carefully removed the gauze and bandages he'd carefully applied the night before. It didn't appear to be infected but his mother applied and few passes of iodine as a precaution.

"I can't even tell what it is," she said.

Lyle noticed the concern on her face and the tears in her eyes. And he hated that. He understood why she was upset but was sure she'd get over it. His dad, on the other hand, would show his disappointment in another way. Glenn never laid a hand on his son and wasn't a fan of corporal punishment. If discipline was required, anything physical like spanking, he'd delegate it to Lillian. Lyle often felt he'd prefer a good beating to the disappointment of his father; it would torment him for days.

As he sat quietly in the kitchen thinking of his predicament upon his father's return from work that night, the solution became obvious. He left the house and entered the garage. While not organized enough to be considered a real shop, there were lots of tools and Lyle quickly went to work searching for the object of his thinking. At last, he found it, a rectangular sanding block with sixty-grit paper. At first, he began timidly sanding away at the still-swollen flesh on his arm. He was right-handed and using his left hand to work felt awkward. Initially, the process was painful, but he was committed. The tattoo had to go. He maneuvered back and forth more aggressively. After a few minutes, the bleeding began, but fortunately, the pain lessened. This allowed for a more abrasive action that continued until he was certain he'd gone deep enough. Suddenly, from behind he heard the voice of his father.

"Lyle, what on earth are you doing?"

Startled, Lyle dropped the sanding block revealing torn flesh and blood, now flowing freely. Glenn quickly grabbed a cloth from his toolbox and applied pressure to the wound.

"It's a tattoo, Dad. I knew you'd be mad so I decided to remove it," Lyle explained.

Remaining focused on cleaning the wound, Glenn continued to gently wipe the blood from the arm. He then reached for a bottle of whiskey he had hidden with his tools. "This is going to hurt."

The pain from the liquid was intense but Lyle was determined to not scream. He clenched his jaw hard and held his breath as long as he could. Gasping for air, he breathed deeply and groaned in pain.

Glenn carefully wrapped his son's arm with materials from his first aid kit. "You know that will still be there after it heals, right?"

"What do you mean? I scratched it pretty deep."

"I don't think much of these so-called friends you've found in Wheat Ridge. They seem like trouble." Glenn paused, then continued his thought, "You'll have a reminder now for the rest of your life. You'd better learn to think for yourself or you're going to experience greater pain than this."

It would be weeks later before the wound would heal and to Lyle's disappointment, he realized the skull on his right arm remained. It would be a constant reminder of a stupid act with a bunch of equally stupid friends.

The school year finally ended and Lyle had survived the ninth grade. He didn't consider himself a great student but did enough to get by. Summer was now around the corner and he looked forward to wrapping up with baseball and jumping into training for the high school football team. Not many sophomores made the varsity team, but Lyle was confident he'd impress the coaches.

Football tryouts went well and Lyle was able to make varsity as a running back. The upperclassmen resented this young kid out-maneuvering them on the field but the coaches saw promise in the young man. Fortunately, Lyle wasn't the only sophomore to make the team. He was thrilled to learn that Tuffy would be blocking up front as he would become a dominant force on the offensive line.

CHAPTER FIVE

Practice ended early as it was a hot August day and the coaches had pushed the kids hard.   After showering, Lyle's friend, Cliff Mason, approached him. "I need a favor," Cliff said.

"You name it," Lyle replied.

"You may want to wait until you hear what I need. It's going to be hard."

Now curious and a bit concerned, Lyle inquired, "What's going on?"

Cliff's voice reflected the emotion he was fighting to hold in. "I have a tough job after school and could use some help. I remember you telling me about your dog when you lived in Lakewood. Well, my dog Tank is sick, really sick."

"Wow, I'm sure sorry Cliff. I know how hard that can be," Lyle replied.

"My dad wants me to put him down today. I don't think I can do it."

"No way. I'll do it," Lyle said. "I remember my older brother helping me out. I couldn't have done it myself."

As the boys approached Cliff's family farm, they saw his father in front of the garage, waxing his prized possession -- a new 1949 Chevy Truck. It was blue and gorgeous. It had a rounded hood with two large, round headlights located above a chrome bumper. Two doors allowed passengers to enter the cab and the truck bed was narrow because of the rounded wheel wells. The bright new paint, along with the new tires and white wheels were a sight to behold. Cliff's father motioned for the boys to come closer. "What do you think?"

"It's fantastic!" Lyle responded.

"Cliff mentioned he was going to ask you to help. Thanks for making a tough job a bit easier."

"Yeah. Not fun. I lost my dog to a trap," Lyle said.

"Well, I'll tell you what, I have another chore for you two. If you help me out, you'll need to use the truck."

Cliff's eyes widened and Lyle couldn't contain his excitement. "You mean we'd drive the truck?"

"That's right. But this job will be hard, maybe harder than putting down Tank."

Puzzled, Cliff asked, "What do we need to do?"

"Our tractor broke this morning and I still have two stumps in the field that need to be removed before planting. You'll need to get rid of them the old-fashioned way."

"The truck?" Cliff asked.

"No. You need to use dynamite. I've got a couple of sticks in the barn. Just dig a hole around the stump, drop in the dynamite, and light the fuse. Then run!"

The boys' faces lit up with excitement. *This doesn't sound like work to me,* Lyle thought.   "I'll grab the shovel," Cliff said.

His dad threw Lyle the keys. "You know how to drive a three on the tree?"

"A what?" Lyle replied.

"It's a stick shift."

"Sure, just never heard it called that before," Lyle said.

Cliff returned with the shovel and Tank, limping slowly behind. They carefully hoisted Tank into the cab of the truck. Lyle got behind the wheel and Cliff walked around to the passenger side.

Cliff's dad walked back to the house and quickly re-emerged. "One more thing, you'll need this," he shouted.

Cliff's father extended his arm with a rifle in hand. Walking up to the truck, handing Lyle the gun, his instructions were clear. "Make it certain. Quick and final. Tank's been a great dog and deserves a painless end."

With that, Lyle, Cliff, and Tank headed to the fields.

"Hey Cliff, I've got an idea," Lyle prodded. "What could be more certain and quicker than to tie Tank to the stump before it blows?"

Almost without a thought, Cliff responded, "Are you nuts?" Pausing briefly, he added, "Let me think about it."

As the work of stump removal began, a stick of dynamite was strategically positioned under the thickest root and covered with dirt, leaving only the fuse exposed.

"Are you ready?" Cliff asked.

Lyle nodded and watched as Cliff lit the fuse. The boys quickly ran to a berm a short distance from the stump and awaited the explosion. It was like a scene from a war movie. Dirt, flames, and debris flew everywhere. Lyle's ears were ringing as he forgot Cliff's instruction to plug his ears. Upon inspection, there was nothing left of the stump. It took ten minutes to move around the dirt to bury the remaining roots and to level the ground. The explosion filled both boys with a rush of adrenaline and they couldn't wait to tackle the next stump.

"So, what do you think?" Lyle asked.

Cliff's response came quickly. "Better than pulling a trigger while looking in his eyes. I could never get that memory out of my mind."

They returned to the truck and retrieved Tank and another stick of dynamite. Cliff knelt to give Tank a final hug farewell. His voice trembled as the tears began to flow. "I love you, boy. Thanks for everything."

Lyle, now questioning his idea asked, "Are we going to do this?"

"Either way, the stumps got to go, and Tank too," Cliff replied.

Cliff lodged the dynamite under Tank's collar and then wrapped the leash around the stump. "Light it," Cliff instructed.

Lyle struck the match and lowered it to the fuse. "Let's get out of here," he shouted.

The boys took off running. They had only gotten fifty feet from the stump when to their surprise, Tank had freed himself from the stump and was chasing them, the dynamite securely lodged in his collar. In a matter of seconds, the dog passed the running boys and was heading for the truck.

"Tank! Tank! Stop, please stop!" Cliff screamed to no avail. Tank had found the open door of the truck and was now inside the wonderfully upholstered cab.

KABOOM!

The sound of the explosion was magnified by the combustion of the truck. The hood of the truck came flying towards the boys.

"Get down!" Cliff yelled.

There was nothing salvageable from the truck. By the time the boys' ears stopped ringing, Cliff's father had arrived at the scene. "What in the world…" He was stunned and after learning the cause of the explosion, was shocked. "What were you thinking? How could you?"

It would take weeks for Cliff's parents to forgive him. He was forbidden from hanging out with that Hileman kid ever again. But Cliff was glad Tank's final moments on earth would live forever in the legendary stories that followed.

For months, the story of the ordeal was the talk of the town. Lyle felt regret for not thinking it through more carefully. But as time passed, he struggled to tell the story without breaking out in laughter. The summer of 1949 had become legendary, but he was now short one friend.

CHAPTER SIX

THE START TO Lyle's Junior year was uneventful, at least until the last weekend in October. Now sixteen, Lyle had the use of his family's car, and a driver's license. With the newfound freedom, he began making the trip south to reconnect with his old Lakewood buddies, including his best friend Dave. Dave's father was a respected businessman in town and he owned a tire shop. He offered the boys jobs, but neither was interested. Lyle had football practice and Dave preferred spending time with some of the rougher kids at his school. One evening, several members of the old gang decided to grab some beer and drink. Lyle had tried beer before and didn't like it.

"Lyle, you just need to acquire a taste for it," Dave said. "Let's just drink two or three and get buzzed."

"I can't stand the stuff," Lyle countered.

"Come on. It will grow on you," Dave prodded.

Lyle was reluctant but gave in to the pressure. After the first few sips, his taste buds faded. Each gulp swallowed was intended to achieve the "buzz" Dave had promised. Three beers in, the boys were getting a bit tipsy and laughter came easily.

"Let's do something exciting," their friend John suggested.

"What do you have in mind?" Lyle asked.

"My jalopy could use some new tires. Let's break into the tire shop."

Dave jumped in. "That's my dad's business, but he'd never miss a few tires. They're lying around everywhere."

With that, the plan was launched.

They waited until they were certain all the workers had left and then slowly drove Dave's car around the back. As they exited the car, snow was beginning to fall and the temperature had dropped significantly. Dave lifted Lyle to reach the office window in the back of the shop. It was open. Climbing through the window, Lyle then walked carefully through the shop and saw his friends waiting by the door in the back. As Lyle opened the door, an alarm sounded. Startled, some of the boys ran back to Dave's car. Undeterred, Dave and John entered, quickly grabbing two tires each.

The young men made their escape and drove west into the foothills. The effects of the alcohol were wearing off.

"We screwed up, big time," Dave said. The other boys nodded in agreement. "We best get home before our parents get suspicious."

"What should we do with the tires?" John asked.

"Just leave them here behind the trees," Dave said. "After school tomorrow, we'll figure out what to do with them."

Lyle jumped in, "Dave, you pick me up in the morning. Then we can get John and we'll see the rest of you guys at school."

With that, they headed for home and quietly made their way back to safety.

The next morning, per the plan, Dave picked up Lyle. "Any trouble?"

"No. My folks never even knew I was gone," Lyle replied.

"Me either," Dave said in relief.

Approaching John's house, something unusual caught their attention. Slowing the car down, Dave pulled over to get a closer look. "Lyle, those are cops."

"John must have squealed. Let's get out of here!" Lyle shouted.

As they turned the car and began driving away, Dave began to shake.

Lyle was scared. "We need to get out of town. They'll be looking for us."

The boys made quick stops at their homes, grabbing all the money they had before heading east. Along the way, they determined they could never go back. Maybe it was from watching too many westerns or perhaps it was the movie they saw in the theater during the summer, *Sands of Iwo Jima*, where John Wayne played the role of a tough Marine Sergeant preparing men for the challenges of war. But whatever the motivation, these two teenage troublemakers decided that adventure on the run would beat facing the consequences of their stupidity.

"You know they'll be looking for your car," Lyle exclaimed.

"That's why we're taking the side roads," Dave replied.

Located nearly 1200 miles from the Denver area is the town of Natchez, Mississippi. The city sits on the Mississippi River and in the post-Civil War era, was the hub of commerce and trade. It gained fame during the era of Steamboats that captivated the imagination of a thriving nation. Natchez was the home to one of these steamboats and the boat proudly carried the name of the city. During the study of history, Dave had marveled at the stories of life on the river. He was especially drawn to photos he'd seen of the many southern mansions that dotted the waters along the Mississippi River. It would be an unlikely selection as a place to hide out. Dave also remembered learning of a famous structure called the Melrose Estate. He was determined one day to see it for himself. That time had come and he needed to persuade Lyle that no one would ever think to look for them there.

"My folks know my girlfriend's family just moved to California. If I ever left home, they'd start looking there," Dave explained. "Also, the town of Natchez is small, and I'll bet we can find work."

It would take multiple stops and nearly thirty hours traveling the back roads, but their new life as Southerners had begun.

Upon their arrival, they spent a couple of days exploring the surrounding area. When they met people, they simply indicated they'd dropped out of school and asked about work. Neither had experienced southern heat nor humidity, and Natchez had both. It was uncomfortable.

They learned a lumber yard in town needed workers and they determined that it would be a good place to begin. In front of the lumber yard was a hardware store. They entered the store and quickly landed an interview. Within a short time, they were employed.

Having found work, they began walking on the main street sidewalk, back toward their car. While walking, they approached a Black man who quickly stepped aside. His head lowered, careful not to make eye contact, he waited for the boys to pass. They had never met a Black man and couldn't understand why he looked so afraid as the boys approached. Walking farther, they saw a water fountain with a large sign that said, *White Only*.

Most of the workers at the lumber yard were Black. Lyle and Dave were treated well and after only a few days, they learned life in the south wasn't easy for their newly found Black friends. The foreman was a giant White man. The workers respected him and called him Big Joe. He took to the new hires and was encouraged by how well they fit in with the crew. "You boys sure work hard," Big Joe said.

"Well, we need the money, and besides, it's better than sitting in school," Dave replied.

Big Joe then shared, "The boss told me to have you boys ready at noon. The local paper wants to interview our newest citizens."

The local paper told the story about the arrival of Lyle and Dave, and even quoted the store owner's statement that they were already two of his best workers.

The boys were flattered by the compliment and became instant celebrities in town, but they knew they were far from the best workers on the crew. The other men were experienced and disciplined. Unfortunately, they were treated like second-class citizens. It would be Lyle's first exposure to racism, and it disturbed him.

Becoming familiar with their new town was an adventure. While work monopolized most of their days, they still had time to explore. On a hot day at work, with temperatures nearing ninety degrees, Lyle noticed Dave looking a bit exhausted. "You okay? Is the heat getting to you?"

Dave quickly replied, "It's not the heat. I'm getting used to it."

"Well, what then? You don't seem like yourself."

"I miss her Lyle. I really miss her," Dave disclosed, referring to his girlfriend Charlotte.

Lyle never understood what Dave saw in her, but he knew they were serious and had even discussed marriage someday. "Well, you can't write her. If you write her, we're done for."

It was at that moment they decided on a plan to conceal their location. All correspondence with family or friends must be sent in an envelope addressed to the Postmaster in Southern California. Once opened, the recipient would find another stamped envelope directed to friends and family.

It would be weeks before the first letter from their son arrived for Glenn and Lillian Hileman. The letter would express his grief and Lyle would go on to share his love and appreciation for his parents and the hope that one day they could forgive him. Before the letter hit the kitchen table, Glenn and Lillian were in their car on a two-day drive to Southern California. Upon arrival, they learned of the deception, notified the local authorities, and begged the Post Office to alert them should another letter arrive. Two weeks later, a letter from Dave to Charlotte arrived at the same Post Office. This time, the return label was found and identified. It originated in Natchez, Mississippi. Dave's parents called the local authorities in Natchez, hoping to confirm the location of the missing boys.

The young men were settling into their new lives. Work continued to go well and they'd even managed to find a furnished apartment that fit their budget. It was early December, but unseasonably warm as Lyle and Dave were hard at work stacking lumber onto the tall racks created to separate the various sizes of timber. Lyle stood on the back of a truck and was pushing the twelve-foot, 2x4 boards off, three to four at a time. Dave stacked the boards carefully as Big Joe warned them of potential warping. Having pushed the last of the boards from the truck, Lyle jumped down to help with stacking, when the noise of engines caught their attention.

Two police cars drove slowly around the store and into the lumber yard. The dirt from the ground rose above their cars as dust filled the air. Anxious, the boys stood frozen. They were frightened. They nearly jumped out of their shoes when the officer turned on his siren, grabbing the attention of the entire crew. An officer exited his car and walked slowly and directly toward Lyle and Dave.

The other officer began searching Dave's car. "You the boys I read about in the paper?"

"Yeah, that's us," Dave replied.

"I need you boys to come with me to the station."

Before either Dave or Lyle could voice an objection, the other officer shouted, "Sheriff, they've got a gun."

The Sheriff's approach changed immediately and drawing his revolver he shouted, "On the ground! Get down on the ground!" He was looking directly at Lyle and Dave and his gun pointed in the direction of the boys.

Immediately, they both fell face down in the dirt.

"Hands over your heads!" instructed the officer.

As handcuffs were applied, Lyle cringed in pain. The cuffs hurt but even worse was the twisting of his arms. With Lyle cuffed, the officer went to work on containing Dave.

"You boys are in real trouble now," the Sheriff stated.

After securing the boys, they were placed in the back seat of the Sheriff's car.

Sitting handcuffed, Lyle looked at Dave in disbelief. "Why do you have a gun?"

"That's just my rabbit pistol. I leave it under the seat for target shooting. I forgot it was even there."

The Sheriff now began treating these "boys" like any other criminals. They knew they were in trouble.

After arriving at the jail, the boys were taken to a booking area. Neither Lyle nor Dave understood the details of their arrest, especially as it would be another sixteen years before the U.S. Supreme Court would make the case Miranda v. Arizona, the law of the land. They hadn't been read their rights - they had none. They knew stealing tires was a crime and hoped to avoid facing consequences. A sick feeling overcame Lyle as he realized his time on the run had ended. The cells were located in a dark basement. Access was through a spring door in the floor and required a ladder to make the descent. As Lyle and Dave made their way down, the two teenagers became fully aware of an even bigger problem awaiting. They were not alone.

As quickly as they stepped on the basement floor, the ladder was retrieved by the officers above. As the door shut, they were rushed by the other prisoners.

"Get 'em," one of the men shouted.

"Help! Help us!" Lyle yelled.

The boys backed into an open cell trying to create distance from the drunk men.

"I get the pretty one," one man shouted.

The other men broke out in laughter as they backed the boys into the cell.

"Help!" Dave yelled.

Not only did their cries go unanswered, but they could also hear laughter from above. There would be no help from the officers.

The largest of the three men entered the cell, closely followed by two other heavily intoxicated men.

Dave saw a bedframe along the wall and used his weight to break a board below his foot. He stepped forward swinging the board and narrowly missed the large man. "Stay away or I'll knock your head off," Dave shouted.

Lyle followed Dave's lead and took another board from the frame. As it broke free, two nails remained protruding from the end. He raised the board and closed in beside Dave.

"Now, now boys. No need for violence," the man responded. "Look here. We just want to get to know you better."

As one man tried to reason with the boys, the others began to circle them.

Lyle jumped forward, now armed with a board that he held like a baseball bat. Dave also used his board to jab towards the face of the men. Seeing the risk of injury, the men backed off a few feet, far enough that Lyle was able to swing the iron bar door to the cell shut. He then removed his belt and wrapped it around the bars while Dave continued to push his board to the face of the men that dared get close.

After a few minutes, the drunks realized their efforts had been deterred and they drifted to the other side of the cell. It was dark, but the moon from the evening sky cast light on the faces of the men. Two of the three men fell quickly to sleep, having lost enthusiasm for the attack. However, the third prisoner glared at Lyle with an evil stare. Nearly an hour passed before all three finally were asleep.

"There is no way I'm sleeping," Dave whispered to Lyle.

"Me either," Lyle replied.

"How about I sleep for two hours while you keep watch, then we'll switch," Dave suggested. Within minutes, exhausted and afraid, he drifted to sleep.

Lyle remained alert throughout the ordeal. He also began to fear the uncertainty of what would follow. Neither Lyle nor Dave would get much sleep that night.

Fortunately, before the three men woke, the door to the basement cell opened and an officer directed them to the ladder he was lowering. "Let's go, boys. You've got visitors," the deputy called.

Standing in the office were Lyle and Dave's fathers. From their appearance, it was clear they'd driven straight from Denver and hadn't slept. They must have left before the boys had been apprehended and they looked angry.

The Sheriff looked at the men. "They're released to your custody, but the judge in Denver will be expecting them."

Back in Denver, Lyle and Dave appeared in court to learn of their fate. The sentencing was lenient and both young men were relieved, vowing to never return to a jail cell again. The judge knew there was little he could do to match the consequences of angry parents who, after a trip to California, drove to Natchez, Mississippi to retrieve their sons. But there would be sentencing. Both were given one-year probation and required to make reparations. They also forfeited their driver's licenses.

Loss of driving privileges was tough, especially as most kids their age were enjoying the freedom that comes with that rite of passage. Without a car, Lyle lost transportation to Lakewood. But his parents took an additional measure and forbid him from hanging out with his former friends ever again.

All the required actions intended to elicit remorse were effective, but none could match the unintended consequence of their choices. At Wheat Ridge High School, in the 1951-1952 school year, Lyle's reputation was damaged and he couldn't get a date. Parents and teachers warned Lyle's classmates he could be trouble. Fortunately, Lyle was well-liked by the gang and his adventure only helped elevate his status as a leader in the group.

Lyle and his buddies were loitering on the steps of the school as numerous students frenetically raced to make class before the opening bell. They were waiting for Tuffy to arrive before they would grace the school with their entrance. The boys were laughing and exchanging stories when Lyle spotted a girl approaching. She wore a bright yellow dress and was the most beautiful girl Lyle had ever seen. His eyes followed the girl as she made her way up the steps and disappeared into the school. The other boys snickered as they observed Lyle's obvious attraction.

"Don, who is that?" Lyle asked.

"Her name is Marylin. I sit next to her sister in biology class."

"That's my girl," Lyle proclaimed.

Don couldn't contain his laughter and looked Lyle directly in the eyes. "Your girl? You have no chance. She's a church girl and when she hears about you, she'll run for the hills!" Tuffy finally arrived to hear the chatter of his friends and quickly recognized Lyle was the subject of the laughter. "What's up?"

"Lyle's in love," Don explained. "He's fallen for a church girl, oh and she's only a sophomore."

Lyle knew his reputation had taken a hit but he was undeterred. He knew this girl was out of his league, but deep in his gut he felt something stir. Something he'd never experienced before.

"Yep, that girl is my girl."

CHAPTER SEVEN

MARYLIN MILDRED MORRIS was born on June 9, 1936. Her parents, Stephen and Amy Morris, felt the struggle of rearing a family. Like most families in the post-depression era, work was a significant concern and both Stephen and Amy worked to support their growing family.

During the summer of 1951, the family relocated to Wheat Ridge, Colorado. Stephen's engineering prowess attracted the attention of his employer and he accepted a promotion that required leaving El Paso, Texas for the prospect of financial gain. Amy found work teaching at an elementary school in Lakewood, Colorado.

Moving over the summer months was tough on the children but with school beginning soon, Amy knew her kids would adapt quickly. After all, this wasn't their first moving adventure.

Amy met Stephen shortly after graduating college. She accepted a teaching assignment in McGill, Nevada. Stephen worked in a local mining operation. McGill was a small town and offered few prospects for young people looking for companionship. When Stephen saw Amy in the town store, he was thrilled. He never expected to find a beautiful girl in the desert, but there she was. Making eye contact, she smiled which was all it took for him to strike up a conversation. Within a short time, their courtship began.

The relationship got off to a rocky start. During the first date, she learned of a story that nearly pushed her away.

"So that's not your name?" Amy asked.

"Well, it's complicated," Stephen replied.

"Complicated? It's your name. Which is it? Stephen or Frank?"

Stephen took a deep breath, realizing he'd dug a deep hole. "Neither. It's Veljko."

He then went on to tell a story of hope, ambition, and regret. Stephen's family immigrated to the United States from Yugoslavia when he was six. Eventually, they landed in Milwaukee, Wisconsin where the family owned and operated a grocery store. The business was successful but required all family members to pitch in.

During Stephen's senior year of high school, a guidance counselor came to the family's home to speak with his parents. "Stephen is our brightest student. He's eligible for a full-ride scholarship at the University of Wisconsin, but he told me he couldn't apply."

"That's right. He's needed here," Stephen's father replied.

ULTIMATELY, THE FAMILY conceded and agreed that Stephen would attend the university, but after graduation, he must return to assist in the store. Graduation came quickly, especially given Stephen's intellect and work ethic. However, without notifying his parents, he boarded a train for Chicago. He decided to not return to Milwaukee but rather he'd pursue his dream to be a chemical engineer.

As the train left the station, Stephen gazed out the window and was lost in reflection. Life as an immigrant was difficult. Upon arriving at Ellis Island his family abandoned their Slavic first names. Veljko would be Stephen, Stephen Novakovich. As memories of his youth filled his mind, he was struck by a large billboard. It was an advertisement for Morris Meat Packing. *Morris. That sounds like a solid American name*, he thought. His name of Stephen helped him during his formative years but carrying the difficult-to-pronounce surname of Novakovich made him the target of teasing. He also knew that failing to return home would initiate a search. His parents would be looking for him. He needed a new name. *Morris, Morris, Morris* he repeated in his mind. By the time he had crossed the Wisconsin border, he had an alias, Frank Morris.

Frank Morris longed for two things: companionship, and professional growth. In McGill, Nevada, he'd found both. His courtship with Amy blossomed and in only six weeks, he proposed marriage. Amy accepted.

"When can I meet your family?" Amy asked.

"I have no family," Frank responded.

"You must have family somewhere," Amy pressed.

"I left home and don't plan to return."

"How old were you?"

"Nineteen, barely," Frank disclosed. "It's been a few years. I don't even know if my parents are still alive."

"But Frank."

"Amy, it's too painful to even contemplate a return. Please leave it alone."

"Well, what is your last name?" Amy asked.

Committed to his new life and with a desire to remain anonymous, he paused, then replied, "Morris, just Morris."

Seeing the pain in her beau's face, Amy decided she'd end the interrogation. "Well, Mr. Morris, your future bride prefers the name Stephen."

"I can deal with that. Stephen it is!" he replied.

Shortly after marriage, Stephen and Amy Morris moved to Utah to be near her family. They also began a family. In only seven years, they had four children.

Marylin was their second child and enjoyed an idyllic life in Utah. She was surrounded by extended family. While a young girl of only eight, her cousin invited her to attend church meetings. Marylin's parents never spoke much of religion and both preferred spending weekends exploring the beauty of Utah's mountains and parks. However, they approved of Marylin spending time with cousins and believed the experience would be good for her.

At church, Marylin felt something. She knew she was loved and embraced the concept that she was a daughter of God. She enjoyed learning stories of Jesus Christ and returned week after week. Eventually, she was baptized a member of The Church of Jesus Christ of Latter-day Saints.

Stephen left his work in engineering to be close to Amy's family. He was employed in the family business, assisting at the funeral home. The work paid well but Marylin recognized they were not nearly as fortunate as her cousins. Her Uncle George and Aunt Mary were wealthy. Not only did they own Jenkins Mortuary, but her Uncle George was the mayor of the town. Marylin wasn't impressed by her cousin's clothes, bigger homes, and things. But what did capture her attention was her Aunt Mary's candy collection. Visitors could find dozens of jars, dishes, and cups filled to the brim with nuts and candy. To Marylin, it was magical.

Stephen was never envious of his father-in-law, but Amy aspired for the finer things. Stephen knew a return to his engineering would allow for significant financial security and he'd been courted by a mining operation in Texas. He dismissed the idea for months but finally decided to test the waters. "Amy, with four kids we're sure working hard, but not getting ahead. I've got an opportunity, but we'd have to move. But I'd make enough that you could stay home with the kids."

Stephen's professional development was only one of the desires Amy had for the family. She had been thinking about change for some time.

"It's been wonderful living close to my family, but I want to meet your family too. I'm in, but with conditions," Amy said.

UPON RETURNING FROM school, Marylin arrived to find her parents in a serious discussion.

"Marylin, sit down please," her father beckoned.

"What's wrong Daddy?"

Her mother quickly got to the point. "Your father has taken a new job. We are moving."

"What? Where?" Marylin cried.

"El Paso, Texas," Stephen explained.

"Not so fast," Amy added. "Before Texas, we'll be spending some time in Wisconsin."

Marylin had no idea where Wisconsin was. Her heart was beginning to ache as she thought of leaving her friends and cousins. Seeing her near tears, Stephen quickly added, "Marylin, it will be fine. Plus, it won't be forever."

Amy then jumped in, making matters worse. "Moving won't be the biggest challenge. We have more news."

"Not now!" Stephen pled. "We'll have time for that conversation on the drive. I'll share the story once, with all the kids together."

The time arrived and the Morris family loaded up for their drive to Milwaukee. Several hours into the drive, Stephen began to share how his family immigrated to the United States in 1911. They learned of a grocery store and family members they had never met. Their father had never before spoken much of his early life, but now was describing events that shaped him.

"You know, I was a great student, but my parents didn't want me to attend college," Stephen said. "In those days, it was expected that everyone would contribute to the family business."

"But you went to college, right?" Marylin asked.

"I did, thanks to my high school counselor. He convinced my parents I couldn't miss a full-ride scholarship offer. They agreed, but assumed I'd return home after graduation."

He went on to explain his desire to be an engineer and his reluctance to return to Milwaukee. He then explained how after graduation, he executed his plan to disappear. The kids were captivated as their father shared the details of his adventures.

"And now you're Stephen Morris, right?" Marylin asked.

"Not exactly. Your mother insisted that I reconnect with my parents. That's why we're going to Wisconsin."

The children were bouncing with excitement realizing they'd soon meet grandparents and cousins they didn't even know existed. Their joy was interrupted as Stephen continued, "We are also changing our family name. Your last name is Novakvich."

Marylin could hardly believe it! Stephen wouldn't try to explain the need to take on his Serbian name as the kids were too young to understand, but he knew it would be important to facilitate healing with his family. If he were to be welcomed back, he couldn't return home with the name Morris. As they neared the city of Milwaukee, Wisconsin, Stephen began losing his confidence. "I'm not sure this is a good idea."

"But you must. You promised," Amy said.

"They'll hate me. How can they ever forgive me?"

Marylin hearing her father's distress jumped in and offered, "But they'll love me. I'm their granddaughter!"

Stephen said, "They will love you and your sister and brothers too."

It was brilliant. Of course, they'd be angry but how better to soften the pain than to introduce the four grandchildren they had never met.

"Marylin," Stephen said. "I've got an idea, but we only have a few minutes to prepare and it won't be easy. Let's get started."

"HELLO, MY NAME is Marylin Mildred Novak…Nov..Novak," She paused and then remembered the rest, "Novakovich."

The elderly couple stood confused and looked at each other in shock.

"What did you say?" Djuro Novakovich inquired.

"I said, my name is Marylin Mildred Novakovich and my daddy wants to come in. Can he?"

Immediately, Djuro and his wife Sofie knew their lost son had returned. Years of anger had faded and after ten years of searching, they'd given up hope of ever seeing their son again. Stunned and speechless, their silence was interrupted by their youngest daughter who came running towards Marylin.

She fell to her knees and slid into the arms of her niece. "My name is Mildred. You were named after me. Veljko is my brother. Is he here? Is he really here?"

Veljko? Marylin thought to herself. "My daddy is Stephen," she shouted over the excitement beginning to stir in the room.

"Oh, that's his American name," Mildred explained. "His real name is Veljko Novakovich."

The reunion was extraordinary and the Stephen and Amy Novakovich family spent the summer with their expanded family. By late August, the time arrived for the family to explore their new home, El Paso, Texas. After a few months, Marylin continued to struggle with her new name. It just didn't roll off the tongue as easily as Marylin Morris. The last name of Novakovich also raised questions of her Slavic heritage, but in El Paso, she found a diverse and accepting community.

The family found a small home in town and while Stephen worked in the mines, Amy focused on helping the kids settle into the area. It wasn't long before the school district learned of Amy's teaching credentials and encouraged her to accept a substitute teaching assignment. She was anxious to teach again after a long break, but with all her kids in school, the time felt right. Two years later, she'd become a full-time teacher again.

During Marylin's fifth-grade year, she was disappointed to learn that her mother would be her teacher.

On a fall morning in the classroom, the boy behind Marylin began teasing her. "Hey, I'll bet your mommy gives you nothin' but A's. Right?"

Marylin quickly turned and gave a quick and stern response. "None of your business."

Determined to get a reaction, the young boy grabbed his ruler and began flipping Marylin's braided pigtails. After the first swipe of the ruler, Marylin rose from her desk, grabbed the ruler, and let the boy have it with several swipes at his arm. Unaware of the commotion that had gotten the attention of the teacher, Marylin was startled when her mother grabbed her from behind and pulled her to the front of the classroom.

"There will be no teasing nor fighting in my classroom!" Amy shouted.

She then sat down, placed Marylin over her knee, and used the ruler to apply a few well-placed swats across her behind. The punishment was barely felt but the embarrassment would be remembered for a lifetime.

Marylin's trouble with her mother wasn't limited to the classroom. Having been invited to attend a classmate's birthday party, she was determined to restore her reputation with the other kids. She needed a gift that was sure to win favor. In her mother's room, she found a jewelry box that contained several items her mother loved. Quickly, Marylin grabbed an item she knew would impress, a pearl necklace. She found a small box and carefully wrapped the item. At the party, the time had come for sharing gifts. Each present was opened and the suspense was growing inside Marylin as she could hardly contain her excitement. Just as planned, the necklace drew gasps of delight from the others. The friend loved the gift and Marylin enjoyed the good feeling she had.

It was several weeks before Amy noticed her pearl necklace was missing. Certain she hadn't misplaced the necklace, she gathered the family. "Has anyone seen my necklace? My pearl necklace is missing."

Annetta was quick to respond. "I haven't seen it. It wasn't me."

Now all eyes were on Marylin.

"Marylin?" Amy asked.

Marylin looked down and pretended to not hear her mother's questions.

"Marylin, did you take my necklace?" Amy repeated.

Looking up at her mother, the expression on her face reflected her anxiety and fear. It was obvious she was the culprit. She then explained, "I needed a gift for a birthday party. I gave it to my friend."

"You did what?" Amy screamed.

By now, Stephen had joined the conversation and knew his daughter was in big trouble. "We did work hard to teach the kids to be kind and generous."

Amy's glare told Stephen that his logic wouldn't calm her anger, so he defaulted to another plan. "This weekend I'll take you downtown and we'll shop for a new necklace."

It wasn't the solution Amy wanted. It wouldn't include the discipline she felt Marylin deserved, but the idea of shopping brought the interrogation to an end. Stephen took Amy as promised and together they purchased a new pearl necklace. It was beautiful but could never replace the sentimental value of the one lost. It was a gift from Stephen during their courtship that she knew was too expensive but had viewed as a gesture of love. Each time she'd put on the new necklace, she'd stand in front of the mirror and while reaching behind her neck to fasten the clasp, reflect on Marylin's motive. Had her daughter given it away as payback? *Had she done it as revenge for spanking her in class?*

One evening, as her parents were leaving for dinner, Marylin spotted her mother wearing the new necklace. "You look beautiful Mom."

Stephen opened the door for his wife.

As the door closed, Marylin stood alone and quietly mumbled, "You used a ruler, but I used a yardstick!"

STEPHEN WAS A great fit in his new job and he quickly secured a promotion to an executive role with American Smelting and Refining Company. The pay increase was significant but required traveling to Colorado to assist with the opening of a new office. Eventually, his work resulted in stable operations and Stephen was offered a position as the new office manager. His family was pleased to be moving as they longed to be closer to their Utah family.

When the Novakovich family arrived in Colorado, they were in the community of Westminster. It was a rural suburb of the Denver metro area and located north of the city near the foothills. Marylin loved it as it reminded her of the mountains in Utah. Shortly after settling in, she was thrilled to learn of another family surprise.

"You're going to have a little sister," Amy shared with her children.

Amy Sue Novakovich was welcomed by the entire family, but for Marylin, this baby was an immediate best friend. Marylin spent hours playing with Amy Sue and loved helping her mother with the challenges of a newborn. By the time Marylin entered the ninth grade, she felt comfortable with her new home and was developing maternal instincts.

"I'll change it," Marylin said when alerted of a dirty diaper.

On another evening, "It's time for Amy Sue to be in bed," Amy instructed.

Marylin eagerly jumped to the task at hand, "I've got it. Tonight, we're reading Good Night Moon. Amy Sue loves when I read to her."

Marylin enjoyed caring for her little sister and she knew she'd want a large family someday.

WITH FIVE CHILDREN, Stephen went to work designing a larger home. He found a wonderful community in Wheat Ridge, Colorado. Just north of the Crown Hill Cemetery, a developer created a unique setting of homes surrounding a lake. Each custom home was stunning, but Stephen wanted a larger parcel with enough land to plant fruit trees and a garden. Plus, he planned to build the house himself. Only a block farther north, he found the perfect site. It consisted of five acres, had a beautiful view to the north, and a stream that ran through the property. It was perfect.

By Christmas of 1950, the home was ready and the family moved in. It was beautiful and reflected Stephen's love of engineering. It also provided for Amy's love of gardening. Stephen created flower boxes on each side of the entrance to the home and Amy had already carefully prepared the soil for a flowerbed. She could hardly wait for spring.

The kids hated moving again, but the excitement of the new house made the transition easier. While much larger than the Westminster house, it only had three bedrooms. Steve and Mike would share the boys room, while Annetta, Marylin, and Amy Sue shared the girl's room. Amy and Stephen had a beautiful room with a walk-in closet that Amy loved. It was a great home, but soon Stephen realized he should have added an extra bathroom. With Amy and two teenage daughters, getting access to the one bathroom nearly required reservations.

The best part of the move for Marylin was discovering two important things. First, the stream that crossed the property had an arched bridge. Marylin spent hours by the stream. During the spring, she enjoyed taking a blanket with her and completing her homework or reading while basking in the sun. The view was extraordinary and there was a sense of peace being close to home, but still alone.

The solitude wouldn't last as the second-best thing about the move occurred early in the summer. A new home was being constructed to the side of the Novakovich property and when finished, she quickly met a new friend, Margie Griffin. Marylin would continue to visit her favorite spot regularly but was rarely alone. This spot was now shared with Margie and together they could talk, laugh, and plan for the upcoming milestone of entering high school.

CHAPTER EIGHT

AUGUST 20, 1951, marked the start of the school year at Wheat Ridge High School. Marylin loved the independence high school offered and especially enjoyed sharing the experience with Margie. They were inseparable. Boys were the most common topic of discussion and there was no shortage of eligible young men for dating. Marylin and Margie would be the focus of countless suitors. During the first week of school, both girls were giggling as they sat on a rock wall in front of the school flag. A group of boys were whistling at them and now headed in their direction.

"That boy is flirting with you, Marylin," Margie teased.

"Me? They are looking your way," Marylin responded.

As the boys neared, Margie reminded Marylin of the pact, "Remember, we play hard to get."

The boys were surprised that these sophomore girls weren't putty in their hands, like so many of the other girls they pursued. "Either of you beauties need help with your books?" inquired the confident young man.

"We're just fine," Marylin replied.

The two girls stood and began to walk toward the school entrance; the boys looked puzzled. This wasn't the reception they'd expected and making matters even worse, Margie looked back and flirted, "You couldn't handle us!"

Deflated, but not discouraged, the boy's interest was only fueled by the brushoff.

Now in the school hallway, Marylin and Margie were discussing plans for the day when they were interrupted by a voice from behind.

"Hi. My name is John," the tall and handsome boy stated. His greeting was to both girls but his eyes were fixed on Marylin.

Noticing a guy making a move on her best friend, Margie jumped to her rescue. "Hey Marylin, we're late for class. Let's go."

The girls had a code and a secret sign to reflect their interest in guys. Marylin's chin dropped, "the sign," and then she spoke the code, "I'll catch up." Margie could hardly believe it. This great-looking guy was making the moves on Marylin, and the interest was mutual.

As Margie walked away she could hardly contain her excitement. "See you after school."

The school day couldn't end quickly enough as Margie was dying to learn all the details.

John suggested going to a movie together over the weekend and the conversation was unfolding smoothly. Marylin quickly accepted. He had just begun sharing with Marylin a little bit about his chemistry project that had gone wrong and Marylin was laughing. This guy's good-looking and funny, she thought.

Before John could finish his story, Tuffy Holland walked up and gave John a little shove to the shoulder. "Hey, that's Lyle's girl. Back off!"

And just like that, John was gone. Marylin stood in shock. Tuffy never spoke a word to her and was already on his way to class before Marylin's senses calmed enough to form a thought. *Who is Lyle and how does he get off claiming me as his girl?*

Her face grew hot as she tried to contain her anger. Marylin then yelled, "I'm nobody's girl!"

Having vocalized her feelings, Marylin stood there as all the students in the hallway turned to stare. Now embarrassed, Marylin ducked into her classroom.

With the school day complete, Marylin and Margie met by the administrative offices.

"I can't believe he would do that," Margie expressed in disbelief. "He doesn't even know you."

Marylin confirmed, "I know. I've never even met him. We need to find out who this creep is and put him in his place. No one is going to tell me who I can and can't date."

As they chatted about the events in the hallway, Marylin noticed Tuffy, walking towards the school parking lot.

"That's the guy. There." Marylin pointed out the giant of a man.

"That's Lyle?" Margie questioned.

"No. Not Lyle, that's the guy who chased John off. He told John I was Lyle's girl and to back off." She jumped to her feet and motioned for Margie to follow. "Let's go, we'll track him to find out who his friends are."

With that, Marylin and Margie began tailing Tuffy. Careful to keep a distance and remain concealed, they navigated the school property, using the trees as cover. Tuffy was approaching a group of guys.

In disgust, Marylin whispered to Margie, "Gross. They're smoking!" Marylin couldn't stand cigarette smoke or understand why anyone would choke down the nasty air.

Margie agreed but also knew that smoking was a big deal in high school, especially among boys trying to look cool. "Let's get out of here."

"No way," Marylin said. "Not until I give this guy a piece of my mind."

Margie was stunned. She'd never seen Marylin angry. At barely five feet in height, she was marching straight into trouble.

"Which one of you idiots is Lyle?" Marylin demanded.

Surprised, the boys smirked and began looking around as if seeking permission to "out" their leader. From behind Tuffy emerged the shortest boy in the group.

Maybe five feet seven inches, but strong and athletic, Lyle confidentially strutted towards Marylin. "I'm the idiot." As quickly as he said it, he wanted to retract the words.

The guys in the gang began laughing uncontrollably. They knew Lyle liked this girl. They also respected him, but did he really just introduce himself to this girl as an idiot?

Lyle turned, and with authority typically only found in a drill sergeant, he rebuked his friends. "Pipe down you knuckleheads."

Now facing Marylin, he made his second attempt to impress her. "What I meant to say is, I'm Lyle and you're the most beautiful girl that's ever set foot at Wheat Ridge High. What are you doing Friday night?"

Marylin blushed for a split second before stiffening her lip and giving him the message. "Friday night? I'm, not sure, but I am sure you won't be a part of it."

Margie raced to catch up and then nuzzled right behind Marylin, her hand on Marylin's shoulder, as a signal of unity and support. By now she'd recognized several of the other guys in the group, and they were cute. Looking directly at Tuffy, Marylin marched in his direction. Tuffy was startled and took a step back as she got within inches of his chest.

Looking up and with her finger pointing close to his face, Marylin shouted, "Don't you ever tell anyone I'm Lyle's girl! I'm nobody's girl!" With that statement, she turned and began a fast-paced walk toward the school. Passing Margie, she grabbed her by the arm and dragged her away, breaking her stupor.

Once out of sight of the boys, Margie couldn't contain herself further. "Did that really happen?"

By now the adrenaline had slowed and Marylin began to crack a smile before stating, "You better believe it."

They then began laughing uncontrollably. While not a fighter, Marylin was tough, just another trait Margie admired in her best friend.

As the school year began, students scrambled to fit in. The boys often gravitated towards sports and the football season was already underway. Training had begun weeks earlier and friendships were already solidified. Those less athletic found a home in band or choir. For Marylin and Margie, navigating the social structure at Wheat Ridge High School was as important as selecting their classes. Their choices were few as neither had an interest in sports, choir, or band.

The Student Body Government Committee established an event in the gym to encourage students to get involved in various activities. As

Marylin and Margie walked through the gym they stopped to consider the Chess Club but passed after learning the club met twice a week for two hours. They weren't that interested in the game and were surprised the club met on Friday night. Friday was considered sacred and there was no way they wanted to be tied down for the start of the weekend. Next, they approached the cheerleaders and pompom girls. Marylin's facial expression let Margie know this wasn't of interest.

"It could be fun," Margie expressed.

"No. They try too hard to impress. It feels phony," Marylin said.

Next, they met members of the Glee Club. This had a real appeal but required trying out. Marylin couldn't hold a tune, and Margie was terrified to sing in front of others. There was no way they'd do that. No, they needed something they could do together.

Finally, they found a great fit. At first, Margie was a bit surprised at the suggestion but after learning from Marylin about some of the traditions and dances she'd learned in El Paso, the decision was made. They joined the Spanish Club. Neither were fluent in Spanish, but both had taken a course in Junior High and Marylin was accustomed to hearing Spanish speakers, almost as frequent as English, while living in Texas. She enjoyed the Spanish culture and persuaded Margie it would be fun.

After signing up for the club, they learned about an initiation. On Monday, all the club members were required to appear in school dressed in gunny sacks. They each received a gunny sack and were expected to tailor it to reflect their sense of style. They only had a few days to prepare but Marylin's mom was a good seamstress and had a Singer sewing machine. This will be fun, she thought. Marylin and Margie arrived at school on Monday looking very fashionable. It made for a fun day and after school, the entire Spanish Club stopped at the local ice cream shop. They enjoyed making new friends at school and especially liked the other club kids. Marylin could hardly wait until spring to share her love of piñatas and cascarones, hollowed eggs filled with confetti. These were traditions she cherished.

On Friday night, the football team held their first home game. It was a big community event and everyone was talking about it. Students got in free but parents were expected to donate upon entrance. As Marylin and Margie took their seats in the stadium, Marylin saw Lyle waving to her from the sidelines. At first, she looked away, but after calming herself, she made a modest gesture back. Lyle smiled and then ran onto the field. During the game, Marylin learned first-hand of his athletic prowess. He was a star running back and was quick. On defense, he was in on nearly every play. Despite her admiration for his abilities on the field, she had little interest in dating Lyle.

As Marylin and Margie were walking down the bleachers, Lyle ran to catch their attention. He knew he'd had a great game and was inclined to share stories of their victory, but he understood he'd gotten off to a rocky start with this girl. He needed to implement a humbler approach. "I'm sorry about earlier," he began. "Will you give me a chance to make it up to you?"

The silence was deafening as Marylin stood carefully in thought. He was cute, but her quick response surprised even her. "I don't date boys that smoke."

As she continued walking towards the exit, Lyle pursued her and then shouted, "If you join me for dinner and a movie, I'll never smoke again."

Marylin paused. He seemed sincere and if a single date could have that kind of impact on a guy's behavior, how could she refuse? "Okay, but you'll need to pick me up at my house. My daddy will want to meet you before we go."

With that, it was set. Lyle got the date he wanted and Marylin would contribute to the rehabilitation of a juvenile delinquent.

CHAPTER NINE

THE NIGHT OF the date arrived. Marylin was excitedly getting ready but she was a bit worried about the interaction that would take place between Lyle and her father. Stephen was small in stature, but stern. She expected her father to establish expectations but couldn't have anticipated the exchange that was about to happen.

Lyle knocked on the door and when it opened, Stephen emerged. Now the door was fully open and Lyle noticed Marylin's father was carrying a military-grade rifle, bayonet attached.

"I never had to use this during the war son, but believe me when I tell you, I was well-trained to kill." Stephen continued, "You mess with my daughter, if she so much as comes home crying, you'll become acquainted with the tip of this bayonet."

Marylin was in the hallway bathroom and could hardly believe her ears. Her daddy had never fought in a war and rarely used a gun. She took one last look in the mirror and then sprinted to the door. "Daddy, isn't that a little dramatic?"

Stephen, keeping his eyes on Lyle, took a deep breath. Pausing for a moment, he said, "You'll have her home by ten or there will be plenty of drama. Treat her well."

Marylin loved her father and knew he'd do anything for her. Putting a little fear into courting boys was expected.

As they walked away from the home, Stephen shouted, "Remember, ten o'clock, or else." With that, Lyle and Marylin picked up the pace as they walked down the road.

"So what show are we going to see?" Marylin asked.

Change of plans."

"You promised dinner and a movie," Marylin complained.

"Dinner for sure but I'll tell you what, if after hearing the plan you'd rather see a show, that's what we'll do," Lyle said.

He then went on to explain that a friend named Cliff was hosting a carnival on their family farm. There would be food, games, a corn maze, and a pumpkin patch. Entry was $0.25 per person. With the minimum wage at $0.75 per hour, Lyle was thrilled when Cliff told him he'd get them in for free. It was the same Cliff that earlier had been told by his parents to stay away from Lyle. Regardless, they remained friends. Given Cliff's parents' encouragement to invite *everyone*, he figured that should include the guy that participated with him in the most memorable disaster he'd ever experienced.

As they walked, Lyle shared a few highlights of his last encounter on Cliff's farm. Marylin could hardly believe her ears as Lyle described the events surrounding Tank and the Blue Chevy Truck. At one point in the story, Lyle described losing Duke and then helping with Tank. Marylin thought she heard a break in Lyle's voice. She quickly looked into his eyes. There were no tears, but he sounded remorseful. *Wow. He's sensitive,* Marylin thought. She'd have never guessed this star athlete and supposed tough guy would have a tender heart, but she was struck by his sincerity. *I think I like this guy,* she mused as they continued the walk.

As they neared Cliff's house, they could hear the noise of a crowd. Music and laughter were in the air. It was a beautiful fall night and the sun was just about to set.

Cliff saw them approach and ran out to greet them. "Hey, Lyle. Who's your friend?"

Lyle's face lit up as he introduced Marylin.

Motioning toward a table, Cliff shared a few of the plans for the evening and then added, "My sister's working at the ticket booth. I told her you'd be coming and she has your tickets." He added, "Oh, and one more thing. My dad is stationed at the fishing pond. You should probably avoid that one!"

Lyle understood.

With tickets in hand, Lyle and Marylin walked around taking in the festivities. They were amazed at the effort the family had gone to in creating this carnival-like event. They had a dance floor and several carnival games. The smell of fried foods filled the air. After a stop for cotton candy, they began walking toward the corn maze when Lyle felt a tug on his arm.

"I want to go there first," Marylin said while pointing towards the pumpkin patch.

"Sure thing," Lyle responded. But he wondered, *Why in the world would she want to start there with so many other fun activities?* It didn't matter to Lyle what they did. He simply wanted to spend time with the most beautiful girl he'd ever met. She was with him tonight and he needed to make a good impression.

As they approached the pumpkin patch, they saw a table displaying a collection of various types of pumpkins.

"Did you know there are forty-five varieties of pumpkins?" Marylin inquired. "See this. It's a Cinderella Pumpkin. Oh, and there's a Big Moon, they are huge! And look there. They have a mini pumpkin collection. That one on the end is called a Munchkin pumpkin."

Of all the hobbies in the world, this girl is into pumpkins? "That one reminds me of you," Lyle teased.

"Which one?" Marylin quickly asked.

Careful to not offend, Lyle pointed. "That one on the end. I think you called it a Munchkin?" Marylin had a puzzled look on her face so Lyle quickly continued, "It's small and cute, like you."

Flattered, Marylin smiled, showing her approval, and then replied, "Good answer!"

Relieved, Lyle swayed, his hands now in his pockets. "Hanging out here in the pumpkin patch with you has inspired me." For a brief moment, they made eye contact and something inside of Lyle stirred.

"Inspired?" Marylin asked.

"Yep, from now on I'm calling you Punk. My cute little pumpkin expert."

Marylin wanted to remind him this was their first date. She wanted to remind him that she wasn't his girl. She wanted to be angry at him for comparing her to a Munchkin pumpkin. But Lyle was nice. He was cute. He was fun. He liked her. *I like this guy, I really like him*, she thought. Marylin hoped there would be more dates in the future.

Over the first semester, there would be many dates. By the time Christmas arrived, Lyle and Marylin were considered an item. Marylin's older sister, Annetta, was protective and often warned her sister about guys like him, but Marylin saw something others failed to see underneath the hard exterior. Lyle had a huge heart. Anything Marylin wanted, Lyle was going to get. If he couldn't buy it, he'd make it. He'd turned over a new leaf and was trying hard to overcome the recklessness of his past.

The New Year's Eve dance was being held in the Wheat Ridge High School gym that year. Anticipation was high. A band was hired to provide live music and the theme, *The King's Ball*, required formal attire. Marylin enjoyed working with her mom sewing a beautiful dress. Lace and delicate fabrics came together with a finished dress that made Marylin feel like a princess. Lyle told Marylin not to expect much as he didn't own a suit, much less a tuxedo.

"I don't care what you wear," Marylin expressed, "Just make sure you're on time."

Lyle wanted to impress. He was excited to learn from a friend that he could borrow a suit that would fit. Relieved, and not wanting to spoil the surprise, Lyle never mentioned it to Marylin. He'd looked forward to seeing her expression as he walked up to the front door, looking like a movie star. However, his biggest surprise had nothing to do with his attire. He couldn't contain his excitement over what he knew would be the talk of the evening. Most of Lyle's friends would borrow the family car for this date, but Lyle knew his parents wouldn't allow him to drive. He was still on probation. It would be a couple more months before his driving privileges were restored and he was committed to completing his penance.

Lyle's friend, Buddy, offered a solution, "Why don't you double with me and Jane? I've got my parent's Studebaker. You guys can go with us."

"Nope," Lyle quickly replied. "I've got other plans."

"But you can't drive," Buddy reminded.

"I know. I won't be driving, but we will be arriving in style!" Lyle smiled with an air of suspense.

For weeks, Lyle had been working late in the evenings on a solution to his problem. His parents had an old wagon behind the garage and Lyle's neighbor offered to lend him their horse for the night. The prior year he'd seen a horse-drawn carriage in the movie Cinderella. The image stuck in his mind and he modified the wagon to create a real carriage for the big night.

As the carriage approached the Novakovich home, Amy spotted Lyle from the living room window.

Marylin was still getting ready in the bathroom. *I love my dress. I look so much older.* Her pep talk in anticipation of the date was interrupted by a yell from the family room.

"You'll remember this night!" Amy exclaimed.

"Mother, I need your help with my dress. Hurry!" Marylin cried out.

Without spoiling the surprise, Amy helped make the final preparations when they heard the knock at the front door.

"Mom, I'm nervous. Would you go answer the door?" Marylin asked.

Amy quickly responded, "Your father will get the door. You've still got a minute. You know he'll want to grill Lyle a bit."

Her response calmed Marylin's nerves and she quickly applied her lipstick, took a final look in the full-length mirror, breathed deeply, and then proceeded down the hall. As she entered the family room, she saw Lyle sitting in her mother's wooden rocking chair. Her daddy's back was to her but she could hear laughter and was pleased that her father was warming up to her beau. She liked Lyle and wanted her family to like him too.

"I'm ready," Marylin interrupted.

Looking up, Lyle was speechless. She was gorgeous and truly looked like a princess. *She's the most beautiful girl I've ever seen,* Lyle thought. He stood quickly and approached Marylin.

She could see he held a corsage, a beautiful arrangement of yellow roses, her favorite color. After slipping the corsage on her wrist, Lyle grabbed her hand and walked towards the door. As they exited the house, Marylin's heart nearly stopped. There on the street was a horse-drawn carriage. She recognized Tuffy holding the reins and he was wearing his marching band outfit but had replaced the shako typically worn on his head with a formal black top hat.

Quickly she turned to Lyle. "It looks like the carriage from the movie." Only weeks earlier, she and Lyle had seen *It's A Wonderful Life* with scenes of cars and carriages intermingling on the roads. Marylin in disbelief asked, "Where did you…"

"I made it for you!"

"It's beautiful."

Lyle was pleased and then added, "I was going for Cinderella, but A Wonderful Life will do."

Tuffy helped Marylin into the carriage. Lyle walked around the carriage, admiring his handiwork. It turned out well and Marylin's reaction was even better than expected. Satisfied, he stepped up to join Marylin sitting on the wooden bench he'd completed only days earlier.

Lyle took another look at Marylin. She was glowing. Then he turned to Tuffy. "To the ball!" Driving away Lyle reflected, *This is a carriage fit for a Queen…and a King!*

As vehicles arrived at the school, the cars were directed to the parking lot. However, Tuffy previously made arrangements to take the carriage right to the front door of the gym. It added to the effect and Lyle and Marylin felt like royalty. The night was off to a great start.

"Let's dance," Lyle said.

He reached for Marylin's hand and they worked their way to the gym floor, near the band. Moments before the New Year's countdown, the band leader announced they would be playing their final number. He announced the song, a slow number that had captivated the nation just months earlier and reached Billboard's number one spot: Nat King Cole's "Too Young."

As the music began, Lyle slowly embraced Marylin and pulled her close. They swayed to the flow of the music and listened to the opening line. "They tried to tell us we're too young…"

They had heard the song dozens of times before but somehow, holding each other closely, it felt as though it was written just for them. Lyle had fallen in love the moment he caught sight of Marylin. It took time, but Marylin realized she was also falling for Lyle. This moment was one to be remembered. The song was nearly over when Marylin heard the closing lyrics, "and then one day they will recall, we were not too young at all." As the music concluded, Lyle slowly moved his head closer and with a tilt of the head, gently kissed Marylin. Her reaction demonstrated she shared his affection. Marylin's heart raced but before she could even catch her breath, the crowd began scrambling towards the stage while the band director rallied the students to prepare. The time had come for the countdown.

"Ten, nine, eight, seven, six, five, four, three, two, one. Happy New Year!"

The New Year celebration had begun. Lyle quickly pulled Marylin close and welcomed the year of 1952 with their second kiss. The year was off to a great start.

CHAPTER TEN

LIKE MOST OF the high school seniors of the class of 1952, Lyle's excitement about graduation was tempered by the reality of war. The Korean War was now in its second year and the possibility of being drafted occupied the minds of all young men. The thought of leaving Marylin worried him.

The United States passed the *Universal Military and Training Service* Act which required males eighteen to twenty-seven years of age to register for the draft. Now in Lyle's senior year, the news was buzzing of another Act of Congress being passed known as the *Armed Forces Reserve Act*. It was intended to strengthen the United States military reserves that would be called upon for a national emergency, as ordered by the President.

Young men now had two options, either take their chances in the draft or sign up for the reserves. The draft required an eight-year commitment to military service, while the Reserve was limited to two years. On March 18, 1952, Lyle turned eighteen. A decision had to be made and it became a subject of regular discussion between Lyle and his parents. Both his brothers had served honorably in the military and Lyle was committed to following in their footsteps. Conversations with Marylin were painful as they struggled with Lyle's options. After eight months of dating, Marylin was in love with Lyle and couldn't imagine being separated from him. Having lived near a military base in El Paso, she'd known many military families, and she had decided at a young age that she didn't want to live a military lifestyle.

"I'll support you either way," Marylin committed.

Lyle, now emotional, shared his decision. "I'm joining the Marine Reserves. That way I can stay in Colorado and be near you."

"But you may not get drafted," Marylin reasoned.

"True, but I might. I'm not taking that chance. I'd be off to Korea immediately and who knows when I'd be back. The reserves feel like the better choice," Lyle resolved.

In April, Lyle formally registered for the United States Marine Corps Reserve. He was required to report for Basic Training on July 1, 1952.

Lyle's pending graduation and assignment in the Reserves led to conversations that required maturity. Lyle's days of carefree, frivolous play were replaced with real-life decisions. Marylin was only fifteen, but her love of Lyle required her to also consider life differently.

Neither Lyle nor Marylin had ever paused to reflect seriously on their futures, but somehow in the spring of 1952, they grew up quickly.

Senior prom was the final school dance of the year. While most seniors were getting excited about the event, Lyle was depressed. Leaving Marylin felt like an ordeal he couldn't survive. Marylin continued to encourage Lyle and confidently expressed her commitment to waiting for him.

"You'll be back by September," Marylin reminded Lyle. "We'll only be apart for two months."

"Longest two months of my life," Lyle replied.

"Stay positive. Think of all you'll learn. It may be fun!" Marylin reassured. "Besides, we have the prom to get ready for and I want your senior prom to be amazing."

Together, they developed a plan. After boot camp, Lyle would return to Wheat Ridge and they could continue courting while Marylin finished high school. Lyle would get work in construction and complete his military obligations on weekends.

"Okay. Enough of serious stuff, let's talk about prom," Marylin said.

Lyle nodded in agreement. He was still feeling down but committed to not spoiling the final weeks of school worrying about things outside his control.

For senior prom, much less effort was made to impress, and more time was spent making their time together unforgettable. The school hired a professional photographer and Lyle and Marylin dressed up for their individual and couple photo shoots. They made an attractive couple and were excited they could capture the memories of Lyle's senior year with a quality picture of them as a couple. The dance was underway and the decorating effects were magical. Even so, Lyle and Marylin were wrestling with the reality of their imminent separation, and the recognition that their time together was short. The fascination and luster of the evening faded quickly.

"Let's get out of here," Lyle proposed.

Together they walked hand in hand past the school playing fields and towards the mountain trail just to the west.

"Let's walk to the viewpoint," Marylin suggested.

"That sounds great," Lyle replied.

Marylin removed her shoes and held them while using her other arm to hold Lyle close. It was a gorgeous night. The temperature was nearly seventy degrees, a bit unusual for an April evening in Colorado. As they sat watching the city lights of Denver in the distance, Lyle noticed Marylin was beginning to get cold. He removed his jacket and wrapped it around her shoulders. As she looked up to thank him, Lyle kissed her gently.

"Punk, I'm going to miss you so much." Then looking plaintive, continued, "You'll be waiting for me, right?"

Marylin didn't vocalize her response but embraced Lyle and held him tightly. Marylin slowly lay back, pulling Lyle closer as they kissed more passionately. Lost in the moment, they acted on the passion that stirred within each of them.

Thirty minutes later, Lyle sat gazing into the distance. *What have I done?*

Marylin remained lying on the ground while looking at the stars above her. *I've never seen so many stars. What a beautiful night.*

Her thoughts were interrupted as Lyle turned his head and looked down. "I'm so sorry. I never intended for that to happen," he whispered.

"It wasn't just you," Marylin confessed. "I love you, Lyle."

Lyle felt a mix of emotions. His guilt was immediately replaced by pure joy. "I love you too, but I know you wanted to wait until you were married."

A smile appeared as Marylin responded, "Well, *I will* marry you one day. So, we got things a bit out of order. It will all work out."

It was getting late. Lyle stood and reached his hand to assist Marylin in standing. Arm in arm, they returned to the school dance and chose to remain teenagers for the time being. Reality would unfold in the weeks ahead.

Graduation Day had arrived and Lyle was making final preparations for the ceremony. Marylin asked her parents to join her in the audience. Over the school year, they'd come to admire Lyle and knew their daughter was smitten. She was going to turn sixteen in just a few days and while too young for a serious relationship, Lyle was the only boy she'd seriously dated. Besides, they understood Lyle would be leaving for boot camp soon. With a summer apart and two more years of schooling ahead, they figured the odds of the relationship lasting were minimal.

"We've got to go." Amy motioned to Stephen. "Marylin is planning on us driving her."

Stephen knew it was important to show his daughter support in this way but he was anxious to finish work in his garden and needed the time as it was getting late in the season to be planting.

"Do this for Marylin, and I'll spend the day with you in the yard tomorrow. We'll get everything planted then."

With that, they were off. They could see the joy in Marylin's face as the principal announced the name of the next graduate to walk the stage.

"Lyle Wayne Hileman," was heard over the loudspeakers.

As Lyle finished his walk and returned to his seat, Marylin leaned over to speak to her father. "Daddy, can I ride home with Lyle and his parents? They offered to take us to dinner after."

"Sure," Stephen responded.

After a great meal with Lyle's parents, Lyle told his folks he planned to walk Marylin home.

"Okay," replied his mom. "But don't be late. Your dad needs your help in the morning."

As they began the walk, Marylin blurted out what had worried her for nearly a week. "Lyle, I'm pregnant." The tears began to flow.

Lyle paused and turned to look at his sweetheart. "Punk, that's great!"

"No, it's not great Lyle. My parents will kill me!"

As they continued the walk, they discussed how to best break the news to their parents.

"Let's get married," Lyle suggested. He then dropped to one knee and looked up into Marylin's eyes. There were still tears. He knew she was afraid but then continued, "Marylin, if you'll marry me, I promise you I'll become the man you want me to be. You won't regret it. I promise."

With that proposal, he noticed her head nodding. "Is that a yes?" Lyle excitedly asked.   Not able to find the words, Marylin continued nodding. They were in love and would be married. Now they had to convince the rest of the world, including their parents.

CHAPTER ELEVEN

"You know, you don't have to keep the baby," Stephen quickly responded. "You're not even sixteen yet."

Marylin responded even quicker, "I want this baby, Daddy. I love Lyle and we want to get married."

Stephen was speechless. The silence, while uncomfortable, gave him time to reflect on a similar conversation he'd had with his parents at nearly the same age as Marylin. In Serbian culture, the parents would select a mate for their children. Stephen's parents had already begun coordination with another Serbian family for what they believed would be a great match. Stephen wasn't in love. He wasn't involved in the decision being made for him. A fixed marriage wasn't for him and another reason he left his home. Looking now at his daughter, his thoughts returned to the matter at hand. *She's so young. She loves this boy.* He was pleased that his daughter was decisive and committed. She would need both traits if the proposed marriage were to work. Not one to look back, Stephen was determined to provide the love and support he knew his daughter would need. Without a word, his head began nodding up and down.

"Do I have your blessing?" Marylin inquired.

"Of course," her dad replied. "Now you better figure out how to break this to your mother."

The moment of excitement was immediately replaced by the dread of knowing the most difficult conversation was still ahead.

"Would you tell her for me?"

"No. You've chosen to move on to adulthood. Telling your mother will be hard, but certainly not the hardest thing that you'll deal with. You'll do fine."

Marylin waited until she knew her mother was busily focused on preparing dinner. She hoped a distraction would ease the news. She entered the kitchen. Amy's head was down as she was aggressively stirring gravy over her stovetop.

"Mom, I need to tell you something," Marylin began.

"What?" Amy turned around, her focus now on her daughter. She could see Marylin was nervous and was now concerned.

"Mom, Lyle and I are going to get married." Pausing to assess her mother's reaction, she then added, "I'm pregnant."

Without a reply, she broke into tears, quickly exiting the kitchen and fled to her bedroom. Marylin heard the door slam closed. Her mother was sobbing uncontrollably. Marylin's heart was pounding and emotion swelled within her chest. While glad it was over, it was only now that the complexity of her situation was sinking in. Paralyzed, Marylin's thoughts were interrupted by her father entering the kitchen.

He embraced his daughter, now also in tears. "Let her be. She just needs some time to digest this. It's a lot. Let's go, I want to walk around the lake. We should talk about what lies ahead."

At the Hileman home, Lyle prepared to break the news to his parents. They had discussed the subject of teen pregnancy numerous times, especially as several friends they knew were dealing with that situation within their own families. *My parents warned me. I should have known better,* Lyle thought. Although he was excited about marrying Marylin, he felt like a disappointment to his parents. A year earlier, he had promised his folks he'd make them proud, but compared to his follies of the past, this news was a huge step in the wrong direction.

Glenn and Lillian sat next to each other on the couch, while Lyle, too nervous to sit, revealed Marylin's pregnancy, and their intention to marry. His parents were calm, showing only concern. It was clear their minds had shifted to the magnitude of difficulties awaiting such a young couple.

Lillian was the first to speak. "Lyle, how could you? She's so young; this destroys her hope for a bright future."

The statement stung, but Lyle knew it was true. Other girls, upon showing signs of pregnancy, were not allowed to attend school. By the fall, Marylin would be showing and there was no chance she'd be allowed to begin eleventh grade at Wheat Ridge High School.

"I'll take care of her, Mom. Her future is with me, and I won't disappoint her," said Lyle, with a sincerity his parents couldn't deny.

Lillian, while troubled and concerned, would assist in any way she was able.

Glenn, being analytical, was focused on the implications of this new reality. "Lyle, you're leaving for Basic Training next month. How can you possibly take care of her?"

GLENN AND LILLIAN Hileman met Stephen and Amy Novakovich in June 1952. Both families had observed the budding relationship unfolding between their children, but neither couple had felt compelled to meet previously. With a grandchild on the way, and Lyle leaving town soon, they made plans quickly, arranging to meet at the Novakovich home. Anxiously, Glenn and Lillian knocked on the Novakovich door. Amy opened the door, forcing a smile, but it was obvious she'd been crying. This would be difficult for both families.

Neither Lyle nor Marylin was invited to participate in the discussion, and Amy asked them to take a walk - a long walk. The two couples sat quietly in the living room. It was strained and uncomfortable.

Glenn broke the ice with an idea he and Lillian had already discussed. "We were thinking Marylin could move in with us for the next year. They'd have a room in the basement. We don't have any other children at home."

Lillian then added, "We recognize you still have young kids at home and it may be easier on your family. We don't live far away and you'd always be welcome." She was clearly in selling mode as the thought of a grandchild on the way was exciting.

"That's very generous," Stephen said.

Lillian then moved on to the other subject of discussion. "We think the kids need to marry before the baby is born and before Lyle leaves."

With the mention of the word marriage, Amy snapped out of a trance. For days she'd been in turmoil over what her friends and neighbors would think and say. The perceived failure as a parent would tarnish the image Amy had so carefully painted as the perfect, model, Christian family. A proper marriage would require planning and elegance, and that was something she felt well qualified for. "Oh my, we don't have much time. We'll need a dress, invitations, food arrangements."

Before she could continue, Stephen burst her bubble, stating the obvious. "Amy, Marylin is pregnant. We don't need to air our dirty laundry to the entire neighborhood. I suggest we plan something less elaborate."

The families opted for a quick and quiet ceremony. Only the couple's parents would be present. Marriages in Denver and surrounding area were always reported in The Denver Post, the main news source. Amy, wanting to avoid local gossip, began looking outside of Denver for a justice of the peace. The challenge would be finding an official that was available on short notice.

The mission began a few days later. With Stephen driving, the three couples headed south to Colorado Springs, only to find that the justice of the peace happened to be in another county that day. Determined to have the marriage performed, the group headed west to Buena Vista. As fate would have it, that justice of the peace was also out of the county. Heading North, the third stop was at Fairplay, where the justice of the peace was currently unavailable. Heading farther north, the fourth stop was in Breckenridge where they encountered even more disappointment; there could be no marriage performed there, either. Finally, heading East, the final stop would be in Georgetown. By this time, it was evening, and they feared another failed attempt. Amy provided Stephen with directions to the justice of the peace. The address led them to a small house and they could see a light on inside. As they approached the porch, a white-haired woman in a green visor appeared at the door. It was after business hours she explained. Exhausted, they begged for her assistance. Moved by their determination, she invited them in. Fetching her husband, they prepared for the less-than-romantic ceremony. Observing the wedding vows, the wife of the justice was touched by the love she saw between the young couple. Now formally married, the parents shared the extraordinary effort that led them to Georgetown.

After hearing about their adventure, the justice's wife exclaimed, "What a great story! I'm going to call the Denver Post and submit it!"

The mothers shouted in unison, – "No!"

Now officially married, Lyle and Marylin each returned to their respective parents' homes. There would be no reception, no family celebration, and no honeymoon on this night. They wouldn't be spending the night together. They were now married, and for the parents, that felt like enough. Lyle and Marylin wouldn't begin their lives together immediately but were informed they'd enjoy some time before Lyle left for basic training.

Glenn had made arrangements for a honeymoon in the small village of Grand Lake, Colorado the following weekend. It was a small, beautiful mountain setting with plenty of summer activities to enjoy. A reservation for two nights was secured so Lyle and Marylin could enjoy a brief break from the reality of adulthood that was quickly approaching.

As the couple began their trek to Grand Lake, they spotted the town they had visited the prior week, Georgetown. They exited the highway and returned to the town square, near the location of their shotgun wedding. Now alone, they had time to walk the charming streets and enjoy a few of the sights.

"Lyle, look there," Marylin directed.

Lyle's eyes were now directed to a beautiful Victorian mansion from the late 1800s.   Marylin teasingly said, "Let's buy that place!"

Lyle knew she was joking but seeing the excitement in Marylin's face, he acknowledged her teasing. "Sure, but does it have to be yellow?"

"Yes. A big, beautiful yellow house in the mountains."

Lyle understood he'd need to provide shelter for his bride and soon-to-arrive child. Living with his parents in a basement would need to be temporary, very temporary. Lyle laughed. "I tell you what, I promise that before I leave for basic training, I'll paint the basement bedroom yellow. Just for you."

Undeterred, Marylin replied, "That's a good start, but someday we'll create a yellow house of our own."

When they arrived in Grand Lake, the town was bustling with activities. Shops lined a wooden boardwalk offering treats and novelties while countless tourists walked the town. After checking into their room, they walked down the street and enjoyed a game of miniature golf. They then discovered a small sandy beach area. There they tested the cold mountain lake by wading ankle-deep in the water. They then soaked in the sun to take away the chill.

"I love this town," Marylin said. "We need to come back after you finish training. Maybe this fall, before the snow comes?"

Lyle too shared in the sense of peace they experienced in this mountain paradise. "It's beautiful. I'm in."

CHAPTER TWELVE

LYLE SPENT EIGHT weeks in training with the Marine Corps Reserves. While only eighteen, he found most of the recruits shared a common story. Troubled was a common thread. It created a bond between the young men, and the stories Lyle heard convinced him he never wanted to be on the wrong side of the law again. His experiences, while difficult, were nothing compared to the problems of others. His drill sergeant was skilled at intimidating and unnerving young men, and it only took a day for all the recruits to grasp the fact that survival required strict compliance with directions. Discipline was a value that Lyle respected, and he genuinely appreciated the structure. He was learning new skills he hadn't considered while in school.

He was anxious to return to Marylin. The time away only deepened his love, and weekly letters were his best outlet for expressing his emotions. He was maturing quickly and spent hours at night reflecting on the sacrifices of his parents. He had put them through a lot and was committed to showing them a better version of himself in the years ahead.

Marylin moved in with Glenn and Lillian. No longer able to attend school, she found work cleaning homes. It didn't pay much but gave her a reason to get out of the house. She also continued to spend time with her parents and began rebuilding the trust of her mother. Amy agreed to put the past behind them and focus on preparation for the arrival of her first grandchild. Marylin introduced her mother to her favorite spot, just over the arched bridge with views of the mountains. It was there that healing began and a different type of relationship emerged. Her mother had celebrated her forty-third birthday earlier in the year and now she spoke with Marylin as a concerned friend.

A week before Lyle's return, Amy suggested they spend some time together. Walking across the bridge to their favorite spot, they spread a blanket and enjoyed an unusually warm fall afternoon. They both lay on their backs, gazing into the sky.

"You know motherhood won't be easy," Amy began. "And marriage isn't all fun and games either."

Marylin had been thinking a lot about Lyle's return and especially about their baby. Now, twenty-six weeks into her pregnancy, she was beginning to show in her belly. "Will it be painful?"

"The connection you'll have with the baby will be like nothing you've ever experienced."

"Yeah, but how painful will delivery be?" Marylin asked.

"Marylin, I've watched you care for Amy Sue and you're going to be a great mother."

"But Mom, how painful will it be?"

Amy paused. She sat up and looked across the panoramic view. Turning to look down at her daughter, still laying on the blanket, she answered, "Yes, it will be painful."

"Well, maybe I can just sleep through the delivery," Marylin reasoned.

Marylin's suggestion made Amy laugh, "You won't be sleeping, but keep in mind more than a few women have survived delivery."

Together, they enjoyed a much-needed laugh and her mother assured Marylin she'd be fine.

Upon his return, Lyle and Marylin decided to take a long drive for their first full day. It would allow them to see the emerging fall colors, take in the beauty of the mountains, and most importantly, time to discuss the approaching changes they were about to experience. They decided on a trip to the town of Estes Park. It would only take an hour to get there, and they'd heard great reports about the beauty of the surrounding area. As they arrived, they were delighted to see elk wandering the streets. It was the rut season and the sounds of bugling filled the air.

"Let's drive to Grand Lake," Marylin suggested.

"Maybe another time. It's just too far away," Lyle replied.

"Actually, we're close," Marylin explained. "Trail Ridge Road is still open and the view is supposed to be incredible. We could be there in a few hours."

With that understanding, they entered Rocky Mountain National Park and began the trek to the top. The drive followed a narrow, winding road and with each passing mile, they climbed in elevation. As they approached the summit, a sign pointed out they'd arrived at 11,796 feet above sea level. They pulled into a parking lot and found a small building offering drinks and snacks. From a sign to the side of the road, they learned of a short hike that would take them to the highest point of 12,183 feet, for a view of the surrounding arctic terrain. To Lyle, each step felt like work, as the air was thin and he struggled to catch his breath. He also noticed a significant temperature change. Immediately after beginning the hike, a strong wind began blowing and the temperature drop had him wishing he'd brought a jacket.

"Hey, slow down a bit," Lyle pled.

"Oh, come on, you just finished basic training! You should be in great shape." Marylin laughed.

Lyle smiled, took a deep breath, then committed to finish the hike. *Even pregnant, my Punk's energy is endless.*

Fortunately, it only took ten minutes to reach the top. They paused to take in the 360-degree views. It was amazing, but with the winds now blowing stronger, it was cold.

"Let's get back to the car, I'm freezing," Marylin shouted.

Back in the protection of the vehicle, Lyle turned up the heater to offset the shivering. After a minute, he reached into his pocket to retrieve a surprise for his sweetheart. "I've got something for you. Something to remember our first day back together." Extending his arm, he opened his hand and revealed a small box.

Marylin quickly unwrapped the box and opened it to find a delicate necklace with a locket. Etched on the locket was a hummingbird. "I love it."

"I knew you would," Lyle replied. "Thanks for marrying me."

They continued to traverse Trail Ridge Road but were now descending a steep, winding road. There were narrow turns that made

Marylin uneasy. The road was so narrow it appeared the car might easily roll off, tumbling to the cliffs below. The views were changing every few minutes as they left the alpine tundra and descended to the thick forest below. The park was beautiful and diverse. With the west side park exit now in view, Lyle was pleased to have discovered a new way to the mountain town that would hold so many great memories over the years that would follow.

"We're getting close," Marylin said.

"Grand Lake?"

"Yes. It's just past the ranger station."

They slowed to navigate the exit and spotted a box containing free maps of the park.

"Let's get one," Marylin said.

Lyle stopped and stepped out of the car to get a map for Marylin. As he did, a Park Ranger handed him the map.

Lyle thanked him and said, "See you again soon."

The ranger quickly replied, "No you won't, we close next week for the winter season. Maybe next spring."

Leaving Grand Lake, they drove over Berthoud Pass, almost as narrow and frightening as the newly completed Trail Ridge Road. It would be another three hours before they would reach home. In one day, they had completed a loop of some of the most magnificent mountain scenery anywhere.

Settling in with Lyle's parents was definitely an adjustment. Marylin found it easier to be there alone. With her husband home, she was now very self-conscious, and very aware that they were not alone. She longed to find a place of their own.

Lyle was anxious to find steady work. His service with the Marine Reserves now required reporting for duty one weekend each month, but otherwise, he was free to pursue whatever he desired. Glenn introduced his son to a contractor in town that was always looking for laborers. Lyle was offered a job, and he quickly proved to be the hardest worker on the crew. He was much more intent on learning than any of the other young men and had acquired leadership skills at basic training that impressed his employer. Like a sponge, Lyle would soak up every detail of the construction drawings. Even more beneficial was the exposure it gave him to a variety of professional tradesmen. He especially enjoyed working with concrete. The process of preparing the ground and setting rebar and wire mesh would never be seen after the concrete had been poured. However, he quickly learned the importance of details, even those not visible.

After the concrete was poured, he could see the evidence of his effort and knew the pad would stand forever. He also enjoyed the challenge, as time wasn't on his side. Execution mattered and it reminded Lyle of his time with team sports. You couldn't do it alone and needed to work together before the mud hardened.

Lyle's attention to detail, and desire to make every project look its best, led him to lead a crew after only two months. Now fully in charge of projects, and with a desire to impress, he needed to motivate others in order to be successful. It came naturally for Lyle. Even though he lacked height, he was stronger than most of his associates. He was very comfortable providing direction and leading others. Lyle embraced the tactics of his drill sergeant and had no problem barking demands during the frenetic pace of pouring concrete. After pouring a driveway, Lyle sent the others home for the day. Grabbing a trowel, he moved slowly around the perimeter looking for any flaw in the finish. Kneeling, he lightly ran the trowel across the concrete, careful not to apply too much pressure but enough to create a perfect edge. Finally finished, he stood and examined his work. *I love this job.* Kneeling, he reached for a screwdriver and carefully etched the letters "LWH" in the finished pad. It was perfect!

With the new year, the arrival of the baby was near. The pregnancy was exciting for Marylin glend while difficult to walk, she hadn't had morning sickness or other discomfort. That all changed on January 26, 1953. The groans and cries of his wife alerted Lyle; their baby was on the way! They had carefully prepared for the event and Lyle quickly grabbed a bag of items Marylin would need. He then assisted Marylin to the car.

Before she could get into the vehicle, a flush of water flowed down Marylin's legs. "Lyle, something is wrong."

Quickly, they drove to the hospital emergency entrance and were met by two nurses.

"Something is wrong," Lyle shouted.

Explaining the situation, the nurse tried to calm him. "Her water broke. It's normal. You're going to be a father today!"

Lyle sat waiting for any news. They had taken Marylin without him even saying goodbye and he wasn't allowed to stay with his wife. The waiting room was properly named. He would wait. What seemed like an eternity was only three hours, but finally, a doctor entered the room.   "How's Marylin?" Lyle asked.

"We need to talk. Marylin has a serious condition known as pre-eclampsia, but we're doing everything we can."

Lyle jumped from his seat and could feel his heart pounding. *What's going on?* The concern and fear he experienced caused him to nearly collapse, and he quickly sat back down. The doctor stepped quickly to assist Lyle, who appeared faint.

"We've already admitted your wife, we don't want to have to admit you too. Stay seated," the doctor encouraged.

What's going on?" Lyle asked

"It's rare. We almost lost her during delivery. Essentially, her blood pressure rose so fast she went into convulsions. We've been able to stabilize her, but she gave us all a scare. She'll need close monitoring before she's through this."

"Can I see her?

"She's sleeping and needs to rest. We've given her a sedative and don't expect her to wake for a few hours."

Seeing the worry on Lyle's face, the doctor injected, "But I can take you to see your son if you'd like. Congratulations. You're a father!"

With that, Lyle was led down a hallway and arrived at an observation area. Behind the window, he saw several babies. They were each carefully wrapped in a white cloth. Some appeared to be sleeping, others crying.

"Which is mine?" Lyle asked.

The doctor directed Lyle's gaze to a resting baby in the front row, nearest the window.

He noticed a blue postcard that read, *Hileman Boy.*

"That won't do," Lyle explained. "His name is Lyle. Lyle Stephen Hileman."

During Marylin's hospital stay, the nurses tended to her every need. When it was time for feeding, they would retrieve her son. Diaper changes were typically handled by a nurse. Her small frame was concealed by edema. Her arms, wrists, legs, and ankles were so swollen it made bending them impossible. The nurses waited on Marylin and she felt like royalty.

After five days, Lyle was informed he could take his wife and son home, but the doctor wanted to speak with them before they were discharged.

"Marylin, eclampsia is rare, especially for someone as young and healthy as you. But it can be fatal. You have a healthy, strong son, but I need to advise you not to risk another pregnancy. The probability of this happening again is high, very high."

The emotion of the news was overwhelming for both Lyle and Marylin. Seeing Marylin in tears, Lyle wrapped his arms around her and held her close. Now Lyle began to cry. He held his Punk even tighter. "We'll figure this out later," he whispered.

The difficult delivery became the subject of conversations over the next few weeks. Marylin's parents spoke with other doctors and Marylin was relieved to learn that the risk of death was far less if under a doctor's care in advance of delivery. They knew they'd want more children, but for now, they were determined to enjoy the one they had.

With Lyle working, Marylin quickly learned how difficult motherhood would be. Feeding, burping, changing diapers, and calming a screaming baby presented challenges. *Where are my nurses?* It was hard and exhausting, yet each day her love for this beautiful baby boy grew stronger. Caring for her baby brought a sense of happiness she'd not experienced before. It was satisfying to realize she'd brought a new life into the world. This felt meaningful.

It wasn't long before Marylin realized another emerging challenge. Naming their child after her husband quickly became a problem as any mention of "Lyle" created confusion. Initially, "Little Lyle" worked to differentiate the two Lyles. However, Lyle wanted to avoid the word "Little" and established a nickname he felt would carry his son confidently through life. At home, his son would be known as Lylo.

Lylo's arrival became the focus for both the Hileman and Novakovich families. He was the first grandchild and everyone's favorite. There were always arms waiting a turn to hold him. Glenn and Lillian enjoyed having their grandson in their home but quickly discovered their house hadn't been designed for a baby. The basement had been designed for storage and had no bathroom. Trips upstairs to the bathroom and the sound of a crying baby interrupted sleep nearly every night. Lyle and Marylin tried hard to soothe their baby, but as the weeks went by, it was clear the baby's primary form of communication would be disruptive.

Stephen and Amy couldn't get enough time with the baby so they initiated a weekly family dinner. It provided them some much-needed time, but also a break for Glenn and Lillian. Each Sunday, Lyle and Marylin would attend church with Amy and then arrive at her home where Stephen would have a meal prepared for the family. Lyle understood he wasn't required to attend church meetings, but he loved spending time with his wife and son. If they were going to church, he was going too.

Easter Sunday arrived, and after a special service, Lyle, Marylin, and Lylo arrived to find an amazing feast had been prepared. Stephen had roasted a pig. He loved spending a day at home and cooking was a fun distraction from the tedious work as an engineer. After a wonderful meal, Stephen was anxious to share an idea he and Amy had concocted over several weeks.

"We have an idea," Stephen began.

"Free babysitting?" Marylin enthusiastically asked.

Amy's emphatic "No!" was barely noted over Stephen's immediate response. "Even better!"

Stephen then shared the details of a plan to divide his large acreage and create a separate lot for Lyle to build a home. It would be only steps away from their home and make for easy access to the grandson they loved. Stephen had built his own home, and with Lyle's experience and construction contacts, it would be a project they could complete together.

Marylin was stunned and couldn't believe what she had heard. "Daddy, how could we afford it?"

"The site is free, and I can help you with the loan." Pausing a moment, he then added, "You can thank your mother. It was her idea."

"Mom? Really? The house can face my favorite view!"

Amy's face beamed with joy. "I know."

CHAPTER THIRTEEN

IN THE SUMMER of 1953, work was underway designing and building a home for the young family. Lyle's employer made available several designs they had recently completed and suggested that using one would save the couple money. Together, they chose a small two-story home they liked and shared the plan with Marylin's parents. All agreed it would be a great fit and they planned to pour the foundation in July.

The excitement of a new home and caring for a six-month-old child, occupied nearly every minute of Marylin's time. For Lyle, while exciting, worries about being able to afford the house prompted him to take on a second job. His work with concrete was completed early in the day and then he'd shift to his role as a carpenter, framing and finishing homes. The increased compensation was essential but the long days of work left little time or energy for being a husband or father. Both Lyle and Marylin were exhausted.

Only a year earlier, the couple had been ostracized by many in their community and neither Lyle nor Marylin had maintained connections with former classmates. Their time was consumed with building their new life. Returning home from a long day of work, Lyle was met by Marylin at the door. She was more excited than he had seen her in months.

"Lyle, guess what?" Marylin began. "We've been invited to dinner with five other couples from school. They're going to Jefferson 440; I've always wanted to go there!"

"I don't know Marylin. Money's tight. That's a fancy restaurant — and anexpensive one. Besides, who'd watch Lylo?"

"My parents will. We haven't been out or done anything fun for ages! Please?"

Seeing Marylin's face beaming, Lyle couldn't refuse.

Marylin rattled off the names of the other couples they would be joining. None of them were married, but all had attended Wheat Ridge High School.

The evening arrived and both Lyle and Marylin were excited to spend time with friends they hadn't seen since Lyle's graduation. As soon as the group was seated at the restaurant, all eyes were focused on Lyle and Marylin as they answered questions about married life and raising a child. The conversation was interrupted by a waiter who handed out menus and took orders for drinks. Lyle and Marylin ordered only water while the others partook of various spirits.

Looking at the menu and prices, Lyle felt a knot in his throat. Determined not to show any sign of concern, he looked to Marylin. "Get whatever you want, Punk."

Marylin had already noted the prices and she wasn't fooled by Lyle's casual sounding comment. This night would be a stretch. Looking again at the menu, Marylin found the least expensive entrée, Chicken Cordon Bleu. She was whispering something to Lyle when the waiter returned.

Lyle pointed to the Chicken Cordon Bleu. Trying to appear collected and relaxed, Lyle said, "We'll need an extra plate. We're going to share." Then looking at Marylin, he added, "I'm not real hungry. I had a big lunch at work."

As the night wound down, one of the more charismatic and vocal boys, Skip, reached for the bill and began figuring out the expenses for each couple. Each passed their share of the meal to Skip.

"I'll take care of this," Skip said. "You guys get the cars warmed up. The night is young; we're just getting started!"

Several minutes later, Skip appeared and jumped into one of the cars. He was laughing and grinning ear to ear. "You can thank me later." He handed each of the boys their money.

The group roared with laughter as he described what he termed "Dine and Dash." He had waited inside the restaurant until the others had left. Once certain they'd had time to reach the cars, he quickly took the cash and rushed out the door, leaving the restaurant tab unpaid.

Both Marylin and Lyle were stunned, as they listened in disbelief.

Lyle said what he and Marylin were both thinking. "Skip, that's not right. It's stealing."

"Since when is that a problem for you?" Skip replied.

Skip's words stung. Lyle's former mistakes were legendary amongst his friends. However, none of the kids knew of Lyle's determination to be a better man.

The group drove to the bowling alley and while neither Lyle nor Marylin said another word about what had happened, a sense of guilt overshadowed what might otherwise have been a fun night out. After bowling, they retrieved Lylo and then drove home without speaking a word. As they reached the front of their home, Lyle sat motionless. Marylin sensed Lyle's pain as he fidgeted with the keys.

"I feel sick," Lyle disclosed.

"Was it something you ate?" she asked.

"No, what happened after dinner was wrong. I need to go back to the restaurant. You take Lylo and get him to bed. I'll be back soon."

Lyle drove to the restaurant and asked to speak with the manager. Confessing the deception, of which he had unknowingly been a part, he apologized and promised to repay every dollar. The manager maintained a stern demeanor, but Lyle sensed he was pleased that at least one of the culprits had the decency to acknowledge the theft and make amends. They agreed Lyle could take as much time as needed to settle the debt.

When he arrived home, Marylin was anxiously waiting.

"What happened?"

"The manager agreed to let me pay it off over time," Lyle shared.

"But we don't have that kind of money. You need to get the others to settle."

"No. I don't want the confrontation, but I'm not a thief."

Over time, Lyle repaid the entire bill. He and Marylin were aware they'd outgrown their school peers but decided not to bring it up with the other couples. They also decided they needed new friends.

During the construction of their home, the need for completion was heightened as the surprising news of another pregnancy added to the pressure of getting into their own place. Marylin's issue with eclampsia was an ongoing concern. During delivery, eclampsia again set in, but this time it was anticipated and the doctors were able to minimize the effects and stabilize her. Recovery was still slow, but they were now parents to a beautiful daughter with dark curly hair. They named her Cherrie Lyn Hileman.

Living with Lyle's parents became even more challenging but the solution was approaching quickly. By Christmas of 1955, the growing Hileman Family was settling into their first home.

Building the home was an adventure and a learning experience for Lyle. It was wonderful having their own space but Lyle was overly aware of every flaw. He enjoyed the process and was determined to build another someday. His list of problems and modifications was growing and he determined if he ever were to tackle a home again, he'd do it right the first time.

His work in construction continued, but his regular income failed to meet the demands of rearing a young family. As a result, Lyle pursued additional jobs after hours. While he was often exhausted, the extra jobs paid cash daily and he discovered he was able to manage with little sleep. Typically, four to five hours was enough as his mind would race through all that was required the next day.

The stress and demands on Lyle were growing. The strain on the young couple was beginning to show. Lyle was tired and irritable most nights. Marylin often felt alone in raising their children and got little, if any, help around the house. After a typical day of hard construction work, Lyle walked in, kicked off his shoes, and fell on the couch.

"You're late," Marylin said in frustration.

Lyle was exhausted but quickly responded, "Somebody's got to bring in the money. Besides, it's not like I'm out late with the boys. I came straight home."

"Well next time, tell me. Dinner is in the refrigerator."

Then Lyle asked, "How about warming that up and bringing it to me in the family room?"

"You need to step it up, Lyle. I've got the kids. You can get it yourself," Marylin shouted.

"Step it up?" Lyle shot back. "I'm working two jobs to provide for this family. All you have to do is spend time at home with the kids. I'm killing myself trying to make ends meet. Maybe you should step it up!"

"You don't do anything around here to help with our kids," Marylin returned fire as she marched to the front door. She slammed the door closed and began her trek to her parents' home. She marched furiously towards the bridge that ran between their houses. Having crossed the creek, she proceeded up the hill. She was exhausted and angry, and her mind raced as she hiked the rest of the way.

I can't do this anymore. I get no help from him. He never offers to help and then he yells at me! Her pace slowed as she approached her parent's back door. *What am I supposed to say to my parents? Is this the end of my marriage? They never expected it to work. How will I ever face my friends? Am I going to let our marriage fail?*

These and other questions began to sink in. She knew she loved Lyle but for weeks she had failed to show appreciation for his efforts. He was changing and not once did she compliment him on the traits she admired. She was so busy with the kids that she hadn't considered how Lyle was dealing with his challenges. Now standing on the doorstep, Marylin took a deep breath. She then turned around and began walking slowly down the hill. Seeing the home her husband and father had built, she began to feel selfish. She wasn't about to fail. She wasn't going to quit. She was determined to change her attitude and show appreciation. Thoughts continued to race through her mind/ I'm not going to prove our parents right - we were not too young. This marriage is not a mistake."

As she neared her home, she spoke out loud, "Things always work out. Everything is going to work out."

WORKING THINGS OUT led to a conversation on a subject that hadn't previously been discussed in their relationship. Lyle knew religion was important to Marylin but never considered himself a religious person. He believed in a God or a Creator, but never really spent time thinking deeply about theology. With the strain on the marriage, Marylin asked Lyle to make a deeper commitment to their religion. He reasoned that any faith that forged a girl like Marylin was worth studying. However, he hesitated to join a church he knew little about.

Marylin's brother Mike had just returned home from serving two years as a missionary for their church. Lyle agreed to have Mike come by and teach him the fundamental beliefs.

"Lyle, you don't need to take my word for anything. I don't want you to. If you'll read and study, you will find out for yourself," Mike testified.

Lyle approached his study of religion like every other interest. He made it a priority to read. He was unafraid to ask questions and with Marylin's support, he learned to pray. Lyle was still learning the basics of his newly adopted faith when early one morning he was reading about the resurrected Jesus Christ. He read how Thomas doubted. *I think I'm a lot like him*, Lyle pondered. As the Savior appeared and invited Thomas to come and feel the prints on his hands and feet, Lyle felt something. Reading more of Thomas's reaction, Lyle found himself weeping. "Marylin, it's true. It happened."

"What are you talking about?" she asked.

Lyle shared his experience and Marylin knew Lyle was impacted by the Holy Ghost for the first time in his life.

Over the next few weeks, Lyle digested everything he could get his hands on and eventually he asked his brother-in-law, Mike, to baptize him.

Lyle's new interest in religion certainly didn't solve all the early marital challenges they faced, but he now had even greater motivation to work things out. One of the teachings he found most fulfilling was the belief that marriage could last forever. He and Marylin could be together, not just "until death," but forever. No other doctrine would be of more motivation than this to Lyle.

Shortly after joining the church, Lyle was asked to serve as a missionary. Not full-time as his brother-in-law had, but for a few hours each week. He reluctantly accepted the assignment with his limited experience and knowledge, but he was bolstered knowing he would work closely with a lifetime member by the name of Jack Messervy. Only eighteen months earlier, Lyle was sitting with missionaries to learn the principles of The Church of Jesus Christ of Latter-Day Saints. He felt inadequate but determined to give his best.

On a summer evening in 1956, Lyle and Jack knocked on the door of Glen and Joan Ryder. Joan remained in the kitchen while her husband went to answer the call. As she listened to the conversation, she could tell it was someone discussing religion. Many missionaries of various faiths that had knocked on their door before. Neither Glen nor Joan had an interest in converting, especially as they remained committed to their current congregation, though they rarely attended.

"My name is Lyle Hileman and this is Jack," Lyle began.

Joan couldn't resist. She recognized the voice and carefully walked towards the family room to sneak a peek at the young man she assumed would have been incarcerated by now. Lyle was dressed in a suit and white shirt and looked sharp. More amazing to Joan was the message he shared about Jesus Christ. She had no interest in changing religion but was astounded that this former troublemaker had changed so dramatically. Glen quickly thanked them for the visit but declined their offer to learn more.

"Glen, I can't believe that's the same guy we knew in high school," Joan exclaimed.

Lyle was changing and in only a few short years, it appeared that the changes were shaping him into a better man.

CHAPTER FOURTEEN

HAVING COURTED, MARRIED, and given birth to two children, Marylin missed out on many of the rites of passage most teenagers enjoy. Also, she had never learned to drive a car. Most youth in the area began driving in their early teens. But Marylin's path had focused her attention on other things. Now eighteen, she sensed the time had come. She needed a car.

"Lyle, I want you to teach me to drive," Marylin pled.

"I can do that."

"And I think we need another vehicle. With you gone so much, I really need transportation."

"We can't afford a car right now. You know you can always borrow my mom's car, right?"

Now getting a bit frustrated, Marylin expressed her real concern. "I need to be able to drive. It's embarrassing always calling friends for rides. I need a car."

"Okay, okay. I may have a great solution. A guy at work is selling a vehicle. I'll see what he wants.

The next day, Lyle returned home, followed by his newly purchased possession, a 1954 Chevy pickup truck.

"That's it?" Marylin questioned. "I thought you'd be looking for a car."

"Yeah, but I got a great deal and besides, she's a beauty, isn't she?"

"But Lyle, it's a truck! And it has a stick shift. I'm already nervous and that looks complicated."

"You'll do fine. I'll have you up and driving in no time."

It took several minutes to adjust the seat and mirrors to fit Marylin. To compensate for her petite frame, a cushion was used to provide a lift to ensure she could see over the dash and hood. The mirrors were moved to provide visibility on both sides. With these tasks now complete, the driving lesson began.

"Okay, put it in reverse," Lyle instructed.

"How?" Marylin responded.

"It's easy. Just push the stick on the column up." Lyle pointed to the shifting stick.

There was a loud grinding sound that startled Marylin, but not nearly as startling as the angry shout from the passenger seat. "Stop! You've got to push in the clutch."

Marylin was now shaking and responded, "I don't know what you're talking about."

Lyle had failed to explain a few of the basics that would be required, and he knew his lack of patience and temper would only get him in trouble. He was relieved when Marylin quickly proclaimed, "Never mind. I'll teach myself!"

After Lyle left for work, Marylin approached the most patient man she knew. "Daddy, can you teach me to drive?"

Stephen's reply was calm and assuring. "You bet."

Her father explained the role of the clutch, turn signals, and breaks. She was told how to slowly press the accelerator while slowly releasing the clutch. Within a few hours, she had a grasp on the basics.

The following day, Marylin had to run errands. There was no need to ask anyone for a ride and the independence felt incredible—until she got behind the seat of the truck. Taking a deep breath, she pressed the clutch and lifted the stick shift to reverse. As she released the clutch and pressed on the gas, the car jerked and the engine stopped. It took several attempts but she eventually got the vehicle out of the driveway and onto the street. Putting the truck into first gear was a success and she slowly made her way down the road. She was making good progress until reaching Wadsworth Boulevard. Ahead she saw the red light and knew she needed to slow to a stop. Successfully stopping the vehicle, she nervously awaited the light to turn green. She put the car in neutral and then noticed several cars approaching from her rearview mirror. As the light turned green, Marylin struggled to get the truck in gear. The man behind her lost patience and began honking his horn. This only added to the pressure, and in her effort to hurry, Marylin accidentally put her vehicle in reverse before hitting the gas. The truck lurched in reverse and bumped the gentleman's truck rather hard. Now further distressed, she tried again but was still in reverse and hit his truck for a second time. Finally, she got her truck into first gear. She crossed Wadsworth and pulled over to assess the damage. As the man followed closely behind, she was surprised as he yelled out the window while driving past her. He never stopped and Marylin was relieved she avoided dealing with the fallout of her first accident…and second! The man most likely determined that stopping would expose him to the risks of what could have been a third accident.

It didn't take long before Marylin successfully met all the requirements to secure her first-ever driver's license. She loved the newly found independence. Her truck was in good shape and while a bit cramped, it had enough room for her children when necessary.

CHAPTER FIFTEEN

MARYLIN HAD ALWAYS wanted a large family. However, after two problematic pregnancies, Lyle felt they shouldn't press their luck. They had a son and a daughter and were already juggling the challenges that came with a young family.

"Lyle, I feel like we need to have another child," Marylin explained.

This wasn't news for Lyle but his silence suggested to Marylin that he wasn't on board.

"I was thinking…"

"Punk, I can't lose you. The doctor told us how dangerous it would be."

"Lyle, I was just thinking we should have another son and name him after your father," Marylin said.

Now completely aligned, Lyle affirmatively nodded. He had never discussed it with Marylin but had often thought it would be a great way to honor his dad. *He put up with so much.*

"Okay. But let's make sure the doctors are good with the decision," Lyle said.

Marylin met with her doctor. While there were concerns over the impact to her kidneys and liver, he felt confident they could monitor her condition and get through another pregnancy. In March 1958, they welcomed a new baby to the family, a daughter, Kim Marie Hileman.

ONLY MONTHS AFTER the birth of Kim, Lyle's father, Glenn, went to the hospital for a routine surgery to remove a growth on his neck. The procedure went well but during the night, Glenn fell from his hospital bed. With no attendant aware, he bled out on the hospital floor and died. The family was devastated. It was so unexpected and left so much undone and unsaid. Lyle had hoped to demonstrate his love for his parents over their senior years and now at only sixty-three, his father was gone.

"Mom, anything you need, you know you can count on me," Lyle consoled.

The grief was overwhelming and all Lillian could do was nod. Turning to Marylin, Lyle added, "I know we just had our third child but I want to try again—for a son."

Marylin's expression reflected her joy. "Absolutely. And we'll name him after your father."

TIME FLEW BY and Marylin was now carrying her fourth child. Again, they consulted with physicians to ensure her safety. Each previous pregnancy presented challenges at birth but none had been difficult to carry. Marylin felt she was born to nurture and raise a large family and she enjoyed the miracle growing inside her, but this pregnancy was different.

Marylin began having morning sickness. She'd heard stories from others about the difficulties associated with the early weeks but hadn't experienced them herself in her previous pregnancies. Now, she could hardly get through a day without throwing up. She was also exhausted. Caring for three other children was a handful on its own, but now feeling poorly, the pregnancy was wearing on her. "I sure hope we get a boy because I won't be doing this again. I'm miserable."

With the third trimester underway, other symptoms of pre-eclampsia emerged. Marylin was experiencing severe headaches and her ribs would ache so much that she'd throw up. Numerous trips to the doctor revealed dehydration so she began drinking a lot more fluids. Of course, her three-year-old couldn't understand why mommy couldn't play. Lylo and Cherrie tried to help, but there were limits to what a nine and seven-year-old could do. Marylin's mom was always nearby and available to help but the greatest aid came from her younger sister, Amy Sue, now fifteen. After school, Amy Sue would run across the bridge and do basically anything she could to help Marylin during her final weeks of pregnancy. Years earlier, Marylin enjoyed caring for her baby sister, and now roles were reversed. Marylin needed the help and Amy Sue was glad to provide it.

On May 17, 1961, Glenn LeRoy Hileman II was born. This birth was by far the most difficult and nearly killed Marylin. Her blood pressure was elevated. She went into seizures and for a moment in the delivery room, the doctors thought they'd lost her. After the delivery, her doctor told her to enjoy her fourth child. It had to be her last. After nine months of pain and suffering, the doctor received no argument from either Lyle or Marylin.

The ordeal brought home just how reliant Lyle was on Marylin. There was no way he could manage four children as a single father. He wasn't about to risk losing his Punk. She required ten days of rest in the hospital. Prior to discharge, Marylin's doctor asked to speak with the couple.

"I'd like to see you in a month. I suggest we perform a tubal ligation."

"What's that?" Marylin asked.

"It's a quick and easy surgical procedure, severing the fallopian tubes and cauterizing the ends. Essentially, it makes pregnancy nearly impossible."

Lyle and Marylin had plans, plans of rearing their family together, and the procedure was understood by both to be essential.

It was a beautiful Sunday morning in the middle of summer. The kids were still sleeping. Lyle awoke and noticed Marylin was already up. Longing for just a bit of relaxation, he paused long enough to enjoy the quiet of the morning. He could hear the birds outside the window, quite the contrast to the sounds that would begin shortly from an awakening household filled with toddlers. For just a moment, he was going to take it all in. The sounds were soon enhanced by the smell of pancakes and bacon. The aroma became too much to withstand, and he decided to help. Entering the kitchen, he saw Marylin busy preparing breakfast. Barely twenty-five, and now having delivered four children, Lyle was amazed at how fit she remained. Motherhood suited her well and Lyle found her even more beautiful as the years passed.

He slowly approached from behind and wrapped both arms around his Punk's waist. "It sure smells good in here! Should I wake the kids?"

"No, let them sleep. I need to talk to you. Have a seat. I'll bring your breakfast to the table."

Lyle was puzzled. It was unusual to eat Sunday breakfast without the kids. *Perhaps she needs some quiet time too.* Marylin watched as Lyle poured the maple syrup over his stack of cakes.

"So, what do we need to talk about?" Lyle asked.

Marylin watched as he reached for a strip of bacon. Taking a deep breath, she reached across the table and grabbed Lyle's hand. The look on her face suggested she was about to share something of significance.

Concerned, he stopped eating and stood. He walked towards Marylin and slowly knelt next to her chair, "Is everything alright?"

"You'd better sit down," Marylin instructed.

"You're making me nervous. What's going on?"

Marylin smiled. Pausing for another deep breath, she spoke, "Trust me. We've got good reason to be nervous!" She went on to share the biggest shock of their married life. Marylin was pregnant again.

"Impossible," Lyle responded, in complete shock. "The doctor said he tied your tubes. He said our fourth would be our last. He said—"

Marylin interrupted, "Lyle, we're having a baby. We need to get ready."

IN JUNE OF 1962, Lyle and Marylin welcomed their fifth and, this time, final child. The boy was named Wayne Evan Hileman and he was considered a true miracle. Not expected, and with no complications, this pregnancy went smoothly. Marylin was relieved and Lyle was grateful to God for not taking the love of his life.

CHAPTER SIXTEEN

Supporting a large family took a toll on Lyle. He loved his work but it required taking on multiple side jobs to make ends meet. While pouring cement, another worker shared that the Denver Fire Department was hiring. The more he learned, the more interested Lyle became. He had little concern over the strength and agility requirements but understood the written exam was challenging. In addition to a basic understanding of emergency medical procedures, it would also require a deep understanding of math, chemistry, and physics. None of these were subjects Lyle studied while in school. The truth was, he was a poor student. However, this job came with full benefits, a decent salary and a chance to earn a pension. And best of all, the work only required nine 24-hour shifts per month. This could leave plenty of time for his construction work. Rather than risk the embarrassment of failure, he decided he'd not tell anyone of his pursuit, just in case it didn't go well.

"Marylin, you won't believe it," Lyle called as he ran through the door. "I got it. I did it."

"What did you do?" Marylin inquired. She then bent down to pick up one-year-old Wayne.

"I tested first in my class. I passed with flying colors."

"Test? What test?"

Lyle then realized he hadn't mentioned his application to anyone. "Punk, you're looking at the newest recruit to the Denver Fire Department!"

Lyle's new work was a good fit - but not perfect. Sure, the pay was better and the benefits were outstanding. However, it would require living within Denver city and county. Their home was only a few minutes from Denver but outside the city limits. They held an emotional bond with their first home but also recognized the new job would provide financial stability previously out of reach. With only a few weeks to secure residency, they began searching in a new development known as Bear Valley. Marylin knew leaving her first home would be hard, especially as her father had sacrificed so much to make it possible. But with a growing family, it was necessary.

The home sold quickly and with the money from the sale, Lyle had the means to purchase a home. Amy and Stephen didn't take the news well but reluctantly supported the decision and acknowledged the benefits it provided the young family. Their new home wasn't ideal but it had only been completed a few years earlier and was in a good neighborhood. Most importantly, it was affordable and in the city limits of Denver. The home was more spacious than the prior home, but it failed to meet Lyle's expectations of quality. Now a Denver resident, he was determined to begin looking for another site that would accommodate his interest in building a new home for the family.

Bear Valley was a thriving community. Marylin loved her new neighbors and had grown especially fond of an elderly couple living across the street. They had no children and "adopted" the Hileman children as their own grandchildren. They loved spending time with Marylin and her children and offered to babysit anytime.

One evening, Marylin crossed the street to retrieve her children, now at play with Grandma Shay. "Wow. Your dining room set is beautiful."

"Why, thank you," Grandma Shay replied. She then shared what seemed unlikely. "You should get one for your empty dining room. The new department store has several models and you don't even need to pay for it now. I bought it on credit! They're having a sale. I'll watch the babies tomorrow so you can check it out."

Marylin could hardly wait to get the kids off to school and to drop off Glenn and Wayne with Grandma Shay. Browsing the department store was exhilarating for Marylin. Having a new and larger home, she enjoyed daydreaming of how each piece could enhance their space.

"Hello, ma'am," she heard from behind.

Turning around, Marylin saw a sharply dressed young man, likely close to her age.

"How can I help you?"

Marylin then proceeded to describe the dining room in her neighbor's home and asked to be shown their inventory. Then she spotted it. It was amazing. Lightly stained wood with white cushioned chairs that featured an intricately designed back. The table first drew her in but then the salesman shared that it came as a set. The table, chairs, buffet, and hutch were the most beautiful in the store.

Marylin loved it. "I understand you sell on credit, is that right?" Marylin asked.

"Of course," came the reply.

Before she knew it, she had filled out a form and made the purchase. No money exchanged hands and it was to be delivered later that week.

The day after delivery, Lyle returned home from a twenty-four-hour shift at the fire station. As he walked in the door, he was stunned by what seemed to have magically appeared overnight in the dining room. "Marylin!" Lyle yelled. "Where did this come from?"

Marylin ran to the dining room to greet him. "We finally have a dining room set. Isn't it beautiful?"

Her excitement was quickly replaced with concern as she noticed the scowl on Lyle's face. His body was tense and his fists were clinched. He then demanded, "It's going back."

"It's not going back!" Marylin shouted.

Lyle's frustration was more than he could contain. "We don't have the money. How did you even buy something like that without me?"

"Since when do I need you to give me permission to buy anything? I don't ask for your permission at the grocery store. I never checked in with you before paying for the diaper service. I didn't even ask you about spending money for the clothes on your back."

Lyle took the argument to another level. "Just what kind of man would sell something like this to a woman? I want to know the store name and salesman who took advantage of you."

"Nobody has taken advantage of me except you! When was the last time you helped clean the house? Or prepared a meal or even did yard work?" Marylin broke into tears.

Seeing Marylin cry caused Lyle to pause. But he wasn't finished with his eruption. "Just how do you expect me to pay for this?"

Marylin felt a rush of guilt for making such a large purchase spontaneously. In hindsight, she wished she'd discussed it with Lyle, but he was rarely home with multiple jobs and had never before questioned her purchases. Their approach to finance was for Lyle to earn the money and let Marylin pay the bills.

Lyle was fuming. The stress of working multiple jobs was taking its toll and he clearly wasn't at his best. Before he said something he'd regret, he quickly changed clothes and left for his construction job. When he returned home late that night, Marylin was already in bed. He wasn't sure if she was asleep but decided to just clean up and get some sleep himself. The next morning, he left for another shift at the firehouse. He left without saying goodbye.

It was a slow day and with no active calls, Lyle had plenty of time to reflect. *I've really screwed up,* he thought while sitting alone at the station house. *I've never seen her so upset.*

The following morning, he arrived home a bit earlier than usual. He quietly opened the door and walked into the dining room to arrange his peace offering. "It looks so much better now! Come take a look, Punk."

Marylin was feeding her five children in the kitchen. Still hurt, her curiosity rose and she began walking towards the dining room where Lyle was standing.

"I really like it; it just needed some added color. I'm sorry. I've just been under a lot of stress." Lyle motioned towards the table where a vase of yellow daffodils adorned the center of the table. "Do you still love me?"

"I'm sorry too, Lyle. They're beautiful. Of course, I love you." She rushed to hug her sweetheart.

"I'm the one who needs to apologize. I should never have jumped all over you to begin with."

Now in tears, the couple embraced for the first time in more than three days. It was clear they had both been bottling up a lot of stress and for a few moments, they embraced as if they could squeeze the earlier episode away.

Lyle broke the silence. "I think we should work on a budget together."

Marylin's smile spoke volumes. "A budget? I prefer my approach. But I'll be more careful and you just make sure we have enough in deposits!"

Lyle laughed at Punk's approach. "That's a given, but if we're ever going to build another house, we need to begin saving."

FIVE KIDS, LYLE thought to himself. It was time he began planning for the new house, a bigger house. And this one would leverage the skills he'd mastered over the past ten years working on countless construction sites. Concrete work, framing, and detailed craftsmanship were skills Lyle had developed and he could hardly wait to get started building another home. After a search, a site was found only minutes west of the current residence. The site was a full acre and surrounded by several other lots. There would be plenty of room to build the house, plus a wood shop for Lyle and a garden for Marylin. The site was purchased and work began. Along with the house, Lyle designed a rose garden for his sweetheart. It was in the shape of a heart and included a small bench where he hoped he'd spend time relaxing with Marylin.

MANAGING FIVE CHILDREN was exhausting. It was especially challenging as Marylin's only transportation was their truck and it was only practical for three passengers. Feeding a family of seven required planning and Marylin had developed recipes and casseroles that simplified the task. One afternoon, groceries were needed and with her shopping list in hand, Marylin asked Cherrie to watch Kim and Wayne, now six and two.

"Lylo, grab your brother, Glenn, and let's go. I could use your help," Marylin instructed.

Now in the truck, they began the short drive to the grocery store. As Marylin left the neighborhood and turned onto Hampton Avenue, Lylo reached to change the station on the AM radio. Suddenly, the passenger door flew open. Marylin gasped, screamed and brought the truck to a stop. In shock, she looked into the rear-view mirror to see her three-year-old son, Glenn, lying in the street. Lylo jumped from the truck to retrieve his brother. He gathered him in his arms and raced back to the truck.

"Mom, I think he's okay."

Paralyzed with fear, Marylin couldn't respond. She sat, gazing into the distance.

"Mom, maybe we should go to the doctor," Lylo said. "Mom!"

Marylin finally snapped out of her trance and turned to look at her toddler. Glenn looked into his mother's face and cried, "Ice cream."

A detour was made. Glenn got his ice cream and every other treat he requested while shopping. That night, Marylin knelt in prayer and again thanked her Father in Heaven for His protection. She had witnessed a miracle she would never forget.

CHAPTER SEVENTEEN

THE HILEMAN FAMILY thrived in their new home. Their son, Lylo, had developed an interest in gymnastics. By the time Lylo entered ninth grade, he had already proven to be stronger and more accomplished in the sport than any of his fellow competitors. It came as no surprise to those who knew him. As the firstborn, his father would relentlessly push him to be his best. In academics, nothing but A's would be tolerated. Early in his sophomore year, Lylo was excited to share with his mother an exciting opportunity at school. He was encouraged by a teacher to participate in school government.

"My friend Stan and I are going to run for the student body presidency. Stan will be president, and I'll be the vice president."

Hearing the excitement in his son's voice, Lyle interrupted. "Why Stan for president? If you run, you should run as president. You're smart enough and will work hard. Never settle."

Lylo had learned it wasn't productive to argue with his father. He had been taught to always excel and to aim for the stars. Rather than argue, he decided to rework the plan. Not only was he smart, but he was also popular, and persuasive. He knew Stan would be okay with the revised plan. As expected, they won the election. Lylo was a lot like his father!

Lylo showed promise as a sophomore and his gymnastics coach mentioned college scholarships would likely be available if he continued to improve. Lyle understood his son had real talent and determined his investment in gymnastics equipment could be the ticket to college scholarships. Lyle had already built his woodshop and installed the rose garden for Marylin. He also created a large garden where the family could grow corn, peas, tomatoes, and many other vegetables. But there was still room for another addition, a complete area for Lylo and his friends to practice. Lyle poured the concrete pad and had a friend weld a framework for other gym equipment.

Together, Lyle and Lylo visited the Gym Master Distributor in Denver. The owner knew of Lylo and his accomplishments. He was a bit surprised that they had an interest in buying an entire gym but when Lyle offered to trade his construction skills, a deal was forged. A trampoline was the focal point and Lyle constructed a shed to hold the other items. Parallel bars, a high bar, a pommel horse, and mats were all secured. But the highlight was the installation of steel rings. "Let's get outside and practice," Lyle invited his son. It was less of an invitation and more of a requirement. "Your job is to be the best and my job is to pay your bills." He then reminded Lylo of the other requirement. "And don't forget, I only pay your allowance if you get A's."

The new home had everything Lyle, Marylin, and their five children could hope for and was the center of family life. As for the investment in the backyard gym, Lylo won back-to-back state championships and secured several full-ride scholarships.

With the expense of rearing a large family, Lyle took on yet another business venture. He founded Arrow Concrete Sawing along with another firefighter. Together, they purchased the necessary equipment and got to work. This was now Lyle's third job and while he needed little sleep, the physical toll on his body was evident. After a twenty-four-hour shift at the Fire Department, Lyle would try to navigate his construction work and concrete sawing business. Demands on time were taxing. The investment in a new business, plus the expenses of a new home were mounting. Even though he was only thirty-five years old, his schedule wasn't sustainable and it finally caught up with him. Lyle suffered a stroke.

"Marylin, he must slow down," the doctor explained. "He's lucky you got him here so quickly or the damage would have been more severe."

"I thought strokes only happened to old people," Marylin replied.

"Generally, that's true. But there are other causes. Has he been dealing with difficult work issues? Is he under any stress?"

"He's been working multiple jobs for years. Stress is what drives him," Marylin explained.

"Not anymore. He needs to slow down a bit."

Lyle's speech was impacted only for a short time. Fortunately, his mobility and memory remained intact. After a few days of rest, he felt good enough to return to the fire station but upon his return home, he found his spouse waiting at the door.

"I want you to sell the business. I need you and it simply isn't worth risking your health by holding three jobs."

Lyle understood his lifestyle wasn't sustainable but was driven by his ambition to provide well for the family. "But Punk, we have so many financial obligations."

Anticipating his concern, Marylin then shared her solution. "I'm going to find a job. With the kids all in school, I've got time and want to help."

Reluctantly, Lyle agreed to support Marylin's efforts. She began with a search through the newspaper want ads. While there were many offers of employment, most required a college degree or minimally, graduation from high school. With neither on her resume, Marylin was drawn to the ads in the restaurant and service industries. One job stood out from the others as it offered a significantly higher wage and referenced additional compensation from tips. Excited to pursue the job, Marylin called and set up a time for an interview. On the day of the interview, Marylin carefully dressed in her Sunday best attire. She was a hard worker and determined to impress the potential employer. She drove about fifteen minutes to East Colfax Avenue to an office building surrounded by numerous restaurants, bars, and motels. As she entered, a young receptionist greeted her.

"I'm here for an interview," Marylin shared.

"Great. Have a seat. Mr. King will be with you shortly."

As she waited, she couldn't help but notice the numerous photographs and awards on the walls. She thought, *Mr. King must be a very important individual.* Marylin recognized many of the celebrities and political figures from TV and newspaper articles.

Now feeling a little intimidated, her exploration of the photographs was interrupted by the receptionist. "Mr. King will see you now."

As she entered the office, she was in awe of the spacious accommodations. Mr. King stood from behind his desk and walked towards Marylin, extending his hand. "So, you're looking for work?"

Marylin energetically responded, "Oh yes, with my five children now in school, the timing is right, and we can use the extra money."

"Hmmmm. I don't think you'd be a good fit for the job."

"I'm very good with people, I work hard and know I could be successful," Marylin persuaded.

"Yes, but," Mr. King began before Marylin interrupted.

"Can you just give me a chance? You really won't regret hiring me."

Thinking carefully, Mr. King paused. Leaning back in his leather chair, his eyes looked up and down, carefully evaluating Marylin's appearance.

Why is he looking at me like that?

"Let me see you dance."

"Dance?"

"Young lady, do you know the kind of work you're here for?"

"Yes, the ad said something about serving in a restaurant."

Mr. King then clarified, "Well, we do serve food and drinks, but were hiring strippers. I can see you're not the type."

Now embarrassed, Marylin realized she was in an interview with the owner of Sid King's Crazy Horse Bar! Later, she was even more shocked to learn of Sid King's reputation as the Sultan of Striptease. Marylin quickly determined she needed to go back to secure her graduate equivalency degree, or GED, a high school general education degree. With a degree, her options would expand.

After six months, Marylin had satisfied all requirements and had her GED in hand and she actively began searching for work. When Lyle returned from work, Marylin was excited to share her news. "I applied for a job at Fort Logan Mental Health Center. They will pay me two hundred sixty dollars each month plus the costs of getting an associate degree in social work. I've accepted the position."

Lyle wasn't thrilled but knew that he needed to slow down. Also, with all the kids now in school, the demands of home life had lessened. Fortunately, Marylin's position offered flexibility in her schedule that allowed her to navigate the various activities of a growing family. The challenge of juggling family, work, and school took its toll, but two years later, Marylin graduated from the Denver Metropolitan College summa cum laude. Her success in school led to a promotion at Fort Logan and Marylin felt a rush of satisfaction reflecting on how far she'd come. She appreciated how hard Lyle worked for the family and now felt empowered to provide some relief for him. The expenses of rearing a family were growing but having Lyle carry the whole load was not worth the risk to his health.

Returning from work one afternoon, Marylin saw something that grabbed her attention. Lyle was playing with the kids on the grass. He was tossing them in the air, rolling around on his hands and knees and genuinely enjoying his children. *That's the icing on the cake. He's having fun being a father.*

CHAPTER EIGHTEEN

BEAR VALLEY WAS an idyllic community. Many new friends were made as homes were being constructed rapidly all around them. Marylin regularly attended church services with the kids, but Lyle's work at the fire department often required working on Sundays. On the days he could attend, he found other options he'd convinced himself were more pressing. Even though getting the family dressed, fed, and to meetings was difficult, Marylin was determined her children would have a solid foundation of faith. She wanted them to learn important values and an hour each week in Sunday School complimented the teaching she did at home.

"Lyle, I want you to start coming with us to church," Marylin said.

"I go when I can," Lyle replied.

"Seriously. When was the last time you attended with us? Besides, the kids look up to you and you should be an example for them."

Lyle understood. He enjoyed the times he would attend, but always seemed to have something more pressing on his mind. Thinking about his influence on the kids, Lyle committed to making church a higher priority.

Lyle hadn't grown up going to church. He felt out of place and inferior to the other members. Most others had spent a lifetime learning stories of the Bible and understood doctrines that Lyle was still only beginning to learn.

One Sunday after a meeting, a stranger approached Lyle and confidently reached out to shake his hand. "Hi, my name is Max, Max Pitcher. You must be Glenn and Wayne's father."

Max was tall, handsome, and highly educated, and Lyle initially thought they'd have little in common. Max was a geologist by profession and was a very organized and a businessman. In addition, he volunteered to serve the congregation in a position referred to as the bishop. Lyle worked with his hands and as a firefighter, he was considered a blue-collar worker. However, he soon realized they shared many interests, especially a love for the outdoors.

A few weeks after meeting Max, Lyle received a phone call from his ecclesiastical leader and new friend, Bishop Pitcher. He asked Lyle to speak at a Sunday service. Now nervous, Lyle agreed and asked what subject he should address.

"Sabbath day observance," Bishop Pitcher directed.

The invitation to speak scared Lyle. He knew there would be more than three hundred in attendance and he had no prior public speaking experience. On top of that, the subject was one that concerned him. The last thing he wanted was to be a hypocrite.

Reluctantly, he agreed and spent two weeks in study to ensure he could get through a fifteen-minute address. On the day of the presentation, Lyle became more nervous by the minute.   "You'll do fine, Lyle. You've prepared and practiced. Try and relax," Marylin coached.

The talk was going well, although Lyle was afraid others could see his leg shaking. He'd practiced speaking slowly but found himself speeding up because of nerves. The time was moving quickly and Lyle was nearing the end of his remarks when he heard loud laughter from the congregation. It startled him. He hadn't included a joke. He wasn't even trying to be funny, but the laughter was impossible to ignore. He paused, smiled, and then went on to finish.

After, he approached Marylin to understand what the cause of the laughter had been.

"Lyle, you kind of butchered a famous Bible story from the New Testament."

"I did? What story?"

Marylin smiled and then explained, "You told the story in Luke where Jesus healed a man on the Sabbath day and was criticized by the Pharisees."

Lyle nodded reflecting his agreement. "Yeah. It's a great example of times when we still have to fulfill obligations, even on the Sabbath. It's a good example of how I'm often required to work at the fire department".

He then returned to the question at hand. "But that's not a funny story."

"You're right. The Savior asked which of them would fail to rescue an ass or ox that had fallen into a pit," Marylin explained.

"Yes. That's what I said," Lyle claimed.

"Well, not exactly," Marylin laughed. "Your notes referred to helping an ox in the mire. But that's not what you said."

With Marylin now laughing again, he again asked, "Why did everyone start laughing?"

"Lyle, it's an ox in the mire, not an ass in a hole!"

The humiliation was instant and Lyle could feel the blood race to his head. He wanted to run and hide, but before he could exit the chapel, a line of members waited to thank him for his comments. Within ten minutes, the compliments diminished the embarrassment and one gentleman broke the ice, allowing Lyle to join in the laughter. "You know, I find my ass in a hole all the time."

Lyle's embarrassment eased in the weeks ahead. Reflecting on the experience, he was grateful. He had learned a lot and enjoyed overcoming his fear of public speaking.

BISHOP PITCHER HAD heard of Lyle's work ethic and knew Lyle's heart was in the right place. "Lyle, can you and Marylin meet with me in my office?"

"As long as you don't ask me to speak again, sure," Lyle replied.

Sitting in the office, Max tried to put the couple at ease by discussing their family and sharing a bit about his. He then got to the point of the meeting. "Lyle, I'd like you to serve as my counselor. You'd be assisting me in coordinating our meetings and providing a variety of services to our members."

Lyle was in deep thought and disbelief. *Doesn't this guy know I'm already working multiple jobs to support my family? What would be required? How much time will the assignment take?* Questions continued to fly through his mind.

Max then stated, "Lyle, I prayed about this and the Lord has told me you're the guy He wants in this assignment."

What! This guy is talking to the Lord? Lyle had gained a basic understanding of his faith but still wasn't very familiar with prayer or inspiration. It seemed like only yesterday he'd been baptized a member.

The truth was, Lyle joined the church ten years earlier, but quickly returned to prioritizing his role as a provider. Over the years, he enjoyed attending an occasional meeting but rarely was he called upon to help. Max must have been sleeping during the Sunday service weeks earlier.

Convinced he was needed, Lyle agreed to accept the assignment.

"I still can't believe he'd pick me," Lyle shared with Marylin as they drove home. "There are so many others more qualified than I am."

Marylin jumped in to end the uncertainty of the calling. "He picked you, Lyle because God knows you have a lot more to learn and to offer. You're needed, and you need to give it your all."

That was a given. Anything Lyle would take on would be done with excellence. His church assignment would not be an exception.

CHAPTER NINETEEN

Volunteer work for his church was much more than Lyle anticipated and required about ten hours each week, hours that stretched him. But the work was more rewarding than anticipated. He was asked to assist those in need and Lyle always felt a warm satisfaction after each assignment. It was also fulfilling to gain exposure to operational tasks like accounting and meeting planning. It was more enlightening and he was forging a deeper understanding of God and His love. Of course, it was more work. However, although Lyle couldn't make sense of it, it seemed that since taking on the church assignment, everything else seemed to go along more smoothly. To him, it was another miraculous example of God's ability to magnify his capabilities.

Max could count on Lyle for anything and knew whatever he asked would be done right. They quickly became great friends and spoke either in person or by phone almost daily. During the summer of 1972, Max asked Lyle if he'd be willing to help him out with a construction project. Max had purchased a small property near Vail, Colorado, and had already begun building what would be a small A-frame cabin.

"Lyle, I'm struggling with getting the foundation level. Would you come look?"

As they approached the property, Lyle looked up the steep grade to see what appeared to be a subfloor for the house. "Max, this hill is too steep to support the structure. It would take a small fortune to build here." Hiking closer, Lyle couldn't believe his eyes. The wooden floor was supported by ten coffee cans, filled with concrete and partially buried into the hillside.

"You can see it's not level," Max explained. What should I do?"

Lyle's response was direct and unexpected. "Tear it down!"

Max was stunned and disappointed. Beyond the failure, he was embarrassed that he hadn't studied building codes. He wanted to build it "on the cheap" and Lyle would have nothing to do with it. More embarrassing, Max had graduated college with honors and attended Columbia University for his master's degree and Ph.D. in geology. While extremely intelligent, construction was something of which he knew very little. Max scrapped the project and sold the property. Months later, he found a modest cabin near Grand Lake, Colorado. It was a beautiful cabin adjacent to a nice lake but a lot smaller than Max had hoped for.

With a get-a-way now secured, the cabin became the destination for numerous weekend breaks for Max and Lyle. Often, they had their children in tow, but they cherished the times they could convince their wives to join them without kids. The cabin had also become the favorite spot for the church youth group and Max enjoyed entertaining the youth and showing them the beauty of the Rocky Mountains.

"Lyle, get a babysitter, and let's take our wives to the cabin," Max proposed.

"I've got built-in babysitters now. When do we leave?"

LYLE, AND HIS new best friend Max, were enjoying the weekend at the Pitcher cabin with their wives. Both families had five children and getting away was a welcomed break. Although Max had another motive for this weekend trip.

"I'm going to take Lyle on a hike and show him around," Max told Diana.

"Okay, but dinner will be ready in one hour, and we're not waiting for you," Marylin responded on behalf of the ladies.

Max and Lyle left the cabin and began the one mile hike up the road.

"Lyle, I found it," Max shared.

"Found what?"

Max was excited. Very excited. He described a property that seemed idealistic. Views of three mountain ranges were extraordinary. The Colorado River meandered through the property creating the property line. On the other side of the river was the world's biggest backyard, Rocky Mountain National Park. The property contained a meadow, and oxbow and the western property line ran along the National Forest. Hearing Max describe the site, it sounded heavenly.

After walking for thirty minutes, Max paused. Turning to Lyle, he directed Lyle's attention to the fields below. "There it is!"

Confused, Lyle couldn't see through the trees enough to notice any mountain ranges. There were no meadows, only willows and streams that looked to be in a floodplain.

Seeing the concern in Lyle's face, Max continued. "Lyle, it's more than one hundred acres. We can clear the meadow and create a large lake from the materials in the field. Imagine the views we'd have. There's room for both families and we'd have a real legacy property."

"What do you mean we?"

"We do this together. Partners, fifty-fifty."

"But Max, how much would this cost? It's a lot of land. Not to mention, there's a ton of work just to clear the willows. We don't have that kind of money."

Max understood Lyle had a lot on his plate and was working multiple jobs, but he had already conceived a plan. "You just finished building three big projects, right?"

"Yes, but…"

"Listen, I haven't shared this with anyone, but I'm accepting a new position with Conoco. The promotion comes with a big pay raise. If you can use the money from the construction projects to buy the land, I'll be able to repay you in just a few months."

Lyle respected Max. Given the trust Max had demonstrated in Lyle, there was nothing Lyle wouldn't do for him. As they walked farther down the trail, they arrived at a clearing in the trees. From that point, a stream crossed the path.

"We'd need to divert this water to dry the meadows but—"

Lyle interrupted. "I see it. I can see the mountain ranges." Lyle was mesmerized by the view. While remote and untamed, it was beautiful. *I've never dreamed of anything this incredible. This could be it, a chance to create something special.* As they talked, a herd of elk walked through the fields.

"Look, Max. There must be a hundred elk in that herd."

"Wait until you see the moose. There's wildlife all around here," Max replied.

"I'm in. But I've got someone in your cabin that may need convincing." Lyle laughed.

Back at the cabin, the couples were enjoying the meal together. Max couldn't sit still and finally jumped into the conversation. "Let's hurry and eat."

Lyle added, "Yeah. We need to show you something we discovered and it will be getting dark soon."

Marylin and Diana followed their husbands up an abandoned forest road that made for easy walking. Unfortunately, after the first half-mile, the road became more of a trail. Fallen trees and spring run-off made walking difficult. Nearing the pre-arranged spot, Lyle's heart raced as he could hardly contain his excitement.

Able to walk no farther, Marylin stopped. "Just where are you taking us and how much farther do you expect us to hike?"

Max smiled and looked to Lyle to take on the challenge of explaining their plan.

"Well, this is it," Lyle shared while pointing to a field of willows, beaver dams, and streams. "We can have it all. Max likes the site to the north, up there by the trees and I want to build our retirement home in the meadow."

"Meadow?" Marylin shouted. "It's a swamp! Diana, let's get out of here."

Together, the ladies left the dreamers alone to dream.

Never one to be denied, Max looked at Lyle and stated the obvious, "You've got a problem."

Lyle laughed. "Oh, Max, she'll come around. She just can't see the vision of what we have planned. But she'll get there."

That night, Lyle snuggled up to his angelic wife, "So what do you think?"

"Are you serious? We've got five kids, a house, and are both working just to make ends meet," Marylin whispered.

"Yeah, but I just got paid for my work on the three church buildings. It's a lot and can easily cover the cost of land."

"How much would it cost to clear the land?"

"I'm not sure, but Max will be coming into some money. He's committed."

"I don't know. It sounds like a giant step for us," she said.

Lyle knew he had an ace in his pocket. "Remember, that yellow house? I can see it clearly. In the morning I'll show you where I think it could be built. The views are incredible. This could be our—"

"Okay. Let's do it."

A month later, Lyle, Marylin, Max, and Diana were partners and proud owners of the land that most just considered a mountain swamp.

WITH THE MOUNTAIN property in possession, their truck was traded for something more suited for mountain travel, a Jeep. Lyle and Marylin were excited to share their vision for the property with four of their five children and a trip was planned for the July 4th holiday. Lylo wouldn't be able to join them as he was spending his summer exploring several college scholarship offers. While disappointed he'd not be with them, his parents beamed with pride over his accomplishments.

In July of 1972, the Hileman family loaded up the Jeep to begin the three-hour drive to Grand Lake. Along the way, Marylin led the family in learning a variation of a new song she heard in a commercial. As they drove over Berthoud Pass, the top was down and the warm summer air felt soothing. Had others been near, they'd have heard the lyrics being shouted from all the passengers assembled in the Jeep.

Beep, Beep
I'm a Jeep
I'm full of Power
And I'm ready to go
With a pack full of Hileman's
I never go slow
I'm one of a kind
On the streets today
And I live on 2710 Chase way!
Beep, Beep
I'm a Jeep

The lyrics were a continuous loop and the family repeated singing, over and over again. They enjoyed a wonderful day exploring the property and learning of their parent's dream of a mountain paradise. It was to be a family project.

During the summer of 1974, the work of transformation on the mountain property began. The first task required building a bridge over a stream that regularly flooded the meadows. Lyle added a concrete diversion with a metal floodgate to control the flow north and south. This was essential, as the next job included clearing the meadows and they'd need to be dried out. Willows and tree stumps were pushed north to create a large wall that would serve as a dam for a lake near the site Max marked for his future cabin. Lyle also had a small pond dug east of his home site in the meadow.

The initial attempt at creating a dam failed. The dam broke, releasing much of the stored water to the meadows below. It took weeks to dry and eventually, an excavator was hired, this time with proper materials to ensure longevity. The final activity of summer was the planting of grass. The meadow was to be a high-quality hay, known as Timothy. It was a more valuable crop but primarily chosen because it grew tall and held a beautiful amber hue during the late summer.   The dreams of Lyle and Max were beginning to take shape. On his last visit before heavy winter set in, Lyle was alone. With no more projects planned for this year, he sat quietly on the bridge he'd built only a few months earlier. The vistas were magnificent. Looking to the north, he could see the Never Summer Mountain Range. To the east, the Colorado River that earlier was the cause of flooding was now contained with an irrigation head gate. On the east side of the river was Rocky Mountain National Park and he spotted the moose Max had once referenced. Looking to the south, Lyle couldn't help but get lost in thought. He was visualizing a beautiful, two-story Victorian house adjacent to the pond. *I love this place. We have something special here. It's just like we planned.*

SPRING COULDN'T COME early enough for Lyle. He spent his entire winter dreaming of various projects he wanted to complete on the property. In May of 1975, Max invited Lyle to join him on a drive to the property.

"Should I check with Marylin?" Lyle asked.

"No, this is just a short trip for the two of us," Max replied.

As they approached the Village of Grand Lake, Max pulled his truck over to the side of the road. "Well, I've got news for you. Something bit. Conoco has promoted me to be the Chief Geologist of North and South America but it requires a move. To Houston, Texas."

Lyle's heart skipped a beat as fear and concern settled in. "But Max, we have plans."

"And we still do."

Max went on to share his idea surrounding the future development of the property. While Lyle would have to complete most of the work, Max would be in a position to fund the improvements. "Nothing changes, other than we can now accelerate our plans. I've got the money and you've got the skills to transform this area for both our families."

"We'll I've already got several ideas on how to spend your money. Let's go!"

"Not so fast. Before you start here, I need you to come to Texas to remodel a house that I plan to buy. I'll pay you well, and then we'll both be positioned to work on our homes here."

LYLE'S PLANS FOR Grand Lake were put on a temporary hold while he successfully navigated the remodel of the Pitcher family home in Texas. While work in Grand Lake was delayed, his mind never stopped thinking of the ideas he had in mind for a mountain paradise.

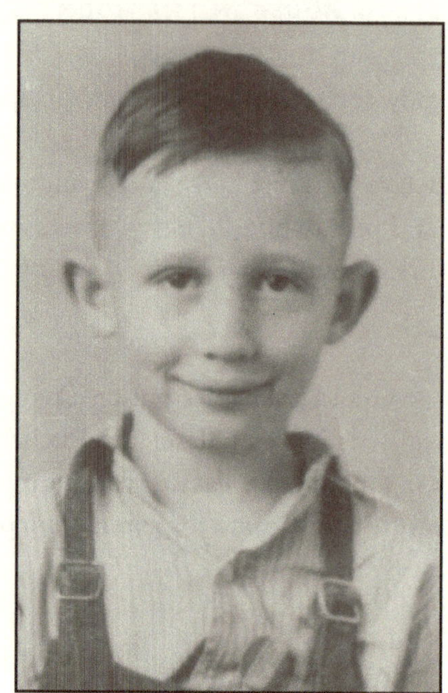

Lyle's school photo from 1940-41.

Marylin 1942 school photo.

Lyle's 1947 All-American Soap Box Derby car was awarded "best in show".

Marylin's 1952 school formal photo.

Lyle and Marylin in front of Wheat Ridge High School. Note, Lyle broke his finger while wrestling.

During the summer of 1952, Lyle enlisted in Marine Reserves and reported for duty.

The Hileman family in 1962. With Lyle and Marylin, from left to right, Glenn, Cherrie, Lyle Jr., Kim, Wayne.

Lyle being recognized by Denver City Fire Chief Merle Wise.

Determined to complete her education, Marylin
secured her GED prior to graduating from Metro
State College in Denver, Colorado.

Together, Lyle and Marylin constructed their yellow house. Foundation work began in 1979, bu
the framing wouldn't begin until 1987. In 1992, their home was completed
and they retired to live in their mountain paradise.

Mountain living was hard, but made possible with heavy equipment. Winter snow removal was a regular part of life in the mountains. Lyle loved it!

Lyle and Marylin celebrated their 50th wedding anniversary on a Royal Caribbean Cruise. They were accompanied by all five of their married children and spouses.

Lyle's love of woodwork led to the creation of countless items. The study in the yellow house showcased his gun cabinet, fireplace and desk area. Oak with walnut inlay was his favorite combination for furniture.

Lyle suffered several strokes that impacted his memory. He loved studying scripture and could be found early each morning deep in study. He was committed to relearning lost knowledge through a disciplined approach. He would never start a day without personal time for prayer and study.

Lyle and Marylin bred their two horses. They named the foal Eclipse. With three horses to care for, Lyle built a coral and barn. Owning horses was hard work, but rewarding.

Married in 1952, Lyle and Marylin enjoyed sixty-eight years of marriage.
As of July 2023, their posterity numbered sixty-one.

CHAPTER TWENTY

Having become a mother at sixteen, Marylin assumed the responsibilities of adulthood early. Now thirty-four years old, she had spent nearly twenty years solely focused on family. She understood the time was approaching but felt completely unprepared when Lylo informed her that he'd accepted a scholarship at Brigham Young University, in Utah. He expected his mother to be as excited as he was, but her reaction seemed less than enthusiastic.

"Mom, isn't that great?" Lylo asked.

Marylin tried to hide her emotions as she felt a sadness begin to swell within her chest. Not able to contain it any longer, she burst out in tears and wrapped her arms around her firstborn son. "I'm so proud of you. I'm just going to miss you."

Lylo was an ideal first son. He was respectful of his parents and established a standard for his siblings to follow. Wanting to cheer up his mom, Lyle said, "Think of the extra money you'll have with me gone. Plus, with my scholarship, you can use my college savings funds to build your house in the mountains."

"No. That money is for you. Besides, you told us you hoped to attend medical school. You'll need it soon enough." Marylin's realization of the upcoming transition hit her hard but looking at Lylo, she couldn't help but feel a sense of accomplishment. *We did well. He's a great son!*

WITH LYLO OFF to college, Marylin's expectations of things getting easier were misguided. Cherrie was still in high school, Kim was in junior high, and Glenn and Wayne were wrapping up elementary school. In addition to her work at Ft. Logan, Marylin tried to keep up with the numerous activities of her children. Juggling her schedule was no less challenging with Lylo having moved out. She remained busy and on occasion felt overwhelmed. However, she was determined to never let her children see her stressed. They already dealt with the frequent eruptions from their father who was less effective at containing frustrations. Lyle allowed little things, like loud noises, running in the house, or clutter to drive him crazy. His stress level was often taken out on those he loved most, and it was hurting his relationships with his kids. To offset her husband's outbursts, Marylin continually reminded her children how much they were loved by both parents.

Often, Marylin would go out of her way to reinforce her love for family. One afternoon, Marylin rushed from work to pick up her son Glenn from baseball practice. When she arrived, she found Glenn sitting alone in the park. She was late and guilt set in.

"I'm sorry I'm late," she began. "I had a hard time getting off work today."

"It's no problem," Glenn replied. "Chipper let me try out his new baseball glove."

Glenn's glove was falling apart. A neighbor had given it to him and it seemed to do the job, but clearly, it was old.

Then an idea surfaced. "Let's go shopping. Dave Cook's Sporting Goods is still open."

"What are you shopping for?" Glenn asked.

"Not me. You!"

Arriving at the store, Marylin took Glenn to the aisle with baseball gloves. "It's time you get a new mitt."

Glenn's face lit up and he raced straight to a glove that was identical to the one he'd admired earlier. It was a red, white, and blue leather Franklin Glove.

Nothing much was said, but Marylin smiled the entire drive home as she looked to her right and observed Glenn caressing his new ball glove. *I love this boy!* Marylin loved all her children and enjoyed finding ways to show them, sometimes with something as simple as a new mitt.

LYLE'S WORK AT the Fire Department continued to be a great fit and he leveraged his off days to pursue construction projects or to work on the Grand Lake property. Developing the property took nearly every penny Lyle and Marylin could spare. Additionally, it required a great deal of time. Marylin was often left to deal with the kids. She did her best to manage the family affairs but now had a problem that required Lyle's less-than-soft touch.

"Cherrie is getting serious with that boy, Bob, and I don't think it's a good thing," Marylin explained.

Lyle, familiar with the risks of young love, tried to console her. "In just a few weeks, she'll be leaving for Utah for college. Once on campus, she'll soon forget about him."

"She says she's not going," Marylin explained. "That's the problem."

"But we've already paid tuition. I even deposited money for her dormitory. She's going!" Lyle pronounced.

"I was counting on that reaction from you," Marylin said while beaming with a smile.

Lyle's discussion with Cherrie failed to diminish her enthusiasm for a relationship with Bob. Nor did it change her mind regarding school. "You can make me go but as soon as you drop me off, I'll be on a plane back to Denver. I'll be back before you and Mom get home."

"We leave on Saturday," her father commanded.

The following day, Cherrie told her mother that Bob was coming to confront her father and demand she stay in Denver. They were seriously dating and he was going to convince Lyle and Marylin of their deep affection for each other.

Marylin called her husband to develop a plan.

"You deal with Cherrie, I'll take care of Bob," Lyle said.

Around eight o' clock in the evening the doorbell rang. Cherri quickly raced to answer the call from her would-be suitor, with Lyle following close behind. Bob was the star catcher on the Lincoln High School baseball team and at nearly six feet tall, towered over Lyle, but Lyle was not intimidated. His body language signaled he was the aggressor and in control of the situation. As an added measure of insurance, Lyle dressed in his fireman blues. He knew the uniform and badge would be intimidating to a high school student, even one supposedly in love.

Bob was the first to speak. "I love your daughter and she needs to stay in Colorado."

By now, the rest of the Hileman children had huddled behind their father to witness what was already a very tense scene. Marylin lurked in the kitchen, close enough to hear but intentionally out of sight.

"Well, Bob, that's not happening. Cherrie is going to college," Lyle firmly stated.

At that moment Bob made a miscalculation and while raising his voice and stepping forward to get within an inch of Lyle's face, yelled, "She's coming with me, tonight!"

Lyle's reaction was swift and powerful. Using only his index finger, he planted it in the middle of Bob's chest with a force that caused him to retreat a step or two. Then stepping down from the doorway, Lyle yelled, "Get off my property, and don't come back!"

Bob was scared. Cherrie was mortified and her crying and objections were dramatic. Dramatic, but not persuasive enough to deter Bob's retreat. The rest of the night, Lyle and Marylin listened to the threats from their teenage daughter and her plans to return on the first plane out of Utah.

As Lyle and Marylin dropped Cherrie off at BYU, Marylin looked at her husband and asked, "Do you think she'll beat us home?"

Lyle's response surprised Marylin. "Nope. She's a social butterfly and with all the other kids around, she'll fit right in."

He was right. On the first day of class, Cherrie was spotted by a young man with ambition, intelligence, and an attraction to this beautiful young girl. Bob was quickly forgotten and Cherrie wed Joseph Kim Wilsted only sixteen months later.

CHAPTER TWENTY-ONE

Mental health issues were not well understood in 1975, and while doctors could prescribe various medicines to control behavior, Marylin preferred extending an abundance of love. The patients loved Marylin and found her acceptance of them unusual. However, the job did have risks. As a mental health worker, Marylin assisted patients in coping with the challenges of living. Most were full-time patients and state-sponsored, given they had significant mental illness. Others were voluntary out-patients. Marylin loved them all, and they loved her.

During a night shift, while assisting a patient with meds, the patient lost control and abruptly kicked the heavy, wooden door closed. Marylin's hand was resting on the door jam and in a split second the door slammed shut. The injury resulted in losing the tip of her finger, and most of her fingernail. Marylin worked hard to carefully conceal the injury by taking frequent trips to have her nails manicured. Careful sculpting of her remaining nail helped offset the constant reminder of the dangers in her workplace. She had been given a month off to recover but was anxious to get back to work and her friends.

"I'm not comfortable with you going back to work; it's too dangerous," Lyle said.

"It was an accident, Lyle. I love my job and my patients. It's sure a lot safer than what you do at the firehouse. Or, even balancing on rafters while framing houses."

Lyle conceded and he knew that they'd both need to keep working to have any chance at building their dream of a mountain paradise. Still, he remained genuinely concerned about his pint-sized spouse. Conversations surrounding her patients was an ongoing reminder of the risks she faced each day.

One day in October, a patient named Robert approached Marylin with an interesting request. A community Halloween costume contest was being held at a nearby mall and Robert wanted to participate.

"I want to dress up as you," he explained to Marylin.

Flattered, she asked, "How can I help?"

"Can I have a dress? Maybe a wig?" Robert asked. "And I'll need help with makeup."

Marylin was delighted to assist. She was shocked when Robert returned from the competition with an award for first place! Not only had Robert won, but he was awarded an all-expense paid trip to Mexico. As a full-time patient, he wasn't allowed to make the trip but proudly bragged about his accomplishment. His parents were thrilled and they gladly accepted the trip on their son's behalf.

WINTER ARRIVED EARLY in November of 1976. The ground of the Grand Lake property was frozen, and work on improvements ended with the first heavy snowfall. However, Lyle and Max continued to talk regularly about the various projects they wanted to tackle in the spring. Max was extremely busy with his work as an executive with Conoco, but his secretary knew that if Lyle ever called, she was to interrupt whatever he was doing and put him through.

"Max, I have an idea." Those words would often cause Max to pause, as many times Lyle's ideas meant more money was about to be spent. Lyle continued, "Let's get all the youth from the church and hold a winter retreat at the cabin."

This time, Max was relieved. "But I've already promised Diana we'd spend Christmas in Texas."

"No problem because I was thinking more like New Year's Eve anyway," Lyle replied.

Max's thoughts then turned to the practicalities of more than thirty young people together in the cabin. "Besides, we only have beds to sleep maybe twenty. How do you propose lodging all the boys and girls on a trip like this?"

"Don't worry. I've got it all planned. The Runyan's offered up their cabin," Lyle added. "And they've even offered to let the youth use their snowmobiles."

With that in place, the youth trip was formalized. The day after Christmas, Max arrived in Colorado with two of his five children, Steve and Shauna. The boys stayed in the Pitcher cabin and the girls were in the Runyan cabin. The entertainment was primarily sledding and ice skating on the lake behind the cabin. The fun outdoors ended at sunset as the temperature dropped to below zero degrees.

As dinner was being served in the Runyan cabin, Max announced, "I just purchased four Canadian-made snowmobiles." Skidoo was a snowmobile manufacturer and the only brand Max would have considered purchasing. As a dual citizen of the United States and Canada, Max retained a love of all things Canadian. "Those Japanese Yamaha machines of the Runyan's just won't do. Tomorrow, we'll celebrate New Year's Eve in style."

The next day was a bit warmer and the youth had an amazing day frolicking in the snow. As evening approached, Lyle and Max shuttled the kids by snowmobile to their property a mile up the road. When they arrived, Lyle went to work positioning the group a safe distance from a huge pile of debris he'd gathered during the working months of summer. A match was struck and flung towards the pile of wood. The bonfire provided the perfect setting to ring in the New Year.

"Lyle, that was amazing. Thanks for suggesting it. Do you realize that is the first real gathering we've had on our property? All the work is paying off."

"It's becoming a beautiful piece of ground," Lyle responded.

"Well, you've lit a fire under me. Literally, and figuratively as well. I want you to build my cabin. I'll need a year or so to get the plans and funds together, but that should give you plenty of time to prepare."

With little savings to begin building his retirement home, Lyle understood that building a new cabin for the Pitcher family would generate enough extra income to maybe get started on the yellow house.

"Are you sure?" Lyle questioned. "If you're serious, I'll be available."

"Absolutely. Our dreams are taking shape," Max proclaimed. "I can't imagine anyone else doing it."

Max couldn't have predicted how quickly his career would advance, but in a short time, he'd been promoted again. Max landed the position as Executive Vice President at Conoco Oil. The money began to flow, an architect was hired, and the design for a new cabin was underway.

CHAPTER TWENTY-TWO

Working at the Fire Department was a good fit for Lyle. Now a fifteen-year veteran, he began to study for the Lieutenant's exam. The test would require an intimate understanding of various subjects and measured leadership potential. If passed, it meant a nice increase in pay and better retirement benefits. When the results were posted, perhaps no one was more stunned than Lyle. He finished the test at the top of his class.

With the promotion, Lyle was assigned to a new station as the leader. His boss, the captain, would alternate shifts. Their responsibilities were similar and Lyle loved being in charge when the captain wasn't working. Many of the firemen enjoyed the downtime at the station. Games of table tennis, exercise, or just relaxing between alarms were common. Lyle used the time to pursue his interests like working with wood but the majority of his free time was spent planning improvements on the property.

The fire station was in a suburban area and considered one of the best locations given the light duty. The guys in the station loved working for Lyle. He was liked by the others but often teased for being so stiff and boring. Lyle never drank. He gave up smoking years ago and regularly attended church. Most importantly, the other firemen knew he was faithful to his wife.

One evening, the captain and Lyle had a shared shift. Given the double coverage, Lyle decided to get some sleep.

"I'm headed upstairs to bed," he told the captain.

"Sure thing, Hileman. It was a tough day."

As Lyle settled into bed, he heard a commotion below with lots of laughter. Are they drinking? But then he heard a woman's voice. Even though that would be a violation of the rules, he knew what he had heard. Throwing a pillow over his head, Lyle tried not to think about what might be going on.

The other firemen knew Lyle was a strait-laced guy and not inclined to join the others in frivolous activities. They figured it would be funny to hire a prostitute to expose Hileman's carnal desires. Lying in bed with a pillow over his head and covers pulled tight, Lyle felt a hand pulling at his blanket. Immediately, he pulled the pillow from his eyes and saw a woman, dressed in a negligee, trying to cozy up next to him in bed. In a split second, Lyle jumped from the bed, slid down the fire pole, and ran into the street. It wasn't until he stood alone on the sidewalk of Federal Boulevard that Lyle realized he was only in his underclothes.

With Lyle outside in his underwear, the captain was afraid someone would call the police to report a crazy guy on the street and he'd end up in all kinds of trouble. "Lyle, get in here."

"Get that woman out of there," Lyle responded.

The captain began begging, "Lyle, come on. It was a joke and if anyone sees you out here, we're busted."

Undeterred, Lyle stood firm. "I'm not moving until she's gone."

They knew he was serious. They also learned that Lyle's commitment to fidelity was firm. It took time for Lyle to forgive his peers but his response heightened their respect for him.

Lyle's work outside the fire department continued on various construction projects. He was hired to lead an effort to create a network of fitness centers, something emerging in the 70s culture. The clubs were called Nautilus Fitness and each grand opening was an opportunity for the owner, Jon Simcox, to sign up hundreds of new members to annual contracts. The approach was effective and the quality of the facility helped in marketing. Jon recognized Lyle's work as exemplary and he quickly expanded, providing Lyle with plenty of work.

In addition to the fitness centers, Lyle also enjoyed small projects. A dear friend, Lloyd Richmond, had called Lyle to consult on a kitchen remodel he'd promised his wife Julie.

"She wants to update the entire kitchen," Lloyd began. "If we proceed, we'll likely need to expand the area by demolishing the adjacent walls."

"That can certainly be done, Lloyd, but what's your budget?" Lyle asked.

"Well, that's going to be the challenge. We want new appliances, flooring and a bigger space. Can you give me an estimate?"

Lyle's experience with this type of project was readily apparent. He explained the basic steps and costs associated with each. After a review, they aligned on each of the components of the project but Lyle was uncomfortable with Lloyd's choice of cabinets.

"Lloyd, those aren't a good option."

Lloyd reluctantly agreed. "I know. But we can't eliminate the appliances and Julie wants the oak flooring. What else can we do?"

"I understand," Lyle acknowledged.

As work commenced, the Richmond family was pleased they selected Lyle. His attention to detail for which he was known was obvious. Every element of the project was completed with excellence and the new kitchen was beginning to take shape. As Lyle was acquiring the cabinets the family selected, he felt a sting of disappointment. He understood they would be functional but they wouldn't complement the quality of work completed.

"Hey Craig, how much for the solid cherry cabinets?" Lyle inquired.

Craig, was a salesman at the hardware store knew Lyle well.

He was also a bit surprised, knowing Lyle, that the lower-cost option was even being considered. "Lyle that's a big upgrade. At least fifteen hundred more."

Disappointed, Lyle paused. "Load up the cherry cabinets and put them on my account." While the workers loaded the cabinets,

Lyle's mind kept repeating over and over, *If it's worth doing, it's worth doing right.*

A few days later, Lloyd returned from work anxious to see the progress. "Lyle, we didn't order the cherry cabinets. They will bust the budget."

Lyle jumped in. "I've got them covered Lloyd. No change to the budget."

For Lyle, completing a project well was a matter of personal satisfaction. He struggled to take shortcuts and his attention to the finished product often took priority over profit. In this case, it meant no profit, but for Lyle, it never was about the money.

The remodel went well, so well that Julie Richmond suggested Lyle also remodel the basement family room. As Julie shared her vision for the space, Lyle confirmed it was a small project, not very expensive and he could complete the work in short order. What he failed to communicate was he'd need Julie's help.

"Hey Julie," Lyle yelled from the Richmond basement.

Julie quickly descended the stairs.

"I'm ready to hang the drywall and need your help."

"Sure, Lyle. What can I do?" Julie offered.

"I need to you hold this sheet up while I hammer in a few nails. I can manage the walls alone but the ceiling has to go up first."

The work progressed slowly. Julie's head and neck would ache for weeks after spending hours using all five foot, two inches of her frame to stabilize drywall, weighing nearly 70 pounds, while Lyle would race to nail sheets to the floor joists. It would be "sweat equity" Julie would have preferred giving to others more suited to the task. To Lyle, she was the perfect assistant in a time of need.

Jon Simcox was thrilled with Lyle's work on the fitness centers. He'd made enough money that Jon was now exploring a possible vacation property. Seeing Lyle hard at work on the latest expansion of Nautilus

Fitness Center in Arvada, Colorado, Jon pulled Lyle aside "I've bought some land - in Grand Lake."

Dropping his hammer and genuinely excited, Lyle asked, "Where. You'll love it there Jon."

"If we go forward, we'd be neighbors. The site is right on the road entering your property. But I can't proceed without a great contractor."

"I'm busy Jon. I already promised Max I'd build his cabin next year."

"Next year? I want to begin now. I've already got the plans approved by the county. You can start as soon as the snow melts."

Lyle paused to contemplate the various commitments he had already in place. "That's a project I'd love to tackle. But Jon, it may take me a while. When do you expect to have it completed?"

"Timing isn't a concern. If you're building it, I know it will be done right!" Jon added.

Smiling at the compliment, Lyle teased, "I may not be able to pick my neighbors, but at least I can make sure you've got a great house."

Lyle stopped taking on new work as he now had two significant projects ahead. Work on the Simcox cabin began in the spring of 1978.

LYLE'S SON GLENN was a junior in high school and had spent the prior summer working with a close friend, Chuck Dubois, installing shake roofs. Lyle had overheard Glenn and Chuck discussing their work and disappointment that while the job paid well, the boss rarely showed up onsite and was getting most of the money.

"Boys, that's the way it works. He's negotiated the contract, purchased tools and materials, and he is trusting a bunch of kids to get the work done right. He's earning his money," Lyle explained.

Glenn responded, "If we had the tools, I know I could find work."

"It will be harder than you think, but I have an idea," Lyle said.

That summer, Lyle hired Glenn and Chuck to complete the work on the Simcox cabin roof. He paid close attention to the detail of their work and enjoyed helping refine their knowledge of how to best complete the job. He also insisted they use hammers and nails on the wooden shake shingles rather than an air compressor and nail gun. While much slower, it would be a perfect way to ensure they understood the process. *This is the way my dad taught me.* On this project, there would be no air compressor, no air guns, or staples. No, his son was going to learn to appreciate the value and risk associated with their former employer's engagement. He also looked forward to teaching his son. He wasn't much help with the books from school, but this was an education he knew how to direct.

The work was nearing completion. Glenn and Chuck were proud of their efforts and ended up making a bit more money than the previous summer. More importantly, they better understood what it meant to be in business.

"Dad, we want to keep going," Glenn said. "Chuck and I are going to start a roofing company."

Reflecting on a time years ago, Lyle fondly recalled his introduction to construction. He was almost the same age as these boys and was pleased to see their ambition. "If you're going to do it, you need to be efficient."

"Dad, we were efficient. And we did it right, didn't we?" Glenn questioned.

Lyle jumped in, "Glenn, you guys did a great job. What I meant to say is that you can't be profitable in this business without the right tools. You had my tools available on this project, but if you move ahead with your plan, you'll need saws, ladders, and a lot more. You certainly can't be using a hammer-and-nail approach on other projects. Too slow."

Glenn and Chuck had been paid well but wouldn't have nearly enough to purchase the long list of equipment they now understood would be required.

"I've already spoken to my friend Don, at Duo-Fast," Lyle shared with the boys. "Take your truck and introduce yourself to Don. He owns the place."

As the boys drove into the parking lot they were curious as to how things would play out.   Don was expecting them. "So, I understand you boys are starting a business."

"That's right," Glenn replied.

Don went into executive mode and began barking instructions to his workers. "We need a compressor, nail guns, hoses, and staples. And get the good stuff." He now looked at Glenn, "Back up your truck to the dock. We'll load you up."

Neither Glenn nor Chuck completely understood what was happening, but as the garage door opened, a forklift pulled up with everything a roofer could need.

"But we don't have that kind of money," Glenn explained.

"Any son of Lyle has credit with me. Just pay me when you can. Your father has been my customer for a long time. It's the least I can do."

As they drove off, they couldn't help but smile. They had nearly $3,000 of tools behind them and hadn't spent a penny. They also better understood the impact Glenn's father had on the people with whom he worked. He had a great reputation and Glenn and Chuck committed to not jeopardize Lyle's character. Within three months, the boys returned after completing a few projects with cash in hand.

Don wasn't at all surprised.

CHAPTER TWENTY-THREE

Growing up in the Hileman home was a haven for their children, but not without challenges. When Lyle was home, there was always tension because he was very strict. Rarely would the kids bring friends home on days their dad was around. It was embarrassing for them. Fear of their father yelling was a constant worry. Not that Lyle was mean, but he had little patience, especially for teenagers. Juggling multiple jobs also created stress that provoked reactions even Lyle would later regret. Demands from him included commands like, take off your shoes in the house, stop running, keep it down, and many other expressions of frustration. If Lyle was home, the kids would often go to their friends' homes.

Marylin observed Lyle's level of stress increase as kids brought friends by. Little things would set him off and it didn't bring out the best in him. She more than made up for it on days Lyle would put in a shift at the firehouse. On those days, she spoiled the kids and their friends.

With Lyle and Glenn building the Simcox cabin, Wayne had his mom to himself. It was a special summer for them because they often would eat dinner, play a game, or watch a TV show together.

Marylin's parents remained in their Wheat Ridge home, about thirty minutes away, and she enjoyed checking in on them regularly. On a Saturday afternoon, Marylin took Wayne with her to help. She planned to do some cleaning and Wayne was going to mow their lawn. Having just turned sixteen, Wayne had recently secured his driver's license but had no car.

"So, you're here to mow our grass?" Grandpa Novakovich inquired.

"That's right," Wayne replied.

"Come see me when you're finished."

While Marylin went about cleaning, her father shared his plan to "sell" Wayne their old car.

With the mowing complete, Wayne sought out his grandfather. "It's all done," he called out.

"I see that. I was thinking how nice it would be to have you mow all summer long, but your mother reminded me you don't have a car. So, you'd need transportation for an important job like that."

He then showed Wayne the Brown 1972 Grand Prix. Over the years, it had limited use and was a great car - but not so much for a teenage boy. It was a power car with a 450 V8 engine, capable of very high speeds.

Wayne's imagination ran wild, "Are you selling the Grand Prix?"

"No. But it is yours to use over the summer. If you've done a good job with the yard, in the fall, it will be yours."

Wayne loved his new wheels. It was a fast car, so fast that Wayne quickly logged two speeding tickets from the neighborhood policeman, Officer Nunez. One night, Wayne and his friend Don were out driving and stopped by the local McDonalds. Upon entering they saw a few of their buddies who had been drinking. It had begun to snow and one of the young men asked Wayne for a ride home.

"Sure thing," Wayne replied. After loading into the car, Wayne pulled away and from the back seat one boy suggested an adventure.

"Let's go ring and run."

Don, sitting in the shotgun seat asked, "Who should we get?"

The answer came immediately. "Officer Nunez."

Wayne knew that could be trouble and that he should have suggested something else. But anger from having received two tickets was lingering. "Let's do it."

Wayne pulled the car slowly up the street and stopped just short of the Nunez driveway. He and Don remained in the car while the three others jumped out and ran towards the house. It was dark outside and Wayne couldn't see clearly what was occurring on the doorstep.

A few seconds later, the boys were running back to the car. "Go! Let's get out of here!"

Wayne began driving forward when a truck pulled out of the driveway, preventing his escape. Putting the car in reverse, Wayne tried backing up to turn his car around but before completing the maneuver, the truck ran straight into the front of his car, bumping him hard.

"It's Officer Nunez, get out of here!" the boys yelled.

The bump from the truck was enough to turn Wayne's car down the street, allowing him to push the accelerator, as the truck sped from behind. After a few high-speed turns, they lost the truck.

"Why was he chasing us?" Wayne asked. "I can't believe he rammed my car."

The boys then disclosed that there was no doorbell. So instead, they kicked the door. They kicked hard enough to put a foot through the screen door. They were in trouble and knew it.

Wayne returned to McDonalds to drop off his friends. Just as they entered the parking lot, a police car turned on the siren and lights. They were busted! Wayne's heart sank and he began to tremble with fear, immediately regretting what he had just been a part of.

Having taken Wayne's ID, an officer approached him. "We know your dad. Get in your car and head home. We'll be following you."

It was a short drive and Wayne felt sick. He'd rather been taken to jail than face his father. As they approached the Hileman's front door, Lyle was waiting.

"Come on in fellas."

They had already called ahead to share the trouble his son had caused. Wayne was shocked at how cordial his dad was around the officers. Wayne expected his father to be outraged, but with the officers in the house, he was unusually tolerant. After thanking the officers, Lyle shut the door and turned to his son. The change in his countenance was instant.

"What were you thinking?" He then moved in close to his son. "You should know better than to be out causing trouble." As he yelled, spit from his mouth sprayed into Wayne's face.

"I, I , I wasn't thinking."

Lyle felt a rage intensifying within, but a memory from his past flashed in his mind. *I was his age when my dad pulled me out of the Natchez jail.* He paused, took a deep breath, and strained to calm himself. *My dad never raised his voice. He never threatened me.* Gaining his composure, Lyle then shared the same sentence once given to him by his father for his son's lapse in judgment. Wayne would lose his car privileges for a month and would be required to return to Officer Nunez's home to apologize and pay for the damaged screen door.

Lyle looked sternly at Wayne and then slowly placed his arm around Wayne's shoulder. "Remember this. If you're ever on the wrong side of the police, you're on the wrong side of me. Never let it happen again. Never."

DREAMING OF THE property continued to occupy Lyle's thoughts. What was once a swamp, had been transformed into a beautiful meadow that produced an abundant crop of hay. The area around the large lake was showing signs of life with numerous pines now growing on its banks. The smaller pond near where Lyle hoped to someday build was in place but with no trees or vegetation. With winter approaching, Lyle wanted to satisfy his itch to make further improvements.

"Marylin, we ought to plant some trees." he proposed.

"We don't have money for trees and besides, there are trees all over the forest."

"You're right, but I'd like some trees around the pond. We'll just get a few."

"Okay. We can plant some pine trees, but we'll need five."

"Why five?" Lyle asked.

"I should've known," Lyle responded after Marylin explained there would be one tree for each of her children.

CHAPTER TWENTY-FOUR

During the start of 1979, Lyle began working through the plans for the Pitcher cabin. He could use his downtime at the firehouse to review the scope of work and to secure estimates for material. As for labor, he secured a commitment from Glenn and a friend to spend the summer on site. However, he needed someone that could manage things when he was required to fulfill a shift at the fire department.

Brent Chick was known from his time building churches, and he was available. He was in his late twenties, single, and most importantly, he was available all summer. He was hired as a foreman. In May, work began. Brent was very familiar with Lyle's work ethic and expectations. Lyle was quick to yell, a habit he refined pouring concrete as a young man. He was demanding and there would be no shortcuts or oversights; however, Brent also knew he'd gain more than a paycheck. On prior projects, Lyle was a thoughtful teacher and willing to share his techniques with his crews. Brent would be paid well, but he knew the knowledge gained working for Lyle was even more valuable.

Lyle's son Glenn and his high school friend, Brian Worster, committed to the summer job and Max's daughter, Shauna Pitcher, was volunteered by her father to be the gopher. The term gopher came as a result of frequent demands to "go for this or go for that." After four weeks of work with no breaks, Lyle shared that he needed to return to Denver for a few days.

There was little time for a social life. The short summer season at this elevation left no time for fun. Lyle understood the urgency of completing the cabin and made sure all daylight hours were utilized. Work began early and ended late. There would be no time for rest, with the exception of Sundays. Lyle was committed to honoring the Sabbath day and looked forward to the day of rest.

By July, great progress had been made on the cabin.

Glenn learned his father would be driving to Denver for materials on Friday. Longing for a day off, he approached Brent with an idea. "We need a break, Brent. My dad will be gone tomorrow. How about we take the canoe and float the Colorado River?"

Brent was intrigued. As foreman, he knew Lyle would be expecting results on his return, but a break for a few hours could be justified. "I'm in. But how do we get the canoe up there?"

Glenn had already figured that part out. Shauna had already volunteered.

Just a half mile south, The Winding River Campground and Sun Valley Guest Ranch hired summer help. In preparation, Glenn stopped by the Winding River Campground store for a few lunch supplies. While shopping, he noticed two cute girls working behind the counter.

"How's it going?" Glenn asked as he approached the cash register.

"Great. We're having a party tonight. You should bring your friends."

"What time?"

After explaining the details, she asked for a favor. "We need a place to hold a few cases of beer. My parents would kill us if they saw it here. Can we use the refrigerator in your cabin?"

Never having been a drinker, Glenn hesitated. He knew his father wouldn't approve, but ultimately agreed. He also reasoned that the beer would be long gone before his father returned. It was destined to be a memorable day, and after weeks of non-stop work, the crew was going to enjoy the night.

As Lyle drove away, Glenn and Brent loaded the canoe in the back of the Pitcher's truck. "Shauna, we've got the canoe in the truck and we're ready to go. Drive us into the park a few miles. After dropping us off upriver, just leave the key in the truck and park it by the campground. We'll load up and get back in time for the party tonight."

Shauna nodded, confirming her understanding, and the self-declared "day off" was underway.

As they began floating the river, all three were struck by the beauty. It was serene, and around each bend, nature would provide a reminder of its glory. Elk, moose, and otters were frequently observed along the shoreline. The sun was out and after nearly two hours, they neared the Pitcher-Hileman property. "Look. You can see it from here," Brent pointed out.

In the distance, the laborers admired their work. With both stories of the cabin now framed, it stood out and was magnificent. The stone fireplace was prominent amongst the roof rafters that had been installed only days earlier. With pride, they looked on until the home was out of sight. Disappointed that their adventure was nearing an end, they looked ahead to the final mile before their unloading point. Looking to the west, Brent saw something more terrifying than a grizzly bear. Dust. In the distance, they saw a white Chevy truck turning up the dirt road leading to the property. It was Lyle.

"Oh no, we're dead!" Brent shrieked. "He's going to kill me."

"You? I'm the dead one," Glenn responded. "I've got the beer in the fridge. If he stops at the cabin, you can just bury me in the woods." Glenn's heart began to pound, and his mind was racing with fear. Missing a few hours of work was one thing, but he knew there would be zero tolerance for alcohol.

The boys paddled with intensity to complete the last leg of the river. Running with the canoe seemed effortless as adrenaline rushed through their veins. Glenn jumped in the driver's seat and raced toward the cabin to dispose of the evidence before it could be discovered. As he made the turn at a corner of the campground, the truck slid. The driver's side mirror was removed by the telephone pole that Glenn failed to avoid. With the mirror dangling, Glenn noticed the other problem. Max's brown truck had a huge dent in the door.

"Now I'm the dead one," Glenn said.

Stopping at the cabin, the beer was quickly removed and relocated outside. The three laborers' hearts were racing as they knew they had some explaining to do.

"Where have you been?" Lyle inquired. "I'm not paying you to goof off."

Brent took charge and pulled Lyle aside. He took one for the crew and said it was his idea and shared we'd only been gone a few hours.

"Well, get to work!" Lyle shouted.

The crew couldn't believe it. Lyle was swinging a hammer, framing away. He never mentioned beer, or even the dent in the brown Ford Truck. He clearly hadn't stopped at the cabin and was completely focused on work. It was like nothing had happened, but the crew knew they'd narrowly dodged a bullet.

Surprisingly, Lyle never objected to the crew mingling with the others that had gathered at the Sun Valley Guest Ranch. Leaving the cabin, they heard Lyle shout, "Don't be out late. You can't stay up with the owls and still sing with the birds. I'm waking you at five-thirty, and I expect you to be singing!"

Before summer ended, Lyle and Marylin hoped to complete the design for their mountain home. A firefighter in Lyle's station, Don Hartsell, was a talented architect.

"Don, we've found Marylin's dream house. I've got some photos as a starting point but need your help. Oh, and one more thing, it has to be yellow."

Don worked fast to complete the hand-drawn plans. It was exactly what Marylin had wanted, with one exception. Lyle was captivated by a mansard roof. The mansard style had four sloping sides that got steeper halfway down. Marylin preferred a more traditional roof line with turrets that pointed to the sky. Lyle justified proceeding with his style preference due to the heavy snow loads but promised to add decorative iron fencing on top that would complement the Victorian style his wife admired.

With plans now complete, Lyle submitted to Grand County for permits. By the time the Pitcher cabin was finished in the fall, the Hilemans had a completed foundation for their future home.

Max invited Lyle and Marylin to join him and Diana to break in the new cabin. It was a brisk September afternoon, but the sky was clear and the views were stunning. Fall color was popping, the elk were out, and with a newly completed cabin, the couples gathered to celebrate.

Sitting on the porch of the cabin, the couples relaxed and took in the view. The dream they'd shared years earlier was coming together and was even more incredible than they imagined.

"You know, until I retire, our family will likely only get up here two or three times a year. We're counting on you guys to keep the lights on," Max shared.

"You can count on that," Lyle replied.

Marylin added, "Keeping Lyle in Denver is going to be the problem."

Max then shared another idea he'd contemplated, "We want to align on the naming of the ranch. I was thinking we should call it The Bar D-M, after Diana and Marylin."

Lyle jumped in. "Great idea. I can make signs to be hung in front or our entries."

Seeing Lyle's enthusiasm, Max interrupted, "Slow down, Lyle. You've killed yourself just getting the cabin done. On this trip we need to relax and enjoy the property. We'll have lots of time for signs and other projects."

They enjoyed the evening and looked forward to spending the next day walking around the property.

While lying in bed, Lyle looked to Marylin and whispered, "See, I told you this would work out. How do you like the name of the ranch?"

"I don't," Marylin stated. "It's not Diana and Marylin. In Max's mind, it's Diana and Max."

"C'mon on Punk, I'm sure that's not true."

"Honestly," said Marylin, "I don't care about the name. You've worked really hard and I'm looking forward to spending time here. Let's figure out how to get our home built."

With the foundation complete, they needed time and money to begin. Unfortunately, they had neither.

CHAPTER TWENTY-FIVE

LYLE AND MARYLIN'S love of family had no bounds. Their daughter Kim married in 1979 and the newlyweds purchased a site for a home in Lakewood. Kim and her husband both had good jobs but getting a home built would require a lot of coordination. Lyle eased some of the burden by offering to construct the home. His love of work made the time spent on the site genuinely enjoyable. Of course, the young couple would need to adjust their budgets to accommodate all things deemed "the best" by Lyle. Solar technology was emerging as a viable source of long-term savings but the large panels attached to the roof were expensive and unproven. A friend had shared with Lyle how the panels would not only provide electricity for the home, but also radiant heating on the floors. Lyle convinced his daughter and son-in-law to give it a try.

In 1980, the home was complete. The solar worked well and Kim was living in an amazing house built by her father. Kim knew her father loved her even though he rarely expressed it in words. His actions though were a constant reminder of his willingness to do anything to help his children.

Kim had a special bond with her dad. Perhaps it was the daddy-daughter dance they attended when she was twelve. Likely, his unrelenting protection of his shy daughter created the connection, but Lyle saw in Kim traits of love and charity that he admired. Kim was kind. She was concerned about others. She had a big heart. His admiration was mutual as Kim looked up to him as the hardest-working man she'd ever known.

DURING THE FALL of 1980, Lylo began his second year of medical school and earned an ARCS Foundation Scholarship. A ceremony was held to honor recipients of the scholarships and the night was hosted by Jimmy Stewart. Marylin was thrilled for her son but especially excited to attend an event with her favorite movie star who was master of ceremony. Students were instructed to walk across the stage and parents were encouraged to join them. As each group neared Jimmy Stewart, the star took time to greet and congratulate the families. Marylin observed the others ahead had brought their programs and Mr. Stewart was signing autographs.

"I left my program on my chair," Marylin expressed as the line continued to inch forward.

Lylo tried to comfort his mother. "Mom, it's okay. It's just a signature."

"It's not just a signature. It's Jimmy Stewart's signature. He's a big star. He's been in all my favorite movies; Vertigo, Mr. Smith Goes to Washington, and my favorite, It's A Wonderful Life."

Lylo had no idea his mother was such a big fan but by this time they were standing only a few feet away from the larger-than-life movie star. As Lylo's approached the dean of the school, he was handed a certificate. Then Jimmy Stewart extended his hand.

Shaking his hand, Lylo stated the obvious, "My mom's a big fan!"

"I can see that," he replied noting Marylin's eyes had opened wide and a huge smile emerged.

"I forgot my program. Would you sign my hand?" Marylin asked.

Rather than an autograph, Mr. Stewart's next move was well suited for a scene in a movie. He grabbed Marylin's outreached hand, slowly bowed, and kissed the back of her hand. She blushed, her heart raced, and she was thrilled.

THE SPRING OF 1981 arrived, and Marylin began working in her rose garden. On a beautiful morning, her planting was interrupted by the kitchen phone ringing. She didn't want to stop working, especially as she was covered in dirt. The ringing stopped, but immediately began again. Coincidence, she thought. However, when it rang a third time, she rushed inside to grab the phone. "Hello?"

"Marylin, I need your help," her mother cried.

"Is everything all right?" Marylin asked.

"No. Your father has died. He's lying on the floor and I can't move him. I need you."

Marylin did what she could to calm her mother and promised she was on her way. She arrived only minutes after an ambulance and overheard the workers acknowledge her beloved father was gone. Stephen was loved by all who knew him and the chapel was filled to capacity for the memorial service.

Wayne and Glenn were asked to pick up Lyle's mother Lillian, and her sister Ruth. The boys each had purchased used MG Midgets. Both cars only allowed for two occupants, so both vehicles would be needed. As they pulled into the church parking lot, Lyle couldn't help but smile as the tops were down and the ladies appeared to be enjoying the drive. After the service, they assisted Lillian and Ruth back into the small cars. When Glenn started his car, the radio was on. He assumed his grandfather must have had a great sense of humor as the song being played on the radio was Queen's, Another One Bites The Dust. Glenn and Wayne shared a laugh but were sure glad their mom wasn't nearby. She was grieving and may not have seen the humor in the moment.

Losing her father was painful for Marylin. It also required a big change in her life as Amy leaned heavily on Marylin. She recognized that soon both Wayne and Glenn would graduate and begin pursuing their goals. As inviting as retirement had always seemed, the thought of coming home to an empty house was depressing. She taught her children important values: honesty, morality, discipline, and Lyle's favorite, hard work. Her commitment to faith included weekly attendance at Sunday services and she felt satisfaction knowing she raised good children who would benefit society. It shouldn't have come as a surprise when Glenn announced he was leaving for Kentucky on a two-year proselyting mission, but it caught Marylin a bit off guard. What was a surprise was that shortly after Glenn left, Wayne indicated he also would serve as a missionary. His assignment arrived and he was to serve in Thailand.

It seemed to happen overnight but now all of Marylin's children were out of the nest and she began feeling a bit blue. After nearly thirty years of mothering, she faced a significant adjustment. She was committed to her family and began to realize keeping the family close would require a different approach.

Now more than ever, she sensed a need to create a gathering place for her children and future grandchildren. The mountain property had always seemed like a good decision, but now it was taking on new meaning. Their home in the mountains wouldn't just be for retirement. It needed to be a place to create memories.

THE COMPLETED PITCHER cabin was beautiful, and Lyle was proud of it. Max sold the old cabin. The Pitcher family continued to live in Texas and made occasional visits to Grand Lake. That left lots of time for the Hileman family to enjoy the much larger and more comfortable getaway. The vision that Lyle and Max had sixteen years earlier had come to fruition. Or, at least partially.

Lyle made a quick trip to Grand Lake to complete some final finish details on the Pitcher cabin. Before leaving for home, he sat for the first time to relax and take in some mountain air. Max had purchased a wooden rocking chair that Lyle carefully positioned on the porch to capture the views. He found the serenity satisfying and emotional. Back and forth he rocked, reflecting on all the work he'd completed over more than thirteen years. He closed his eyes as the sun engulfed his entire body, feeling like a warm blanket. The moment was important. A sense of joy overwhelmed him.

As he rose from the chair, he scanned the meadow when something caught his attention. The reflection from metal strapping on his foundation flashed in the sunlight. Suddenly, a deep sadness overcame him. *I'll never be able to get our home built,* he thought. Even with Marylin's income and the side jobs Lyle took on, the expense of rearing five kids was brutal. With their children now grown and pursuing their interests, they still provided financial support for two missionary sons. Also, Marylin was quick to send money to her kids. Birthdays and holidays always included a card and check. Never huge sums, but enough that they were spending what they brought in. Reflecting on the home he desperately wanted to build, Lyle began walking across the meadow toward the foundation he'd completed earlier. Standing atop the foundation wall, he noticed something that snapped him out of his funk.

BACK IN DENVER, Lyle explained to Marylin "We have to start. The foundation wall is showing signs of distress. I need to at least get the subfloor down, or all the money we already spent will be for nothing." Tears were flowing down Lyle's face.

Marylin had rarely seen him cry.

"We ought to just sell the property," Lyle cried.

"That's ridiculous." Not knowing exactly how they'd pull this off, Marylin then wrapped her arms around her broken husband. "It will all work out." Marylin had great faith and an amazing sense of optimism.

Lyle was typically upbeat, but if ever feeling down, he appreciated the way Marylin could lift his spirit. He knew Marylin was right. He was discouraged but couldn't give up on their dream.

LYLE HAD A great relationship at the local lumber yard and decided to lean into his line of credit. Almost as if a fulfillment to prophesy, only two weeks later Lyle secured a contract to build a local church in Granby, the neighboring town to Grand Lake. He was overwhelmed. The money he'd earn that summer would be more than enough to not only pay for the subfloor but framing as well. Plastic sheets would serve as a temporary roof but by the summer of 1986, the couple had saved enough to completely enclose the home, including the most satisfying addition, yellow siding.

Lyle and Marylin began preparing to move to their dream house in the mountains. Now fifty-two and fifty years old, retirement was still a few years away. However, as their yellow house took shape, the excitement was building. Every minute and dollar they could spare went toward completing their dream. With funds tight, Lyle leaned into "cheap" labor…Marylin. While he didn't pay her for work, the real cost was high. As a difficult taskmaster, Lyle had previously only worked with men. He could yell or shout demands and the crew jumped into action. Marylin would have none of it. She welcomed the chance to help but wasn't about to have Lyle barking orders. Despite the strain, they eventually found their rhythm and worked together, side by side, making their dream a reality.

"Lyle, let's get a swing for the porch," Marylin suggested.

"I think we need two. One for each end of the patio," Lyle replied.

"We've worked so hard, I want to slow down just a bit, and relaxing on the swings will be Heaven."

Lyle hung the swings as planned and on a beautiful summer evening, they put down the tools, grabbed a blanket, and cuddled. The views were extraordinary. From the porch, they looked beyond their pond. A herd of elk was settling in for the night in the meadow, only a short distance away. Gazing up, they were overcome by the setting sun over the mountain range. The sky was an assortment of colors.

Comfortable and relaxed, Marylin stated the obvious, "It's happening. Our dream is taking shape."

CHAPTER TWENTY-SIX

In August of 1987, Lyle and Marylin prepared to participate in Lyle's thirty-fifth high school class reunion. Five years earlier, the number of participants had dropped, but early indications were that attendance at this reunion would be high. The event was planned over a weekend in Vail, Colorado. The first evening was filled with reminiscing over past times. There was a lot of laughter and while most were intoxicated, the group had learned through the years that neither Lyle nor Marylin would drink alcohol. Regardless, with the passing years, the bond of a common school experience brought unity and camaraderie and it was fun for all. The following day included a variety of activities in the mountain area.

While hiking a beautiful trail, Marylin shared with Lyle what she'd been thinking since their arrival. "We look a lot younger than the others."

"You're the prettiest girl in the school. Always have been," Lyle boasted.

Marylin quickly returned the compliment. "And you have the most hair!"

Given the hard work over the years, neither Lyle nor Marylin had put on much weight. They did look good. Marylin attributed it to the absence of alcohol and tobacco but Lyle chalked it up to hard work and genetics. Regardless, their youthful appearance conflicted with the normal aches and pains associated with aging. Years of construction work left Lyle with back pain and Marylin occasionally struggled with kidney infections and migraines, a complication from her difficult pregnancies. Spending time with former classmates reminded them they were getting older. It was also eye-opening to see some of their friends had retired. Retirement had always been a milestone that seemed so far off, but now, it seemed a bit closer.

WORK ON THE mountain home increased and just as quickly, balances in their bank accounts were reduced. Money was running low and there was still a lot of finish work needed before the home could be occupied. Lyle and Marylin decided the time had come to sell their Denver home. Their equity would provide enough cash to complete the mountain home plus leave a small emergency fund. The Denver home was listed and sold quickly. For a short time, Lyle and Marylin moved in with Marylin's mother, but in early 1990, they finally moved into their yellow house in the mountains.

Lyle completed over twenty-five years of service with the Denver Fire Department and was eligible for retirement. He couldn't stop working, and would never want to, but retirement from the Fire Department would provide him the time necessary to pursue construction work and free him up to work on the Bar D-M. Max wanted a barn and convinced Lyle they should buy horses. Lyle wanted a large wood shop to hold his tools and allow him to create. Max funded the cost of materials and Lyle committed to the labor. Once complete, it satisfied both of their needs.

MARYLIN ALSO HOPED to secure a full pension but would need three more years of service to qualify for her state pension. She regularly spent weekdays with her mother while she worked and then weekends with Lyle in Grand Lake. Lyle was as busy in "retirement" as he'd ever been. With the barn completed, Max wanted another barn built closer to his cabin that would provide an additional kitchen, bedrooms, and bathroom. Of course, no one but Lyle would be selected as the contractor.

But then the unexpected occurred. Max suffered a stroke. The stroke was devastating and impacted his mobility and speech. It also led to his decision to retire from Conoco Oil. Recovery would take time. Max was never one to sit still and was determined to spend his time recuperating at the Bar D-M. There he could engage with Lyle in conversations surrounding future improvements on a property he'd dedicated time and money to develop. He wanted to get his hands into the dirt and with Lyle's help, work became his therapy.

Their time together consisted of completing various small projects in the Pitcher's new barn and exploring their interest in horses. Adjacent to the original barn, they built a tack shed to hold saddles, reins and other items that were needed for horses.

Early one morning, Max and Lyle paused long enough to sip some hot chocolate Max had prepared. They sat together on the porch of the Pitcher cabin and rocked slowly, observing the moose strolling through the morning fog that had set in on the meadow. The calmness was interrupted by the phone ringing in the kitchen.

Lyle quickly stood and jogged to the kitchen.

"Lyle, you need to get to Denver quickly. Marylin is in the hospital," the voice on the other end of the phone call frantically stated.

Lyle stood frozen in disbelief. "What? The hospital? What happened?"

Max could hear the exchange and saw the fear on Lyle's face. He walked into the kitchen, grabbed the keys to his truck. "I'll drive. Let's go."

When they arrived at the hospital, they learned that two mental health patients had attacked Marylin and another nurse in an escape attempt. Earlier, the courts had accepted the claim of diminished capacity for the two offenders and placed them in the mental health facility as an alternative to prison. Fort Logan was a secured facility and had lockdown procedures, but it was managed by nurses, not guards. On the night of the planned escape, Marylin heard screams for help from down the hall.

"Marylin! Help me! I need help!"

Marylin ran to the doorway and upon entering a bathroom, was overtaken by one of the men. He strangled her until she passed out, leaving both nurses for dead as they made their escape. Emergency crews rushed the woman by ambulance to the hospital. Along the way, they provided oxygen and took measures to resuscitate them.

"She's going to make it, Lyle," the doctor assured.

As Lyle walked into the room, he saw the love of his life lying unconscious. Nearing the bed, he could see the bruises across her neck and abrasions on her face. Tears turned to anger as he contemplated the evil men that could do something so heinous. *How could they? I'm going to…*

Lyle's thoughts were interrupted as Max entered the room. "She needs a blessing. Lyle, help me."

Lyle anointed Marylin's head with oil, something his church taught was a part of healing in the Savior's way. Max then stood next to Lyle and together they placed their hands on Marylin's head as Max pronounced a blessing and promised healing.

THE NEXT MORNING, Marylin opened her eyes. She saw Lyle, asleep on a chair in her room. "Lyle," She struggled to whisper.

He immediately rushed to her bedside. Tears returned, but now they were tears of gratitude to his Heavenly Father for answering his prayers that rose to the heavens late into the evening.

"How's the house coming along?" Marylin asked.

The house. He couldn't care less about the house. All he wanted, all he needed, was his Punk. "You can't go back to Fort Logan."

While Marylin knew he was right, her love for her patients tugged at her heart. "I don't need to go right away. We can discuss it later. I'm glad you're here. Fill me in on what you've gotten done."

When Marylin returned to work, she learned that the two fugitives had been captured and were now in prison. When she lost the tip of her finger years earlier, it scared her, but this shook her to the core. She couldn't understand what would drive someone to the point of attempted murder, but she was now a victim and would never be the same. Still, she wasn't ready to retire. Her work with the mentally ill patients was gratifying, but serious retirement planning was underway.

Living in her yellow house in the mountains was a welcomed oasis, and now Lyle and Marylin were together every day.

"Can you believe it?" Lyle exclaimed. "We haven't spent this much time together alone since we were in high school."

Leaning in to hug her husband of forty years, Marylin replied, "And I still love you! Thanks for my yellow house. I love it!"

CHAPTER TWENTY-SEVEN

With the house complete, they weren't alone for long. Lyle joked that he should have put in a revolving door due to the non-stop arrival and departure of family. They had five children, and now grandchildren were arriving. Lylo and his wife adopted their first two children because of difficulties conceiving, but then proceeded to have three successful pregnancies.

Cherrie had seven children. She had planned to stop after their sixth, however, while attending a church service, she made a decision that would bless them with another. A doctor had recently returned from Belize and was reporting on his humanitarian trip during a church service. While describing the challenging circumstances associated with life in that country, he told the story of a Mayan Indian girl living in a thatched hut. Now seven, the girl needed health care not available in her country. The doctor went on to explain that the only way the girl could receive help in the United States would be if a family were to adopt her. Cherrie sat listening but couldn't stop reflecting on the image of this young girl in need of assistance. *I have been so blessed. We need to do something.* Leaning towards her husband, Cherrie whispered, "I feel like we should help."

It would take time, but ultimately the Wilsted family adopted the girl and brought her to the United States where she received the medical care she desperately needed. On each Wilsted family visit to Grand Lake, Lyle and Marylin marveled at the love they witnessed from Cherrie and her family.

Kim had two children but soon after divorced her husband. They remained friends and shared responsibilities in rearing their children. Glenn and Wayne had only begun having children but already had two each. Only forty-six, Marylin had ten grandchildren. She loved to entertain visitors, especially family. Much of her day was spent in the kitchen where she prepared carefully orchestrated meals. Her kitchen was the main gathering point in the yellow house and many conversations were enjoyed standing around the island range top while Marylin worked her magic. Her meals and desserts, particularly her pies, were legendary. The aroma of her cooking would entice the entire household and it was common for guests to sneak a taste of the culinary masterpieces. When she caught someone nibbling, Marylin would shoo the intruder away, adding to the anticipation of another memorable meal.

They didn't leave empty handed. Marylin collected a variety of unique dishes and bowls and made sure they were always stocked with all varieties of candies, cookies, and nuts, a tribute to her Aunt Mary. They were always on display and positioned on her kitchen counter. Over time, the collection of dishes grew, requiring an expansion of counter space dedicated to the treats. Given their prominence in the kitchen, it was the most heavily traveled path through the home. Children and grandchildren would run through, stop momentarily to reach for a handful of their favorites, then run into the family room. After they passed, Marylin would open the cabinet below, pull out replenishments, and ensure each container was always full. To the family, it seemed a never-ending supply of sweets. For Marylin, pleasing her family and other visitors was fulfilling and gratifying. Lyle was no stranger to the candy counter and over time, he consumed more than his share.

When the family arrived for visits, the noise and commotion of children playing and running through the house drove Lyle crazy. In retirement, Lyle hoped to exhibit more patience. Throughout his life, he was known to be kind, loving, generous, and fun to be around…except with family. At home, things tended to cause him stress and those he loved most were often the ones to deal with his release of frustration. He wanted to change but found it sometimes overwhelming.

Glenn and Wayne had arrived with their children for a winter stay. Sitting at the kitchen table, they were enjoying a conversation with their parents when they heard their children bouncing down the metal, spiral staircase that connected the playroom to the hallway outside the kitchen.

"Hey, hold it down," Lyle yelled. The volume and intensity of his voice froze the kids in their tracks. "Stop running in the house!" he shouted.

The grandkids were scared.

"Don't yell at the grandkids," Marylin scowled.

"I'll yell if I want to," Lyle responded. He looked at his sons. "They're your kids, keep them under control. In my day, kids were to be seen, not heard."

Now Marylin was angry. In exhaustion over her husband's lack of tolerance, she rose from the table and walked to the family room where the grandkids had gathered around the television. Taking a deep breath, Marylin knelt. "Grandpa is having a bad day. Don't mind him. Come back and get some candy." Now walking back to the kitchen, she looked at her boys, said goodnight, and then directed her stare at her husband. "I'm going to bed."

The wrinkles around Lyle's eyes deepened as he was now angry at his sons. With a scowl on his face, he exclaimed, "I'm always in the doghouse after you leave."

Lyle would spend countless hours "in the doghouse." He loved his family, and he loved the visits, but his tolerance and patience with children, and the chaos that accompanied them, he had yet to master. Now leaving to join Marylin upstairs, he paused long enough to turn to his sons. "I'm sorry. I'll do better.

CHAPTER TWENTY-EIGHT

Dᴜʀɪɴɢ ᴛʜᴇ ꜰᴀʟʟ of 1993, Marylin was experiencing health problems attributed to a hiatal hernia and a tumor in her esophagus. Treatment for the tumor would require a daily series of radiation treatments, only available in Denver. She would wake early and leave her home at five o'clock and usually be back by early afternoon. Lyle was busy with projects around the property and while Marylin appreciated his hard work, she was feeling somewhat alone in her struggles. Truth was, Lyle and Max had a long list of priorities, and she wasn't currently on the list.

Feeling a bit alone and jealous, Marylin reasoned with her husband that they could use some time together. "Lyle, I think you should come with me to Denver for my doctor's appointment tomorrow. I could use your support. Besides, you've been working so hard and you could use a break."

"Marylin, I already promised Max I'd help him build the corral. Besides, you mentioned it was a simple treatment. It will take the most of the day by the time you make the round trip."

Marylin's feelings were tender. Undeterred, she again asked, "Can't you just take one day to be with me?"

"Punk, I promise I'll join you next week but we only have so many good weather days left and we've got a lot of posts to place. Next time."

The morning of October 11, Marylin began her trek alone, upset that Lyle didn't show more concern for her. *I'm always taking care of him, I wish that he would slow down enough to help take care of me.* The more she pondered, the more upset she became. Eventually, she shifted her thoughts to Lyle's more positive traits. *He works so hard. He's always tried to provide for our family. He's honest. He's faithful to me.* Contemplating even further, Marylin continued to count her blessings. Lyle was at the center of her world and while it appeared his passion for work took priority, she recognized his efforts as his way of demonstrating love. Nearing the hospital, Marylin spotted her mother waiting in the parking lot. "I'm so glad to see you."

Amy replied, "Anything for you."

WITH MARYLIN NOW in Denver, Max and Lyle would have much of the day to tackle the work of building the corral. October in the Rockies is magnificent and there are numerous signs that winter is on the way. On this particular day, the entire area of Grand County was covered with fog as Grand Lake, Shadow Mountain Lake, and Granby Reservoir had not yet frozen and they emitted a vast amount of steam into the air. The Colorado River ran adjacent to the property and contributed to the thick fog. Lyle and Max sensed the urgency to complete the project as it wouldn't be long before snow arrived. Given the size of the job, Max purchased a tractor and auger. It made for easy work in digging the forty post holes and would come in handy on countless other projects around the Bar D-M.

Materials arrived the day prior and the men got to work digging. They were frustrated by the terrain that contained a heavy concentration of gravel. Additionally, the cold evening temperatures had begun to freeze the ground.

"This is why we bought the auger," Max explained.

Lyle was quick to recognize the benefits. "Yeah, otherwise you'd be directing the work while I throw my back out!"

They both laughed and took in the realization that they were blessed.

Max backed up the tractor and aligned the auger with the spot Lyle indicated would be the northwest post. As the auger met the ground, it failed to break the surface. "It's not heavy enough. The ground is frozen," Max yelled over the noise of the diesel engine.

"Not to worry, I've got this."

Lyle leaned into the auger and applied the weight of his body. The spinning auger caught hold of a string that dangled from his hoodie sweatshirt. In a split second, his arm was pulled into the drive shaft that connected the auger to the tractor.

"Stop the tractor," Lyle screamed.

Lyle's arm spun around and round until it was completely twisted off from his body.

Max quickly turned off the tractor, but it was too late. Lyle was in trouble.

"You need to cut me loose quickly or I'll bleed out."

Max used his pocketknife to cut away at the materials pinning Lyle to the auger. As Max cut, Lyle noticed something extraordinary. Looking down, he saw his left arm lying on the ground. His wristwatch was pointing towards the air. Lyle couldn't make out the time but realized his arm was completely removed from his body. *That's my arm, but I don't feel anything. I'm going to bleed to death.*

"Grab me some rags. Towels. Anything. I need to pack the wound."

Max helped Lyle as he worked to control the bleeding. Using his right hand, Lyle reached deep into the cavity near his left armpit and grabbed hard. Turning to his side, he leaned into the auger, using his weight to assist in adding pressure. Adrenaline was flowing and he knew he was in a state of shock. *Stay alert or you'll bleed to death.* The pain began to intensify.

"Max, you need to call 911. Now." Fortunately, only weeks earlier, a phone line had been installed in the barn, just behind the scene of the accident.

"They need to send a Flight for Life helicopter," Lyle screamed as Max was explaining the emergency.

The emergency operator explained, "Sir, the nearest helicopter is in Fort Collins. We're sending an ambulance now."

As a senior executive with Conoco, Max knew how to demand action and he was now in executive mode. With the seriousness of Lyle's injury and the initial shock now fading, Max screamed, "Listen to me.

I need that helicopter now. The arm is severed and he'll bleed to death driving to Denver. Get me the Flight for Life. Now!"

Lyle continued applying pressure around his armpit. The shredded material from his jacket had bound him to the auger, making it difficult to breath.

After hanging up the phone, Max ran back to assist Lyle.

"Can you free my neck?" Lyle asked.

Using his pocket knife, Max cut the material away. With Lyle's neck now clear, breathing became easier.

"Now what?" Max asked.

"We wait. And pray."

It felt like an eternity, but twenty minutes later, the paramedics arrived. They found Lyle pinned to the machinery fighting to control the bleeding. Many of those that came to help knew Lyle from his volunteer service on the Grand County Search and Rescue Team. As they worked to free him from the tractor, Lyle overheard the radio communication with the Flight for Life helicopter. It had left Fort Collins and was navigating the mountain passes.

"They're on their way, Lyle," Sheriff Zellars shared.

"Let us give you some morphine," the ambulance nurse suggested.

"No!" Lyle groaned. "No drugs yet." He was fully in control of his senses and knew that as soon as pain medications entered his bloodstream, he would drift into a deep sleep. He insisted that he remain alert as he trusted his experiences as an EMT. His insights could prove helpful as lifesaving efforts were being made. Additionally, he needed God's help and wanted a clear mind as he asked for divine assistance. Once Lyle was completely freed from the auger, the medics carried him into the ambulance, being careful not to disrupt the lock Lyle had on arteries and veins.

With Lyle still lying on his side to add pressure, the next radio message sent a chill over the team. "The entire valley is socked in with fog."

The weather conditions made it impossible to land. The pilot then spoke the most devastating blow. "I'm low on fuel, and if I can't land soon, you'll have to drive him to Denver." It was a death sentence, and both Lyle and Max knew it. Both men offered silent prayers, pleading with their Heavenly Father for help.

Lyle's prayers were interrupted by the pilot. "We see a small opening in the clouds. We're landing, but you'll need to bring him to us. We have no idea where we are."

Deputy Sheriff Carl Zellars would later share publicly that miraculously, "A small hole opened in the fog, directly over where the ambulance carrying Hileman was parked." He would also report to the newspaper. "It probably was the only break in the fog in the whole area."

As the Flight for Life neared the ground, no one could believe their eyes, but it was less than one hundred feet from the ambulance.

Over the years, Lyle's faith had strengthened and became a primary focus in his life. He had been taught about Jesus Christ's power to heal. He had experienced healing, both as a recipient and as one providing a blessing. The ordinance was much like a prayer and included anointing the recipients head with oil and then pronouncing the individual be healed. Through faith, Lyle believed miracles could occur. Now, he needed God's help more than ever. As they prepared to depart, Lyle shouted to Max, "I need you to give me a priesthood blessing."

Max climbed into the helicopter and anointed Lyle's head with a drop of consecrated oil he always carried in a vile attached to his key chain. Then, he placed his hands on Lyle's head and began to offer a prayer. Both his and Lyle's eyes were closed, but the two medics continued to work on preparations for leaving. As the blessing was pronounced, the medics paused and looked at each other with puzzled expressions, never having seen anything like this before.

Now finished, Max stepped away and lowered himself to the ground. Moments later, the helicopter lifted off and the flight to Denver began. Only when the medics notified Lyle that they were ten minutes from the hospital did he determine to seek relief.

"Okay, I'll take the morphine now." He knew at this point he could let go of the situation and place his life in the hands of the professionals and God. Seconds later, he could feel the medication taking its effect. *Punk, I'm sorry. Punk, forgive me.* Then he was asleep.

Located east of Denver are two adjacent hospitals, St. Anthony's and Presbyterian-St. Luke's. Marylin's mother helped check her in and waited with her until the doctors were ready to begin her procedure. Amy then returned to her home, only ten minutes away. The procedure was about to get underway at St. Anthony's when a nurse emerged to notify Marylin that Lyle was involved in a terrible accident. The nurse then handed the phone to her. On the line, Marylin heard the voice of her mother.

"I don't have the details yet, but Lyle's in trouble. Flight For Life will be arriving soon across the street at Presbyterian. I'll be by in ten minutes to pick you up."

Fear and concern flooded Marylin's mind. She needed to be there when Lyle arrived.

"Mom, I'll meet you there. I'm running over now."

Marylin's oldest son, Lylo, was an anesthesiologist at Presbyterian-St. Luke's Hospital. As Marylin arrived, she asked the emergency room attendant to page her son.

While she waited, her thoughts raced about her feelings of neglect earlier in the morning. Her thoughts were now completely on her husband. He was in trouble and there would be nothing Marylin wouldn't do to help him.

She was directed to the Intensive Care Unit. As she entered the ICU, she saw the faces of her daughter Kim and son Wayne. Moments later, Lylo and Amy arrived.

"Lylo, you and Wayne need to give your father a priesthood blessing as soon as they arrive," Marylin instructed.

Soon after, a rush of emergency workers ran into the ICU. Lyle was unconscious, but the ambulance attendant explained to the family that while he had lost a lot of blood they were able to control the bleeding during the flight.

"We're going right to surgery," a doctor explained to Marylin.

Lylo knew the doctor and interjected, "I just need a minute."

Lylo and Wayne then stepped to the side of their father. Marylin listened to the wonderful prayer of faith but was disappointed that while promises of life were given, there was no mention of saving Lyle's arm. Lyle had spent his life working with his hands and she feared the pain and difficulty associated with the loss of a limb would be too much for him. Silently, she offered her own prayer, *Heavenly Father, you know he needs that arm. Please, please let him retain the use of his arm.*

It would be several hours later that Max arrived at the hospital. Upon questioning Lyle's condition, Wayne shared what they knew.

"Dad is in stable condition. They believe he'll live."

Looking toward Marylin, Max could see the tears rolling down her cheeks. Walking close, he placed his arm around her shoulder and asked, "How are you holding up?"

"He's going to live Max, but he needs to keep that arm. He'd be miserable without it," she cried.

Max quickly responded, "No worry, I took care of that in the helicopter." Max then shared the inspiration he felt upon giving Lyle the blessing that led to him promising Lyle he would live and that his arm would be restored. Marylin felt peace in knowing the Savior was looking out for Lyle and that all would be well.

During the first few hours in the hospital, countless efforts were made to stabilize Lyle's life. In the waiting room, a surgeon approached Marylin. "Mrs. Hileman, I represent a team of surgeons that are in Denver to explore strategies to reattach severed limbs. While still unproven, we would like to perform a procedure known as limb replantation surgery."

She interrupted, "Yes, please, yes!"

The doctor went on to explain the low probability of success, but then shared the incredible coincidence that some of the world's premier experts were gathered in Denver and that Lyle could benefit from some of the latest techniques available.

Updates came every fifteen minutes and early in the evening doctors confirmed the arm was being re-attached. Even though the arm was severed, the nerve bundle was stretched and remained intact. Surgery would last for many hours.

On one occasion, the nurse commented, "Miracles are occurring and angels are present in the room."

The day after surgery, Marylin and Wayne sat with Lyle in the recovery room. Lyle tried to speak, but with a breathing tube, all anyone heard was mumbled words.

Observing the motion of his hand, Marylin questioned, "You have an itch?"

Lyle's response confirmed his irritation. Assuming an area around his face, Marylin leaned in and gently scratched under his nose and around his cheeks. Lyle muttered in frustration, but again, neither Marylin or Wayne could understand.

"What are you saying Lyle, where do you itch?" Marylin again inquired.

Listening carefully to Lyle's mumbled response, Wayne interjected, "Mom, I think his balls itch."

Immediately, Lyle's response came as a confirming groan "AGH!" The unthinkable task fell to Marylin who lovingly attempted to satisfy and relieve his discomfort. Lyle's frustration was vocalized and while the words were not understood, only one other person in the room could appreciate the dilemma and the needed solution.

"Mom, you're not doing it right. You need to scratch harder," Wayne instructed.

"Then you do it!" Marylin replied.

Without thinking, Wayne aggressively assumed the role of digging in for a real scratch.

"Ahhhhhhhhhhhhhh," Lyle responded.

For the first time since hearing of the accident, Marylin was brought to laughter.

Caught in the moment, and with his hand surrounding his father's private parts, Wayne immediately withdrew from the unpleasant task. "I assume my share of the inheritance has increased, right?"

Marylin and Wayne giggled and noticed Lyle crack a smile.

LYLE SPENT SIX weeks in the hospital and each day brought miraculous news of progress. The hospital staff went to extraordinary measures to make Marylin comfortable as she rarely left her husband's side.

Eventually, Lyle stabilized enough to be moved into a rehabilitation facility. Blood was flowing to his arm and hand and recovery looked promising. Typically, only the patient would be allowed in the room at the rehabilitation facility. However, given the circumstances and with many of the doctors being friends of Lylo, an exception was made for Marylin. She longed to remain near her spouse and was grateful for the exception made to accommodate her.

During the first week in the rehab center, Marylin was concerned over what appeared to be an unusual amount of blood in Lyle's dressings. "Nurse, would you take a look at his dressing? It doesn't look right."

"It's fine. I just checked it. By the way, visiting hours are long past; you need to leave!"

Not wanting to jeopardize the exception and accommodations given, Marylin began to leave the room but stopped at the doorway when she spotted a familiar doctor across the hall. "Excuse me. I need help."

Annoyed by her overstep, the nurse assured the doctor entering the room, "I've already checked it. It looks normal."

As the doctor examined the arm, he quickly shouted, "Get the surgery room prepped, now."

In only a few seconds, several doctors and emergency room personnel surrounded Lyle and quickly began to move him. The nurse moved to the far side of the room to assist in lifting Lyle from the bed. Now standing next to Lyle, she felt something wet beneath her feet. Looking down, she saw a pool of blood she hadn't noticed in the previously darkened room.

"It's serious, Marylin," the doctor said as they began pushing Lyle out of the room. Looking back to Marylin, the doctor then yelled out, "You just saved your husband's life!"

Hours later the nurse approached Marylin in tears. "I'm so sorry. They have stabilized Lyle, and I just learned the bleeding was from a torn suture in the artery. If you hadn't persisted, Lyle would have died."

Marylin felt a tug of compassion for the nurse and assured her that she had no hard feelings.

Eventually, other family members would be allowed for brief visits. On his first visit to the rehab center, Wayne rushed in to embrace his father, now awake and clear of the anesthetics. "Dad, I understand your arm is doing great."

Lyle's response caught everyone by surprise. "Why did it have to be my left arm? At least it could have been the one with my tattoo."

Marylin and the kids in the room smiled as they had often been told by Lyle of his disdain for the constant reminder from his youth.

After several months at the rehab center, Lyle was stable enough to continue treatment and rehabilitation from home. Given the drive to Grand Lake was nearly three hours, they chose to stay with Marylin's mother in Wheat Ridge. This made the daily trek for Lyle's recovery more manageable and provided Marylin with precious time with her mom. Lyle's arm continued to show promise as he attacked his exercises like everything else he committed to - with full force.

While the arm was healing, a different, darker problem emerged, situational depression. The doctors assured Lyle and Marylin that this condition was common after trauma, but with each passing week, fear occupied Lyle's thoughts. Years earlier, he had lost a brother to suicide, and while he'd not shared with anyone, thoughts of ending his life were frequent.

"Punk, I need your help," Lyle finally shared.

Not anticipating a disclosure of this magnitude, Marylin replied, "What can I do?"

Lyle then slowly expressed his fears out loud. "I'm having thoughts of suicide. I can't shake the blues and I'm exhausted from the recovery."

Having worked in mental health for years, Marylin jumped into action. "Let's go!"

Together, they drove to the doctor's office and spent considerable time with a psychiatrist discussing the options for help. It was decided that Lyle should begin taking a medication that showed promise with patients experiencing deep depression. Prozac. It would take some time, but Lyle's thoughts cleared, his countenance brightened and his zest for living was restored.

The early summer days in Grand Lake are magnificent! June of 1994 was particularly special. Walking on the deck of her yellow house, Marylin spotted Lyle, carefully working the concrete that would become the permanent front steps to their home. Less than nine months had passed since Lyle's accident and already he was back doing what he loved most, working. As the healing continued, Marylin marveled as she'd watch her husband reach down to pick up one of his grandchildren for a toss into the air. The same air that months earlier, angels had parted to allow for lifesaving help to arrive.

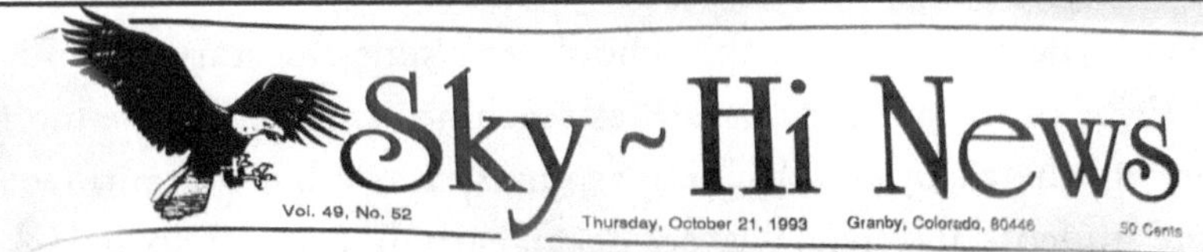

Sky ~ Hi News

Vol. 49, No. 52   Thursday, October 21, 1993   Granby, Colorado, 80446   50 Cents

Severed arm nearly saved?

by Cece Krewson

His arm nearly severed in an agricultural accident on Oct. 15, Lyle Hileman, 59, of County Road 491, Grand Lake, appeared a week later to be well on the way to regaining almost full use of the limb.

On the morning of the mishap, Hileman was helping his neighbor, Max Pitcher, dig post holes on the Pitcher Ranch. Pitcher was operating the tractor, while Hileman was manning the auger.

Suddenly, the cuff of Hileman's jacket became caught in the auger, with his arm being drawn into the machine.

Hileman drew upon his courage and skill with emergencies to take action that probably kept him from bleeding to death.

His arm was nearly severed at the shoulder, with ruptured arteries spurting blood.

A retired Denver firefighter, Hileman drew upon his courage and experience in dealing with emergencies to take immediate action that probably kept him from bleeding to death.

According to Deputy Sheriff Carl Zellars, who responded to Pitcher's 911 call along with Deputy Mike Krueger, Hileman pulled himself up against the drive shaft connecting the auger to the tractor and pressed his wound against the shaft, effectively stopping the flow of blood.

A Flight for Life helicopter responded immediately, but encountered dense fog enroute to the scene. Deputy Zellars said that as the pilot reached Corona Pass he reported that the fog was so heavy he couldn't see the ground and was unable to locate the town of Grand Lake.

But suddenly, Zellars said, a small hole opened in the fog directly over where an ambulance carrying Hileman was parked. "It probably was the only break in the fog in the whole area," Zellars said.

In the meantime, ambulance personnel had managed to bandage Hileman's wound to permit his transfer from the auger to the ambulance. Zellars paid particular tribute to EMT Wayne Kerber for packing the wound in such a matter that blood loss was minimal during the transfer.

Once aboard the helicopter, Hileman was rushed to Presbyterian/St. Luke's Hospital in Denver where a team of doctors from the hospital's unique Institute for Limb Preservation was waiting.

The medical team re-attached the limb and "revascularized" it, restoring the flow of blood. On Monday a hospital spokesperson said that the operation appeared to be a success although the first few days following the surgery are crucial.

She also said the arm seems to be viable and promises to be more useful than would a prosthesis that would have had to be used had the arm been amputated.

She said that additional surgery is scheduled for later this week. "Mr. Hileman will be with us for some time," she added.

Brave man

In the upper picture, emergency workers prepare to move Lyle Hileman of Grand Lake to a waiting ambulance and then a Flight for Life helicopter that transported him to Presbyterian/St. Luke's Hospital in Denver. The lower picture shows how Hileman's jacket became caught in a post hole auger, dragging his arm into the device. Although his arm was nearly severed, Hileman held his shoulder against the drive shaft between the auger and tractor to stem the flow of blood until help arrived. (Sheriff's Department photos)

CHAPTER TWENTY-NINE

The summer of '94 was less productive than hoped, but to Lyle, it was wonderful to be alive and back home. While he was able to work, Lyle still lacked the strength he'd previously enjoyed, and fatigue set in quickly. However, by fall, he was feeling good, not 100% but functional.

With the beginning of the school year came the start of seminary. Prior to the accident, Lyle was teaching seminary to the high school youth at church. Teaching seminary was a big commitment for the students and Lyle. Classes began each morning at six o'clock sharp and lasted about an hour. By seven o'clock the kids were off to school and Lyle returned to work on the property. During his recovery, he was sorely missed. The study for the year was the New Testament and the kids loved the way Lyle could bring the scriptures to life. He also had the best stories and could tie them to nearly any spiritual subject.

When told of Lyle's accident, the youth met with their church leader and begged him not to release Lyle from his assignment. They didn't want another teacher. They promised to teach themselves and report on their progress throughout the year.

During the long winter months, the seminary students made frequent visits and shared the things they were learning. Listening carefully, Lyle thought, *These kids are amazing. They're teaching me.*

With a new school year, and Lyle's health restored, he again was teaching the seminary students. As Lyle walked into the room, the entire class broke out in cheers.

"Brother Hileman, we love you. Great to have you back," one student proclaimed.

Balloons and a banner adorned the classroom. And there was cake, a bowl, and milk. The kids knew Lyle's favorite was chocolate cake. Marylin had told the students many times about the first cake she made for Lyle. It was a work of art. As soon as she presented it, he cut a piece, placed it in a bowl and covered it with milk. Using a spoon, he then smashed the cake into a mush. Seeing her labor of love destroyed brought Marylin to tears. Now, years later, the students were prepared. The milk, bowl and spoon were the perfect complement to the cake they brought.

Deeply touched, Lyle stood trying to find the words. They never came. The tears that flowed freely spoke volumes. The love was mutual.

By December, winter had arrived in Grand Lake and Lyle wanted to celebrate his seminary students' accomplishments. "Max, I need to borrow your snowmobiles."

Max was quick to respond. "Anytime. You sure you can ride?"

"Not yet. I'm still working to regain strength in my arm, but I invited the seminary students up on Saturday to play in the meadows."

As the youth arrived at the Hileman home, Lyle met them in the driveway. It was cold, about twenty degrees. After giving the kids instructions, he turned them loose.

"Just come in before noon. Marylin's made us a great lunch," Lyle instructed.

Lyle returned to the comfort of his warm home and was pleased so many of the kids had shown up. He knew they'd have a great time. Only a few minutes later, Lyle and Marylin heard a knock on the door.

"I've got it," Lyle said.

"Brother Hileman, we can't get the blue machine started," Randy explained.

"I'll be right out."

Stopping in the garage, he grabbed a few necessities. With starter fuel, a new spark plug, and his favorite new tool, rubber bands, Lyle walked through the deep snow to find the kids actively taking turns pulling the starter cord on the machine.

"Hold on, hold on," Lyle shouted. "It's flooded."

After changing the spark plug, Lyle explained the way the carburetor worked and how their efforts likely allowed for too much gasoline to enter the engine. Lyle then shared his best trick. "These things are tough to start with one arm, especially if it was ripped off just a year ago. Rather than holding the throttle with one hand, I hold it down with these rubber bands. That way, I can use both arms on the cord."

The youth were listening carefully and admiring the strength and wisdom of their teacher and friend. Giving the carburetor a quick shot of starter fluid, Lyle closed the hood and confidently related how this had worked every time. Carefully, standing aside the snowmobile, Lyle grabbed the cord with his right arm. Slowly, he added his left arm, the arm that only one year ago had been ripped from his body. With both hands now in position, Lyle placed his left leg on the machine, leaned back, and initiated the first pull.

In an instant, the machine took off. The kids stood in shock. Lyle was lying on the ground, but none of the kids even noticed Lyle had fallen. They were captivated by watching the machine fly across the meadow. Running at full speed, they watched helplessly, the throttle held down by rubber bands. The top speed for a sled is around seventy miles per hour, but in the deep snow, it likely only reached fifty miles per hour. Regardless of the speed, after a direct slam into a large tree, it came to a complete stop.

The machine was totaled. The burst of adrenaline was still rushing through the veins of the kids, and Lyle. "That made for an expensive adventure. I'm sorry guys but you'll have to get by with two sleds today."

Jeremy spoke first. "Brother Hileman, we are so sorry."

"Sorry? What do you have to be sorry about? That was all me. I didn't consider that I was starting a warm engine."

Repeatedly, the kids retold the story recalling every detail of the mishap. Randy waved to the others to stop talking so he could share a thought. "Brother Hileman. Do you remember the lesson you taught last year about Jacob?"

"Huh?"

"Yeah," Jeremy said. "Remember. God changed his name. He was no longer called Jacob. Moving forward he was known as Israel."

Randy then paused, took a deep breath and proclaimed, "Brother Hileman, from here on you will be known to all as The Rubber Band Man."

Instantly, the entire group broke out in laughter. Lyle loved the name and found humor in the experience, even though he knew he'd need to replace the machine.

Inside the warm yellow house, the youth enjoyed telling Marylin all about their experience. Lyle was embarrassed but pleased the time together would never be forgotten. He didn't mind being the target of the laughter and chuckled every time he thought about the adventure.

In the spring of 1995, Marylin and Lyle felt a surge of gratitude. It had been eighteen months since the accident and life had returned to near normal. Lyle's rehabilitation was officially over, although he would continue to work on his own to build strength. They had their health and were determined to enjoy every moment in their yellow house in the mountains. Most importantly, Marylin still had Lyle and he still had his arm.

"We need to do something special to ensure we never forget God's blessings," Marylin suggested.

"What do you have in mind?" Lyle asked.

Marylin shared the idea she felt inspired to carry out. "I want to plant two spruce trees. One for each of us. Follow me."

Together they walked, hand in hand, across their yard to the north of the house.

"This is the place. Look, Lyle. From this point, you see all three mountain ranges. It's beautiful. You can see our home and the flagpole. I want our trees planted here."

Lyle never wanted to disappoint Marylin and he loved her suggestion. A few days later, he arrived with two blue spruce trees in the back of his pickup. Lyle and Marylin dug the holes, prepped the soil, and carefully positioned the trees to ensure they were straight.

"I love them," Marylin exclaimed.

"Me too, Punk."

Marylin then said something that caught Lyle off guard. "When I die, this is where I want my ashes spread."

Lyle quickly added, "Okay, but you better not be leaving anytime soon."

"No, but when I do, I hope we'll go together."

CHAPTER THIRTY

Retirement was everything Lyle and Marylin dreamed of and more. After having spent more than twenty-five years building their yellow house, they now turned their attention to enjoying their creation. Between Max and Lyle, they now had five horses roaming the meadows. Marylin loved watching the horses play but was too afraid to saddle one up and go for a ride. When expertise was needed to care for their horses, they could count on their neighbor, Ken Bruton at the Sun Valley Guest Ranch. Ken was a real mountain man and spent his life around horses.

One day while changing the shoes on Lyle's horses, Ken had a suggestion. "Lyle, you've got two beautiful horses. Have you considered breeding them?"

"I wouldn't know where to begin," Lyle replied.

Ken offered to help breed their mare in exchange for bales of hay cut from the fall harvest. Soon they had three horses, Comanche, Playgirl, and a newborn foal they named Eclipse. Caring for the horses was work, but neither Lyle nor Marylin minded. Ken eventually helped Marylin get comfortable riding and Lyle purchased new saddles in anticipation of the coming summer. The saddles were beautiful and had their names engraved on the leather.

On horseback, they were able to cover a lot more ground and during the summer of '97, they began exploring the beauty of Rocky Mountain National Park. They could cross the Colorado River from their property and head up into the high country. They loved mountain living, and the horses accentuated what was already for them heaven on earth.

Winter dependably brought heavy snow. Lyle enjoyed keeping the roads clear for all the neighbors. He would spend hours on his tractor and rarely complained. His only frustrations occurred when he'd occasionally break a shear pin, or even less frequently, drive the tractor into a ditch. Getting his tractor stuck was occurring a bit more frequently than in years past, but fortunately, there was always a neighbor nearby to assist. Having the snow to remove gave Lyle purpose. For Marylin, clear roads were essential as she lived for visitors during the winter months. Besides, she loved Lyle and if he didn't have his tractor and a project, the time in the house would likely drive them both crazy.

For years, Lyle and Marylin dreamed of retiring in their yellow house, but they rarely discussed the details of what it might entail. Another hope they had in retirement was to volunteer as workers in the nearest temple of their church, The Church of Jesus Christ of Latter Day Saints. The temple was located in Littleton, about a three-hour drive from their home.

When the time arrived for them to work, they agreed to serve a six-hour shift every Friday. Initially, it required rising early in the morning and making the treacherous drive over Berthoud Pass in the dark. On their return home, again the drive would be challenging as nightfall had arrived. Eventually, they came up with alternative plans. They would drive to Denver on Thursday and spend the night with one of the children. Their daughter, Kim, and her husband enjoyed having the weekly visits, but their home was a bit out of the way. Wayne lived very close to the temple but was in the chaotic stage of rearing a family. He wanted to better accommodate his parents, so much so, that he remodeled a room in his basement so they could escape the chaos.

Week after week, Lyle and Marylin repeated the same schedule to ensure they had their day in the temple. One evening, Wayne pointed out the mileage they were putting on their vehicle driving to Denver and back weekly. "Mom, I just calculated that you guys are driving more than 12,000 miles each year, just for your temple assignment. With the cost of gas, that's got to hurt."

"Not only that," Marylin responded, "but the maintenance is expensive. We get new tires almost every year."

Lyle added, "But it's a good excuse to get your mother a new car every few years!"

The expense of volunteering in the temple was nothing compared to the satisfaction they received in return. The first benefit they recognized was a broadening network of friends. They quickly became close with the other couples that volunteered on Fridays. But even more special were the occasional encounters with friends and loved ones from their past that would show up to participate in a service. It seemed to happen frequently, and they loved it.

Another real benefit for them was the intellectual stimulation. Working in the temple required a different set of skills than they developed in their careers. Organizational skills were developed and importantly, memorization. Lyle loved the challenge of trying to memorize lengthy dialogues from scripture that he would recite in helping others.

The greatest return, however, was the weekly reminder of their purpose in life. They felt a sense of appreciation to God for blessings and their service was a small way of showing gratitude. Their time also was a constant reminder of their love for each other and family.

ANOTHER ASPECT OF retirement that they had yet to pursue in a meaningful way was travel. For more than fifty years, vacation meant driving to Grand Lake to work. They loved it but it was far from relaxing. Working in the temple, they heard countless stories from friends that had visited locations around the world. Lyle and Marylin hadn't even visited many of the beautiful areas in the United States.

Marylin began to itch for an adventure. "Lyle, I'd like to travel and I have an idea of where."

"Travel. Why would you want to be anywhere other than Colorado? It has everything we need."

"I agree. But there are places I'd like to see and even more important, people. I haven't seen my brothers or sisters in a long time. They always visit us, but I want to visit them."

It was agreed. Lyle and Marylin began carefully planning trips that wouldn't break the budget but allow them to experience family in different settings. The first trip planned was to visit Marylin's brothers, Steve and Mike.

"Alaska is so far away," Lyle complained.

"Oh, it's just a day of flying. You spend more time on your tractor than you'll spend on the plane. I've got everything planned."

Both of Marylin's brothers lived and worked in Anchorage and they were thrilled to share the beauty of their state. Lyle was spellbound by the beauty. He knew the Rocky Mountains, but here he was seeing extraordinary mountains. They jetted out from the ocean into the sky above and the contrast of colors was captivating.

Steve operated a fishing expedition company and owned a cabin in Homer, Alaska. In addition to his lodge, he owned two of the largest fishing vessels on Kachemak Bay.

"Lyle, you're going to love this. The salmon are amazing, but wait until you reel in a halibut," Steve said.

"I don't even like fish, let alone fishing, but I'm happy to give it a try," Lyle replied.

The day on the water was magical, other than a bit of seasickness for Marylin. Even that was overshadowed by the thrill of the experience and beauty. That night, Lyle was exhausted. Previously, his idea of fishing had been to sit by the pond or river and patiently wait until there was a bite on the line. Today, he experienced something entirely different. Reeling in a halibut took every ounce of energy he could muster. The work was worth the effort. Upon returning to Grand Lake, he and Marylin had enough frozen halibut and salmon to feed guests for a year!

After enjoying a beautiful fall back in Grand Lake, Marylin began to crave another vacation. Plans were made to visit her sister

Annetta in the spring. Annetta was living in the Washington, D.C. area.

It had been more than five years since Marylin had seen her sister. Annetta married a military man and his assignments in the United States Air Force required regular moves around the country. Now retired, they too enjoyed volunteer work in a temple. But their assignment was full-time and for three years.

Located just north of the Capital Beltway stands a landmark that is distinct and unmistakable. The temple was impossible to miss, as it rose 288 feet tall and included six spires, three on each side. Making the facility even more majestic was the exterior finish. The entire edifice was encased in white Alabama marble and when contrasted against the trees or night sky, it glowed.

Neither Lyle nor Marylin had ever been in the area and they were drawn to the history. Annetta and Don took time away from their duties at the temple to be tour guide. The couples spent a week together visiting numerous historical sites. Walking the fields of Gettysburg felt like being on sacred ground. The war memorials tugged at Lyle's heart, having several classmates who had been lost in war. The visit lasted for ten days and was wonderful.

"I needed that," Marylin expressed to Lyle as they sat on the first leg of their return flight.

Lyle agreed. "I'll never forget it."

"The changing of the guard was my favorite," Marylin said. "The respect shown at the Tomb of the Unknown Soldier was something everyone should experience."

THE FLIGHT FROM D.C. to New York City was short and they only had a few minutes at LaGuardia Airport to grab lunch before boarding their flight home.

"Mr. Hileman," they heard over the loudspeaker in the airport. "Mr. Lyle Hileman. Please come to the ticket counter."

"I'm Lyle Hileman," Lyle indicated to the agent.

"We have upgraded your seats to Business Class, but only have two window seats. They are in rows ten and eleven. Would you like me to make the change?"

Marylin's expression told Lyle all he needed to know. "That would be great, thank you."

As they took their seats, both were thrilled as neither had spent much time in the air and not only would they have great views during an afternoon flight, they would also benefit from the perks of business class. As the flight reached altitude, Marylin listened to the gentleman sitting next to her in conversation with the man in the aisle seat.

Waiting until they'd finished their brief pleasantries, Marylin reached to touch the man on the arm. "I don't mean to intrude but I overheard you talking. Did you say you worked for Kraft Foods?"

"Why yes," the man confirmed.

"Well, my son works for Kraft Foods."

The man, Bill Mihal, responded quickly. "I'm the Vice President of Sales. I'll bet I know him. What's his name?"

"Glenn Hileman," Marylin proudly disclosed.

"Yeah, I've heard great things about Glenn. He's doing well."

Marylin could barely contain herself, "You should know, he's brilliant."

"I don't think I'd go that far," Bill laughed, "but he's proven to be a hard worker."

"Oh yes, you even said he's doing great things. He's brilliant," Marylin concluded.

The man next to Bill jumped in, "She's right. Your comment confirmed what she said. The kid must be brilliant."

It would be a long flight for Bill. Nearly three hours sitting next to the mother of a young and promising employee. He did enjoy the discussion and finally promised to work with Glenn in the near future. And he did. Three months later, Glenn was promoted to the NYC office.

CHAPTER THIRTY-ONE

Christmas of 1999 was especially joyous as all the Hileman kids and grandchildren visited Grand Lake over the holiday. It was everything Marylin hoped for. They could sit back and watch the interaction amongst their family, and they took great pleasure in their growing posterity of now twenty-two grandchildren. However, the holiday wasn't all bliss. With a house full of kids, it was impossible for Lyle to relax. He could retreat to his tractor to clear snow but eventually, found himself agitated by the noise and movement of a large family gathering.

Marylin was quick to scold him if he ever yelled at the grandkids and Lyle tried hard to avoid being in the doghouse. Rather than letting his frustrations out, he'd learned it was easier to escape to his room and watch his favorite TV show, Gunsmoke. Marylin recognized the signs as she'd seen them through the years. Lyle struggled with anxiety when their home was filled with energetic kids, even though it was built precisely for these occasions. Still, it was taking a toll on Lyle.

A few days later, the Hileman and Pitcher families gathered for their annual barn dance. Five years earlier, Max had created a loft above the barn and a New Year's gathering was now a favorite tradition for both families. Dancing was mandatory. Even Marylin couldn't get out of the obligatory festivities. Having suffered numerous strokes, Max would sit in his rocking chair, smiling. A look of accomplishment emanated from his countenance as his children and the Hileman crew ran through the annual tradition. First came the Chicken Dance, then the Hokey Pokey, and finally the bunny hop. Max's daughter, Marcia, led the group through several square dances, including the Virginia Reel. The final dance of the night was the Limbo.

After the dancing, there were two remaining traditions. First was the New Year's Eve Piñata. Kids lined up from youngest to oldest to take a whack at the piñata that hung from the rafters of the barn. Tom Pitcher would control the string to ensure everyone had a chance. The older kids were blindfolded and Tom took pleasure in making the teenagers miss. With every swing of the stick, parents and grandparents would gasp, concerned that a youngster would walk too close to the activity. Fortunately, no one was ever seriously injured, but there were many close calls.

Finally, the entire group dressed for the cold and walked outside to enjoy the lighting of the annual bonfire. As they prepared to welcome the New Year, this bonfire created a small problem. Over the summer, all the debris and dead trees were piled up in the meadow, as in years past. This year's pile was enormous.

"Dad, it's too big," Wayne observed. "We'll never get it to light."

"Grab some fuel. Ten gallons of diesel and some regular," Lyle instructed.

Glenn and Wayne took the tractor and gathered six five-gallon gas containers. Two were filled with diesel and four with regular. Glenn navigated the bucket of the tractor to position his brother over the woodpile. Wayne opened each container and distributed over thirty gallons of fuel. When the rest of the group arrived, Wayne and Glenn were discussing their concerns over having used too much fuel.

"You can't light that now," Max said expressing his disappointment.

"We've got to light it. Besides, it's freezing out here," Glenn responded.

Wayne had an idea. "Give me a minute. I'll be right back."

When he returned, Wayne had a roll of toilet paper. Max instructed everyone to get back, way back. Wayne took the toilet paper and slid it over a long broom handle. Putting a bit of gas on the roll, he then struck a match. In one smooth motion, the flaming roll of toilet paper was hurled toward the pile of wood. In the dark of night, it caught the attention of the entire group.

When the flaming role of toilet paper was fifteen feet away, the gas fumes ignited and an explosion of fire erupted. The heat pushed everyone back farther. It was dangerous. It was foolish. But it was also never to be forgotten. Smoke from the fire was billowing towards their neighbor's cabin and was so thick, visibility of the cabin was lost.

"Grab the glasses," Max called out.

They proceeded to open the bottles of Martinelli's Gold Sparkling Cider and freely began pouring. Once everyone had a cup of juice held high, in unison they proclaimed, "Happy New Year!"

"To good friends, hard work, and many great years to come!" Max shouted.

A new millennium had begun.

CHAPTER THIRTY-TWO

IIT WAS BARELY five o'clock in the morning when Glenn heard the bedroom door creak open "Glenn, wake up. We need to go," Lyle whispered trying not to wake Glenn's wife, Michelle, still sound asleep next to him.

"Dad, I wasn't feeling great last night after the bonfire. I picked up a bad cold and besides, we need to drive twelve hours back to Phoenix today."

"Okay," Lyle conceded. "I'll let Max know. But he won't be happy!"

"I told Steve last night," Glenn said. With that, he fell back to sleep in hopes of getting another hour or two of rest before making the long drive home with his family.

Steve Pitcher was Max's oldest son. Steve and his brother, Tom, worked late into the evening preparing for what would be another epic adventure. Max initiated the New Year's morning snowmobile ride years earlier and participation was mandatory. Riders were expected to be dressed and ready to leave by five-thirty in order arrive at Blue Ridge in time for the annual traditional. The temperature at 12,000 feet would be frigid and stoking a fire was part of the lure. Fire would provide warmth and also heat the long-established breakfast fare, hot chocolate and breakfast burritos. After eating, the group would await the rising sun of the New Year.

Learning that Glenn was still in bed, Max marched into the yellow house.

"Get up!" Max barked.

Glenn tried to whisper but spoke loud enough to wake Michelle. "Max, I'm not going."

"You're going!"

"No, I'm not. We're driving home today, and I need the sleep."

"You have five minutes," Max spoke with authority, then took a seat in the chair next to the bed. "After that, I start waking up your kids."

Michelle was shocked that Max had walked into the bedroom fully dressed in his snow gear. Her two youngest were asleep on the floor. Not wanting them to wake up, she elbowed Glenn in the shoulder. "Get out of here. Just be back by nine. I'll pack up."

Angry and frustrated, Glenn rolled out of bed and began to dress.

As Max left the room, he looked back at Glenn, "I'll have your machine started. Let's move."

The ride to the top was about thirty minutes and all six of the riders had made the trek countless times. It really was a favorite tradition, but Glenn's thoughts raced, nearly as fast as his sled, *I still can't believe he made me come.*

As they arrived at the top, they located a cluster of trees and began unloading the wood for the fire. Once lit, they threw in the foil-wrapped breakfast burritos that Steve and Tom had made the night before. Next, Max pulled out his large tea kettle and filled it with snow. He then carefully began adding packets of hot chocolate mix. Within twenty minutes, the group was actively engaged in trying to stay warm, eating, and enjoying the hot beverage.

Lyle looked at his son, now huddling close to the fire and sipping his chocolate. "Now aren't you glad you came?" Enjoying the camaraderie and experience, Glenn was feeling a bit guilty for nearly breaking with tradition, especially as his cold symptoms seemed to vanish in the cold mountain air. "Yeah, thanks for encouraging me."

"Here it comes," Tom said while pointing to the east. Quickly the sky turned from black to dark blue and within minutes, light blue. The rays of sun began expanding up and over the mountain in the distance, Mt. Baldy.

Max looked around, and to memorialize the moment exclaimed, "In all the years we've come here, I've never seen it this clear."

It was true. There was no wind and not even a cloud in the sky. After enjoying the time on the mountain, Glenn reminded the others he needed to begin heading back.

"Glenn," Max said, "slow down. It may never be this warm and clear again. How can you resist the fresh powder? We need to stop by Hatchet Park first and enjoy the meadow."

Arriving in the meadow of Hatchet Park, everyone engaged in boondoggling, a maneuver where the rider counter-turns and then lays the sled on its side while accelerating at full speed. When done properly, the tail of the machine whips around, and the rider has an exhilarating thrill. Done wrong, digging a stuck machine buried in snow could take the help of several others. On this magical morning, each rider would rely on the others for assistance as the snow was so deep getting stuck was inevitable.

Checking his watch, Glenn noticed they'd been playing for nearly an hour. "Max, I've got to go. It's already nine, and I have to drive twelve hours to Phoenix. I've got work tomorrow."

"So, you're already in trouble. I've got another plan." Max laughed.

By now, Glenn was feeling better and anxious to learn of Max's next adventure.

"This summer, I took the horses from Hatchet Park to the property. I've tied an orange ribbon along the trail. It will be fun and it's a shortcut," Max explained.

As the riders reached the edge of Hatchet Park, they saw a steep mountain. Before anyone could discuss the danger of the descent, Max and Lyle were over the edge and flying straight down the mountain. It was steep, very steep. Glenn, Wayne, Tom, Steve, and Marcia were left looking at their aging fathers acting like kids.

"Who's next?" Tom asked.

One at a time, the kids took their turn trying to follow the tracks of their fathers. As the riders reached the bottom they observed a creek. While frozen, the previous riders had broken the ice which required the others to accelerate enough to avoid getting stuck. Wayne was the last one down. As he crossed the creek, he joined the others. They turned off their machines and Max directed everyone to walk around to find the first orange ribbon.

"We need to find it because there is no way these machines can climb back out of here," Max explained.

"I've got it," Tom yelled to the others while pointing to the bright orange tape.

With that, they began navigating the thick forest looking for the orange markers Max had placed every quarter mile. They began making progress but after forty-five minutes, the next marker couldn't be found.

"I know it's this way," Max stated.

Lyle wasn't convinced. "Max, that's north. It can't be that way. We need to head east."

"You're turned around. Trust me," Max said breathing hard.

"Max, you're wrong. We need to be heading east," Lyle volleyed.

It was clear to the boys that neither Lyle nor Max would concede. They had dug in and were certain they had the right orientation.

"Hey, a debate isn't going to solve anything," Steve injected. "We need to hike up this hill to get our bearings."

Glenn, Wayne, and Steve waited with the machines while Lyle, Max, Marcia, and Tom made the difficult walk through the snow and towards the top. As they reached the summit, the big yellow Hileman house with its sixty-five-foot tall flagpole could be seen. It was many miles away but at least they now had settled the debate.

Max yelled to the boys at the bottom of the hill. "We'll take Tom with us and you guys try to get the sleds back to the base of Hatchet Park."

Lyle added, "If we start walking now, we'll get back by around four Then we'll grab the truck and pick you up at the park." He then couldn't resist the opportunity to reinforce his superior sense of direction. "Oh, and we'll be walking east, not north!"

Taking three machines at a time, the boys rode about half a mile, then walked back to retrieve the other machines. Over and over again they repeated the effort until they reached the creek with all six machines.

Now barely two o'clock, Wayne shared an idea. "We can't just wait here, we'll freeze. You guys walk up the hill. I'll throttle the machines and climb until I run out of steam. Together, we may be able to get one of these out. We can beat the others home."

The plan was thrilling, hard, and it worked. In fact, so effectively, that within another two hours they had all six machines sitting in the meadow of Hatchet Park. The sun had fallen behind the mountains and it was getting cold, and dark.

"Let's go," Steve said. "We'll come back for the other machines tomorrow."

Glenn and Wayne walked into the yellow house and found Lyle resting comfortably by the fireplace.

"Dad, you were supposed to come to get us," Wayne said.

"We only beat you by an hour. We figured we'd warm up first and then leave at six to find you," Lyle explained.

Glenn found Michelle in the kitchen helping Marylin with dinner.

"I guess you didn't need to be to work tomorrow after all," Michelle said.

Glenn noticed she was smiling. Relieved, he couldn't help but respond, "It was Max's idea and nobody can say no to Max."

The New Year's ride took the entire day. Michelle was a little worried but understood Max's adventures rarely went as planned. For Michelle, having another day in paradise was a blessing.

CHAPTER THIRTY-THREE

After fifty years of marriage, a celebration worthy of their commitment to each other was in order. The family planned a cruise to celebrate together. Neither Lyle nor Marylin had ever been cruising but had heard from others that it would be fun. Nothing could have prepared them for the wonder of seven days together with their children and their spouses. The family met in Miami and boarded a Royal Caribbean ship named Explorer of the Seas. It was massive with twelve levels, two dining rooms, a rock-climbing wall, and a spa. In addition to the amazing food and service, the entertainment on the ship was fun. On the first night at sea, the family was introduced to their cruising staff at dinner. Each night they'd have the same table and servers. After the first dinner together, the couples walked to the ship's auditorium to watch a comedian perform. During his act, he requested volunteers from the audience and Wayne was quick to volunteer. He was brought on stage to interact with the comedian.

Marylin's thoughts quickly drifted to a time when Wayne had been a toddler. Even then, he liked to entertain. As a baby, he'd sit in his highchair, take any food or drink within reach, and pour it over his head. The other kids would break out in laughter which further fueled Wayne's attempts to entertain. Ultimately, it would lead to a rule in the Hileman household. "Anyone who laughs at Wayne will get spanked." As the rule was not strictly enforced, Wayne would continue to make others laugh throughout his life, and now on stage with a comedian, laughter was okay, even encouraged.

The next morning, the family awoke and found themselves in Jamaica. Jamaica was extraordinarily beautiful. The highlight for Lyle was holding Marylin's hand during the entire ascent of Dunn's River Falls.

Another meal, another show, and the next morning they were in Grand Cayman. There they swam with stingrays. Marylin was a bit nervous about the excursion but found it exciting to experience something so unique.

Cruising was fun for the family and the seven days passed quickly. On the final evening, the family gathered for a formal dinner and presented Lyle and Marylin with a gift. The girls had purchased a necklace and earring set and presented them to Marylin along with a 50th Anniversary cake prepared by the ship's chef.

The final night at sea concluded with a talent show. With a little persuading, Marylin convinced her sons to enter. At their appointed time, the three Hileman brothers walked on stage and performed the song "More Than Words" by Extreme.

"That was good," Lyle said.

"Good? It was great!" Marylin proudly corrected.

Nothing could have celebrated the night better for Marylin than to witness her sons walk back on stage to accept the trophy for winning the competition. She was proud of her family and having spent an extended time together, Marylin was filled with joy.

"We need to do this again," Marylin said.

Lyle's nod confirmed his approval. He was beginning to realize the joy of travel and there was so much they had yet to experience.

It wouldn't be long before the couple's next trip was underway.

"Mom, we want you to join us on a vacation," Lylo said over the phone.

Marylin's response came before Lylo could even say where. "When do we leave?"

"Mom, this will be epic. We'll be gone for two weeks," Lylo said. "Pack your bags, we're going to China."

Lylo loved his parents. As their oldest, Lylo experienced many of the growing pains associated with having young and inexperienced parents. His father always wanted the best for his son, but sometimes pushed so hard that Lylo felt he had little input into the choices being made for his life. Regardless, now in his fifties, he was the beneficiary of his parents' sacrifices. His career as an anesthesiologist paid well and he longed to demonstrate his love by spending extended time with his parents.

For two weeks, Lyle and Marylin explored a world they could never have imagined. They were amazed by The Great Wall of China and spent hours one night discussing the effort and time required in its construction. Spending most of their lives in Colorado, they were in awe of Hong Kong. It was enormous. Each day presented insights into a land and culture they never expected to experience and they were grateful Lylo had made the trip possible.

Marylin discovered a passion for adventure and even Lyle got the travel bug. They made plans to visit their children, now scattered all across the country. Over the next few years, they visited Hawaii, Alaska, Vancouver, Arizona, New York, Ohio, North Dakota, Illinois, Missouri, and Arkansas

After every adventure, Lyle and Marylin felt an itch to return to the mountains. There was still nowhere they'd rather be than Grand Lake.

Now a seasoned traveler, Marylin was determined to knock off a "bucket list" trip. Her sights were set on a visit to the Holy Land. Marylin's sister, Amy Sue, wanted in on the adventure and they collaborated in convincing their husbands the time was right.

Jack was eager to go and worked to create the itinerary. The trip would be epic and last for two weeks. They began in Turkey and then moved south through Greece, Italy, and finally, they arrived in Israel.

Each day in the Holy Land included walking tours. Exploring the sites of the Mediterranean was thrilling but as they returned each night to the ship, they were exhausted.

"I think we're getting too old for this," Marylin confessed to Lyle.

Lyle's response pleased Marylin. "You sure don't look or act old. But standing all day at the Vatican about killed me."

They both felt the effects of aging as they pushed themselves to see everything they could. They understood they'd never return to these sights and didn't want to miss anything. Exhausted, they retired to bed early. The following morning, a lifelong goal was achieved as they walked the streets of Old Jerusalem.

The following day they visited Bethlehem. Returning to Jerusalem, they then saw the assumed location of Christ's Last Supper. Outside of the Old City, they stopped in the Garden of Gethsemane. Surrounded by the olive trees, the guide explained, "Christ likely walked amongst these trees."

Jesus likely suffered near these trees, Marylin thought. She recognized they were on sacred ground. For years, she had studied the events surrounding the Savior's atonement but now she was sitting on the very ground of one of the most significant events in the history of mankind.

Finally, they arrived at the last stop of the tour. They stood in a garden cemetery and were directed to a tomb where historians believe the body of Christ was placed following his crucifixion. A large round rock was rolled back to provide visitors visibility into the tomb. As she looked in, Marylin was overcome with emotion. It was empty and yet, the moment she stepped in, her thoughts began to race. *He lives! Jesus Christ was raised from the dead. He is resurrected.* Suddenly, tears began to flow and Marylin was lost in the moment. As she turned to look at her husband, she noticed he was also caught up in reflection.

"Lyle, I feel so blessed to be here," Marylin shared.

That night on the ship, the conversations revolved around the day's events. This was no ordinary trip. The locations they visited were historic, but even more, they were influential in shaping the lives of countless individuals committed to the teachings of Jesus Christ.

As the dinner concluded, Lyle leaned over to whisper in Marylin's ear, "Can we call it a night? I'm exhausted."

There was no argument as they both were physically and emotionally drained.

They were settling down for the night as Lyle leaned into his wife "I'm beat. I'm ready to get back to the mountains to relax."

"I agree. But you better recover quickly. I'm planning another family reunion!"

CHAPTER THIRTY-FOUR

In 2007, Lyle and Marylin organized a family reunion to celebrate fifty-five years of marriage. Each of their children and all twenty-five grandkids planned to attend. The Pitchers offered the use of their cabin.

To accommodate the entire group, Lyle called his neighbor Rick Richmond. He owned a cabin that was more like a mansion. It slept thirty-six! He loved the Hilemans and was more than thrilled to offer his "cabin" for their family reunion.

Now in their seventies, Lyle and Marylin were slowing down. Much of the heavy lifting needed for a crowd of this size would require their grown children to take responsibility. Lyle and Marylin made arrangements for lodging but delegated assignments for food and activities to their children.

Lyle loved having his family around. After all, this is what he'd envisioned for years. But with a large group, the running, yelling, and commotion would be more than he could handle. Marylin knew this gathering posed a risk for Lyle's anxiety to surface again. Rather than chance an outburst, she decided to take preventative measures.

"Doctor Reid, I need your help. Lyle's getting irritable and we have a huge family gathering coming up," Marylin explained.

"What can I do?" he asked.

"You know, he's been on Prozac for years and I've found that on occasion if I give him an extra pill it really helps."

"I know that can be effective, so what's the problem?" the doctor asked.

"I need to increase the prescription, so he doesn't run out, especially when we have family around."

The doctor laughed out loud and then consented. Marylin now had an adequate supply for those times she sensed Lyle might be short on patience.

Sitting at the kitchen table, Lyle was deep into his reading.

"Lyle, take your pills," Marylin directed.

There were pills for blood pressure, pills for strokes, aspirin, and on occasion, an extra pill Lyle never questioned.

"The kids are arriving soon and we have a big day ahead."

It became Marylin's secret weapon, and it worked. On occasions with large groups, she'd make sure he benefited from an extra dose of defense. Lyle never paid enough attention to know.

The entire family was gathered and seeing their posterity together brought joy to Lyle and Marylin.

"It's incredible," Marylin said looking at Lyle who snuggled next to her on the bench.   Lyle didn't speak. He simply soaked up the warmth of the sun and held tightly to the hand of the woman who made it possible. There was running, laughing, and loud noises all around, but Lyle remained calm…the extra Prozac worked!

After several days together, the time for departure arrived. Before anyone could leave, Marylin insisted on a family photograph and directed the family to gather just north of the pond. Lyle and Marylin were surrounded by their children and twenty-five grandchildren. Collectively, their entire posterity now numbered forty-six. The backdrop for the photo was her favorite mountain range in the distance, the Never Summer Range. The portrait was framed and took a prominent place inside the yellow house. Lyle and Marylin looked at it daily.

AT THE CONCLUSION of the reunion, the quiet peace of the mountains returned. Having spent so much time away from their home, Lyle and Marylin returned to their various tasks around the house and property. Marylin focused on most of the household duties, along with cleaning up the Pitcher and Richmond cabins. Lyle was busy mending fences that had fallen or been knocked down by elk over the winter months.

Marylin had just finished folding laundry and while putting Lyle's clothing in the dresser, she saw it. It was hidden beneath the other items in the drawer, but she recognized the object instantly. "Lyle!" she shouted. She could hear him climbing the stairs to the bedroom. He was moving slowly which was a good thing as Marylin was more than angry. The few minutes of waiting allowed her to calm down a bit. "What's this in the drawer?"

"Oh, I bought that a long time ago," Lyle answered.

A long time was likely only a few months as Lyle had found interest in gun collecting and now Marylin was regularly uncovering new guns, nearly every month. Years earlier, Lyle studied and received his Class 3 Federal Firearms License. It allowed him to purchase and sell machine guns and ammunition. It was a hobby for Lyle and a strain on the budget.

"Marylin, it's an Israeli Uzi," Lyle explained.

"I don't care what it is. The last thing you need is another gun."

Lyle reminded her, "Marylin, they're an investment. Someday I'll sell them."

True to his word, Lyle began depleting his inventory of weapons. He still had his handguns and rifle collection, but over the next few years, he sold his inventory of machine guns. To Marylin's surprise, they had appreciated and the profits were used to make improvements around the property.

IN ADDITION TO Lyle's interest in gun collecting, he spent much of his time pursuing his passion for woodwork. Over the years, there was nothing he couldn't build from wood.

"I'm headed down to the shop," Lyle said.

Marylin knew he'd be gone for hours, lost in the creation of another piece of furniture or more knickknacks. Alone now, Marylin was strolling through her house and noticing the number of creations her husband had made. In her kitchen, every cabinet was handmade from oak. Lyle even built a special railing that held her plate collection. In the hallway, she paused to look at a shadowbox that was built in the early 70s. It held many precious objects she'd collected over the years. In it she saw Lyle's graduation ring, Lylo's gymnastic medals, Wayne and Glenn's scouting awards, a tiny set of dentures that Kim had worn at the age of five, and many other small items that would otherwise have been thrown in a drawer and never seen. Pictures on the wall were surrounded by Lyle's frames. *He's built this house and nearly everything in it.*

Marylin now entered the study and immediately her eyes were drawn toward the grandfather clock. It barely fit in the room as it approached nine feet in height. Adjacent to the clock remained the parts he'd purchased earlier but never got around to installing. She stood in front of the entertainment center he created and was reflecting on the day it took six men just to move it into the house. It was solid oak and walnut and held a sound system that had rarely been turned on.

She then saw a barber chair Lyle had purchased from a farm that was destroyed by fire. He had all the parts cleaned and chromed, and he rebuilt the framework from wood. It was then reupholstered. *Incredible.* She turned to her right and saw displayed on the wall a wooden box that held razors and barber scissors he'd been given from his father. She then looked closely at the gun cabinet, which was impossible to miss. Again, solid oak and walnut with glass windows to allow visitors to look in, but not touch, his prized collection. Marylin then smiled as she saw the small key, intended to keep people out, still protruding from the keyhole. *A lot of good that will do.*

Finally, she sat on the chair in front of his desk. Nothing Lyle created was ordinary but this desk was likely his most remarkable work. Lyle spent more than two years building a roll top desk. Of course, it too was solid oak and walnut but most amazing was that each one of the sixty-two rails of the roll top was made of oak, with a walnut inlay. The rails were only an inch wide and about five feet in length. And yet, each had a 1/4 inch walnut inlay set perfectly in the middle. She remembered Lyle describing the process. Each rail required eleven cuts.

Marylin began to calculate the total number of cuts but quickly gave up knowing it would equal more than six hundred. *Wow! The patience this took is unbelievable.* Marylin's astonishment was even greater as she contrasted this with how Lyle struggled in showing patience with his kids. But clearly, he had a gift that couldn't be rushed.

Marylin's musings were interrupted by the ring of the doorbell. It was Max.

"Marylin, Lyle said you had photos of the lake."

"Hundreds."

"No. specifically, I need photos from nineteen seventy two that show there was no groundwater in the lake prior to our improvements."

Max looked worried, but Marylin knew exactly where to locate the pictures. As she handed them to Max, he thanked her and ran off to his car.

Over the years, their water rights to the Colorado River had been challenged and both Lyle and Max were required to show use of their claim annually. But now, the water commission was challenging the water rights of everyone with access to the river. Lyle and Max hired a water attorney, and the defense of their rights required a great deal of time. Fortunately, the photographs documented the development over the years and proved to be essential to helping ensure the water rights would be deemed absolute. This meant they could rest assured that their access to water for the fields, lakes, and ponds was no longer at risk.

After the water project was complete, Max returned to his second home in Utah. Soon after, he suffered a stroke. Max had several strokes over the years. Fortunately, the effect of this one was mild; however, he became more concerned over his health and was especially concerned about the transition of the Colorado property.

"We need to divide the property," Max said over the phone.

"There's no need for that. We share everything," Lyle reasoned.

"I'm not sure how much time I have left, and we can't leave something this important undone. I don't want our kids needing to figure it out."

Lyle hired a surveyor and the Bar D-M was divided into two equal parcels. In more than forty-three years, there had never been a disagreement between Lyle and Max. They often marveled that two people so different could become best friends. They were always aligned and the division of property would be no exception.

"I guess we can rename the ranch now," Marylin reasoned.

"Rename. What do you mean?" Lyle asked.

"Let the Pitchers keep Bar D-M. We'll come up with another name, a name of our own."

CHAPTER THIRTY-FIVE

ONE OF MARYLIN'S favorite activities in retirement was hiking the trails surrounding Rocky Mountain National Park. For years, Lylo and Kim had been her hiking buddies. Each year, Marylin would train to make long hikes over the continental divide with them, but now in her seventies, her energy for long hikes had diminished. However, she still enjoyed the trails and delighted in taking two or three-mile walks.

A favorite short hike began just north of Grand Lake. After only a half-mile walk, hikers could arrive at Adams Falls. Marylin had visited the spot dozens of times and never tired of its beauty.

"Lyle, I want to hike to Adams Falls. Want to come?" She knew it would be unlikely as Lyle found his solace in work.

"No. I'm determined to assemble the grandfather clock that's been collecting dust in the study." Lyle had begun building the clock in 1974, but more pressing projects always seemed to take priority.

Marylin was pleased he was thinking about it. For years, she assumed it would never get completed. "Wonderful! When I get home, I want you to show me the progress."

That day, Marylin felt a sense of peace. There were no other hikers on the trail as the summer season had ended. Most visitors to the area now were hunting and hunters were not allowed inside the park. Arriving at the falls, she positioned herself on a large rock perched high enough to allow a view of the waterfall. The warmth of the sun felt especially comforting as the fall temperatures had arrived. She took a deep breath and slowly exhaled. She felt a surge of energy and again drew in a slow, deep breath. Her heartbeat had now slowed to a normal pace and she began reflecting on her life. *Heavenly Father, thank you. Thank you. Thank you.*

Returning to her yellow house, she saw Lyle standing near the kitchen window. As she drove near the house, Lyle emerged from the doorway and walked quickly toward the moving car. Marylin knew something had happened.

Lyle reached to open the door. "Max has died. Max is gone," he cried.

Heartbroken, they drove to Utah for the funeral service. Just as Max would have expected, the service was an event. The day consisted of over two hours of speakers, a horse-drawn hearse, a parade down Center Street in Alpine, Utah, and finally a traditional Navajo Indian Dance at the graveside. It was over six hours before family and friends departed.

"Wow," Marylin said in exhaustion. "When I go, that is not what I want. Just spread my ashes by our trees."

"Max always did things big," Lyle commented. "I'm sure he loved it."

Marylin sat down to relax. "I agree. But please, keep my service simple."

In 2012, Marylin received a phone call from her grandson, Pat Casey, Kim's son and an accomplished musician living in New Orleans. He met and fell in love with a beautiful and well-known singer, Robin Barnes. Robin was a featured performer at Jazz Fest each year and was known as The Songbird of New Orleans. Pat was an accomplished bass player with a regular gig at The Spotted Cat Lounge. Pat and Robin were courting and he wanted to share the beauty of Grand Lake with her.

"Grandma, I want you to meet Robin. You'll love her."

What Pat didn't share was that on the trip, he planned to propose marriage. Before arriving at the yellow house, they stopped in Grand Lake to hike Adams Falls. Arriving at the falls, Pat dropped to one knee. "Will you marry me?"

After the hike, Pat and Robin drove to the yellow house. Robin had heard countless stories of Pat's memories on the property but now she was going to see for herself. It was even more grand than she'd imagined. Before they could exit the car, Marylin had already reached the driveway to greet them.

"Grandma, this is Robin," Patrick said. "We're engaged!"

After a pleasant visit, Pat and Robin began walking the property. With every step, Pat recalled another story of adventures he had growing up.

"We should get married here in the mountains," Robin said.

Pat couldn't believe it. It's what he'd hoped for but given the distance from Robin's family in New Orleans, it seemed improbable.

"Pat, will your grandparents allow that?"

He smiled and nodded, knowing his grandmother would be thrilled.

Returning to his grandparents' home, Pat and Robin shared their idea and asked for permission. It was settled. The yellow house in the mountains would be the location of their wedding.

A YEAR LATER, the family gathered for the wedding celebration. On the day before the service, Marylin began feeling sick. Now seventy-six, her health was a concern. But this wasn't a typical illness. She felt extreme pain in her lower back and had a high fever.

"Lyle, I think I have a kidney infection. Something is wrong."

Her pain increased and she asked Lyle to take her to the hospital. A few hours later, they learned Marylin's kidneys were failing, likely due to several battles with eclampsia in her child-bearing years. She needed to be admitted to the hospital. The tests revealed her kidneys were functioning at less than thirty percent.

"What does that mean?" Marylin asked.

Her doctor replied, "Unfortunately, it means you'll miss the wedding."

After the rehearsal, Pat and Robin stopped by to visit Marylin.

"Grandma, I'm so sorry," Pat began. "They tell me you won't be there tomorrow but we'll stop by afterwards."

Robin then added, "We'll sneak some cake in for you."

The events of the next day unfolded perfectly, except for the missing family member. The setting was ideal and the ceremony by the pond was memorable. Later in the day, the family returned to the hospital to visit Marylin. She looked exhausted but at least was out of pain and in good care. Lyle on the other hand was showing signs of distress.

"You okay, Dad?" Kim asked.

"I miss your mother," Lyle said. "What would I ever do without her?"

"She'll be fine, Dad. Just keep praying."

They prayed, and prayers were answered. A few days later, Marylin returned to her mountain paradise.

Marylin began taking antibiotics to reduce the risk of infections, and as the summer progressed, so did her health. She began feeling better and was able to engage in various activities she'd put on hold. With Marylin feeling better, Lyle was anxious to begin another project. But he was running out of ideas. *What's next?*

CHAPTER THIRTY-SIX

IN 2014, LYLE and Marylin's youngest grandchild, Charlotte, known as Charlie, was turning six. Lyle was now eighty years old and he felt the effects of aging. Even simple tasks, like getting out of bed, required effort and concentration. Regardless, he continued to keep up with his practice of morning study before finding tasks to occupy his day.

To provide Charlie with memories of her grandparents, Terri and Wayne frequently made the trek to Grand Lake for extended weekend trips. In June, his parents would celebrate their sixty-second wedding anniversary and he had something special in mind. Arriving at his parent's yellow house, Wayne shared his plan to take them to Marylin's favorite place of indulgence, The Broadmoor Hotel in Colorado Springs. It had become an annual tradition and Wayne knew his parents loved it. It also provided Charlie with time to hear stories from her grandma and grandpa and learn more about their lives.

The next morning, Wayne woke early to join his father in an early conversation. He went to the kitchen, fully expecting to find his father immersed in reading. It was already six, and the lights weren't on. Lyle wasn't there. Surprised, he decided to wait until his father joined him. While sitting, Wayne couldn't help but reflect on the beauty all around. To the east, the mountain peaks were beginning to be illuminated by the sunrise. Outside the kitchen window, he observed the numerous hummingbirds, busily engaged in drinking from the feeders that Marylin kept located in the aspen tree adjacent to the house. The deck displayed flowers that Marylin had arranged, adding to the beauty. *It's no wonder they love this place.* His pondering was interrupted by the flash of sunlight that penetrated the window. The sharpness of the sunlight caused Wayne to turn his head.

He saw Lyle approaching the table. He was wearing a green bathrobe and walking slowly. Wayne was struck by his father's movement. *He's getting old.*

Later that day, Lyle was found taking a nap on the carpeted floor in the family room. Wayne was again reminded that Lyle didn't seem to have the same enthusiasm as usual. Seeing his father beginning to stir, Wayne said, "Dad, let's go to work."

Lyle perked up immediately. "Work? What do you have in mind?"

"I want to build Charlie a playhouse. It needs to be a replica of your yellow house. What do you think?"

Immediately, they began drafting sketches of a potential design and discussing the materials they'd need. Lyle was invigorated. He found new energy. Sleep now became a burden, and that summer there were fewer naps. At night, he'd lie in bed thinking about the details of the day's work ahead. And getting to work with Wayne on the project was the best part.

By the end of the summer of 2015, Lyle and Wayne completed a nearly exact replica of the yellow house. All the grandkids would love it, but Charlie was especially thrilled as it fit her small frame perfectly and became a favorite spot to gather for tea parties with Marylin. Not surprisingly, the quality was extraordinary. What was surprising was that Lyle spent nearly $15,000 in materials, money that they didn't have for something Marylin considered unnecessary. However, for Marylin, it was worth every penny. Lyle had a newfound spring in his step. He enjoyed hours with Wayne and now as she looked out her kitchen window, she saw another incredible attraction for her grandchildren. It was a perfect complement to the other projects Lyle had constructed over the years - a giant swing set, a teeter-totter, a horseshoe pit, and the dock in the pond. The Hileman family property attraction continued to expand.

Marylin remained in awe of her husband's talent. To her, his handiwork was perfect. Keeping Lyle busy provided him with purpose and a rebirth. He was hard at work and happy doing what he loved. She'd need to find another project for the years ahead.

I₩ 2016, it was Marylin's turn to reach the age of eighty. For this milestone birthday, the kids arranged to be in Grand Lake. What was to supposed to be a special celebration, instead became the cause of family worry. Marylin was suffering from kidney stones. For weeks, she'd been taking antibiotics for an infection, but the stones wouldn't pass. She had a procedure to try and break up the large stones but no relief came.

Marylin looked tired. She'd lost a lot of weight and lacked energy.

"Mom, isn't there something more they can do?" Cherrie questioned.

"We've tried everything but the doctor says I just need to be patient," Marylin explained.

"Lylo, you're a doctor. Is there anything else that can be done?" Cherrie asked.

Lylo shared that while Marylin remained uncomfortable, the shock wave lithotripsy she received days earlier should do the trick. However, only time would allow for the stones to pass. Until they did, fevers and discomfort were expected.

The birthday celebration wasn't the joyous reunion for which the family had hoped. Marylin was suffering and there wasn't anything that could be done. Rather, the gathering forced a discussion about the realities of mortality.

"Mountain living is hard," Lylo stated.

With all five children gathered in the family room, Lyle could sense where the conversation was headed. "Yeah, but it's the only living we're interested in."

"We were thinking you should consider finding a small place in Denver," Cherrie stated. "The winters here are brutal and if you ever needed something, access is impossible if you can't plow the road."

Lylo then added, "It would sure be nice to have you living closer."

Weak and still feeling worn out from battling kidney stones, Marylin said exactly what Lyle was thinking. "As long as we're able, we're staying in our yellow house."

THERE WERE OTHER, smaller gatherings in the yellow house over the next year. Each of the Hileman children made frequent trips to visit and lend a hand in managing the work on the property. Nothing was more meaningful for Lyle and Marylin. They were blessed with longevity and overall good health. Sure, age brought with it various aches and pains, but sharing the beauty of their mountain home was fulfilling.

THE NEXT BIG family gathering came when Lyle turned eighty-five. In March 2019, the Hileman kids and their spouses gathered again at the yellow house. To everyone's surprise, Marylin looked great. She was energetic and looked vibrant. Lyle on the other hand was showing signs of decline.

Lyle suffered his first stroke as a young man, and while he'd never noticed, his doctors indicated he'd had several transient ischemic attacks or TIAs. The "mini-strokes" reduced blood flow to his brain and, over time, impacted his balance. Years earlier, Lyle had a more serious stroke that impacted his memory and speech. The lingering effects of strokes, in addition to the trauma with his arm, had taken their toll.

After dinner, the family gathered around the dining room table to share gifts and to light the birthday cake. After a photo with his birthday cake, Lyle retired to bed.

"Mom, Dad is slowing down," Kim observed.

Marylin shared, "I'm worried about him. He seems exhausted all the time and even small projects are wearing him out. His cramps at night are getting worse."

That night, the five kids stayed up late discussing the challenges associated with aging parents. The reality was that living at 9,000 feet above sea level was tough, and if either of their parent's health failed, staying in the yellow house would no longer be a viable option. Also complicating things, money was tight for Lyle and Marylin. They were making ends meet but a significant health challenge would put an end to their mountain living.

"If Mom passes first," Kim said, "Dad will live with me. I'll take care of him."

Wayne added, "We could take care of him, too."

Kim quickly countered, "You'll have to fight me for it – I called it first."

"I can't imagine Dad without Mom. He'd be miserable," Lylo said.

Everyone agreed. If Mom left, caring for Lyle would be a huge trial.

"Well, what if Dad dies first?" Cherrie questioned.

Glenn had worried about that as well. "There is no way Mom could live up here alone. The maintenance alone is too big of a task."

Having to discuss the potential loss of their parents wasn't a subject any of the kids wanted to accept, but they knew changes were coming. In fact, they were closer than anyone could imagine.

CHAPTER THIRTY-SEVEN

THE YEAR 2020 began with a bang, or perhaps more like a rumble.

"Mom, you won't believe it," Glenn shared by phone. "It shook the house like nothing I've ever experienced." Salt Lake City had experienced a 5.2 magnitude earthquake and the aftershocks continued for days. "This has us shaking, literally!"

"Glad you're okay," his mother replied. "Are you sure you and Michelle want to live here one day?"

"Absolutely," Glenn replied. "It's been our dream for years."

Marylin then asked, "Do you think you can buy it now? I can't stop feeling like it's important to get it done."

"We'd hoped to wait a few more years, Mom. We've still got two kids in school and besides, I don't want to buy it unless everyone is aligned."

By everyone, Glenn was referring to his siblings. Over the years, the property had grown in value and while he desired to preserve the legacy property, Glenn didn't want it to become a wedge between him and his brothers and sisters.

"I've already discussed it with them," Marylin said. "They're all supportive, if it's what you want."

"Well, we do, but let me just confirm with Michelle and I'll get back to you."

"Okay, but I'd like it done soon. Oh, and we plan to stay here as long as physically possible. We'll pay you rent."

Glenn spent the next several days in discussion with Michelle and each of his brothers and sisters. He was still a bit concerned over the financial obligation it would entail, but like his mother, he knew things would work out.

On a call with Wayne, Glenn learned more about what may have prompted Marylin's desire to complete the transaction. "You know Mom has a bucket list, right?" Wayne asked.

"No. I didn't. What's on it?"

"Mostly vacations, while they still can travel. She specifically mentioned an extended cruise she's been planning. They're rich in land, but to travel, they need the money."

Glenn and Michelle went to work securing the necessary loans and insurance to complete the sale. Lyle and Marylin now had the financial means to travel and deal with any emergency expenses that might arise.

UNEXPECTEDLY, THE SPRING of 2020 bought another significant change. The world had shut down due to a virus that began in China. COVID-19 was unlike anything seen in over one hundred years. It was contagious, very contagious. City by city, America was brought to a halt. Businesses were closed and across the nation, people prayed for relief and a vaccine.

Having sold the property and yellow house to Glenn and Michelle, Lyle and Marylin now had the resources to travel but given the pandemic, they were grounded. As summer approached, Marylin shared with Lyle an alternative plan. It was something on her bucket list and wouldn't require any travel.

"I have one more project I want you to complete for me."

"Anything, what would you like?" Lyle responded.

"I want a park and pavilion built in the oxbow."

The oxbow was an area of their property surrounded by water and generally inaccessible. It was forested in the early 1900s and overgrown with willows. It had always been considered beautiful, but not of any value for development.

Lyle began immediately. Each morning he would wake early, head for his tractor, and begin work clearing stumps and willows that littered the ground. He knew the project would require additional equipment and enlisted a friend, Clive Smith, to join in the fun.

OVER THE NEXT several months, Lyle experienced an unusual surge of energy. He and Marylin were both healthy, they had money in the bank, and most importantly, Lyle had a project that would occupy each day. He loved it. For Lyle, COVID meant more time on the property and less travel away from the place he loved most.

WITH THE CLEARING of the oxbow progressing, Marylin became excited thinking about her park and pavilion. Visualizing the future gatherings that would be hosted on the grounds, she decided to name the newly developed area. Grabbing a pen and notepad, Marylin began scribbling potential ideas. The first idea she'd contemplated for naming the new park was "Mountain Oasis." After writing it down, she quickly scratched a line through as it didn't feel right. Next, she wrote down "Winding River Hideout." She liked it but then recalled there was already a Winding River Campground just down the road. Not original enough. Striking the idea with another line, she continued to think. Then it came to her. *There are so many trees, I can't even see through them. It will be "Hileman Hide-a-way."* After seeing it written down, she felt a rush of excitement. It was perfect!

Selecting a name for the pavilion was much easier. It was the only option considered, and nothing else would do. *PUNK'S PAVILION* was written in all caps. It would be an exclamation point on their years of work. This ground was sacred to Lyle and Marylin and they would leave their fingerprints all around. Reviewing her notes filled her heart with satisfaction. Carefully, she folded her page of ideas and placed it in the drawer next to her candy counter with all her other important documents.

GIVEN THE VIRUS that had limited travel for the world, they had an entire summer of family visits planned. As each family arrived, Marylin prepared her traditional meals. Prime rib the first night, pork roast the second. Her famous lasagna was always the favorite and would be offered on the third night. For all other meals, the kids were on their own, but dinners at the Hileman home were legendary, and Marylin would never disappoint.

One by one, the children came, grandkids and great grandkids in tow. Nearly every week during the summer of 2020, the family visited. In all the years living in the yellow house, neither Lyle nor Marylin could ever remember having more guests in such a condensed time-frame. Marylin's brothers, Steve and Mike visited. Her sister, Amy Sue, along with her husband Jack, spent multiple days relaxing in the mountain paradise. Having visitors filled Lyle and Marylin with joy. They had little time for boredom. Marylin enjoyed hosting while Lyle continued clearing land in the oxbows and enlisting his guests to help whenever possible. It was magical. We have been so blessed, Marylin thought.

In July, Cherrie brought her entire family to visit. The house was packed and they used the Pitcher cabin to accommodate grandchildren. Lylo had heard about the gathering and called his mother. "I know you're full, but would it be all right if Brenda and I drove up for the day? We'd love to see Cherrie's family, and you and Dad too."

"Of course," Marylin predictably replied.

When Lylo and Brenda arrived, they were struck by just how large Cherrie's family had grown. They were moving about the property so quickly that Lylo was unable to get an exact count.

Lylo noticed his father happily pushing kids on the swing set. He looked good. "Mom, is Dad still taking Prozac?"

Marylin's head lowered. She grabbed some dirty dishes and began washing, "He is, but he doesn't know it."

During the summer, conversations regularly included discussions about fire. California was ablaze, and in Colorado, there were already four fires that had yet to be contained. While not close by, smoke from the fires could be seen and smelled from miles away. Neither Lyle nor Marylin was concerned as forecasts indicated the area of Grand Lake was not in danger. Regardless, during their visits, the children and their families helped in clearing the property of dead trees. With Lyle driving the tractor, children and grandchildren worked together gathering wood and taking it to the meadow where a pile was prepared for what would be another grand New Year's Eve bonfire.

In August 2020, Glenn's family made another trip to visit his parents. With school about to begin, they wanted to enjoy a final summer weekend in the mountains. They especially wanted their children to have more time to create memories with their grandparents. The late summer temperatures were ideal for hiking, riding ATVs and canoeing on the pond. But most of the time, the family relaxed at the house and engaged in playing games. Marylin always enjoyed a card game or two but Lyle rarely participated.

"Come on Dad, come play a game," Glenn encouraged.

Surprisingly, Lyle nodded and sat at the round kitchen table that for years had been the site of countless games and conversation. The game Sequence was selected. The afternoon sunshine was now warming Lyle's back and after two games, he stood from his chair, walked a few feet toward the porch sliding door, and slowly lay prone on the soft brown carpet. From this position, the sun engulfed his entire body and in only seconds, he fell fast asleep.

"That didn't last long." Glenn laughed.

"I'm amazed he lasted that long," Marylin remarked.

As evening approached, Michelle offered to help Marylin with preparations for dinner. "Mom, do you remember our discussion in two thousand ten?"

"I don't remember what we talked about yesterday, let alone back then." Marylin laughed.

Michelle continued, "Well, you told me you planned to live here for ten years. I asked you to make it at least thirteen."

"And I told you I was sticking to my ten-year plan," Marylin replied.

Michelle couldn't help but laugh out loud. She loved Marylin and admired her directness and determination. "I was just hoping to get our last kid through high school. Glenn's getting closer to retirement and in three more years, we'll be empty nesters. It would have been easier to handle the expenses if we had waited a bit longer to buy the property."

"You'll be fine," Marylin assured.

"Yes, but we're counting on you and Dad to live here for a few years, hopefully even longer!"

"We're not going anywhere. My yellow home is the only place I ever want to live."

GLENN AND MICHELLE continued to travel to Grand Lake every other weekend. As the new owners of the property, they enjoyed making numerous improvements and repairs. Glenn spent one weekend on the roof patching up the gutters. On another visit, he helped his father paint the fence posts that were strategically placed in the developing park area. On each trip, a priority was clearing the dead trees around the property. Glenn operated the chainsaw, while Michelle would gather the trunks and branches. Lyle followed with his tractor. After filling a bucket load of debris, Lyle would drive the dry and brittle remains to the meadow. By the end of September, the pile was large. The New Year bonfire would certainly be memorable in 2021!

With projects out of the way, Glenn and Michelle were back in the kitchen playing a game when Marylin asked Glenn to follow her outside.

"I need to show you something." Pointing to the barn, she explained, "The barn roof needs to be replaced before winter. It's leaking on Dad's tools."

"I'll get on it," Glenn responded.

"There's more. The septic tank has failed. And there are leaks in the bathroom plumbing." Marylin went on to describe several additional repairs that would be needed.

Glenn understood there would be numerous maintenance needs for a house that had been built thirty-four years earlier.

While walking around the yard, Marylin shared one more issue. "Look. Your dad backed the tractor into the corner of the house."

It was obvious Lyle had tried to repair the aluminum siding but it would need to be replaced soon.

"That can wait until next year," Glenn reasoned.

"It can, but look at my car."

Walking towards the garage, Glenn saw a significant dent on the back of Marylin's SUV. "Yikes, The tractor?"

"Yes. I think it's time for a new car."

Knowing his parents were now financially comfortable, Glenn excitedly responded, "Let's go inside and look online. I'm sure we can find you a good deal on a new car."

Once in the kitchen with his laptop open, Glenn went to work exploring the various options for a similar SUV to the one now in use. It was a Hyundai Santa Fe and had been purchased new only a few years earlier. But given the weekly six-hour round trip to Denver for Lyle and Marylin to complete church assignments, the vehicle had over 100,000 miles on it. With Lyle's cosmetic enhancements to the vehicle, a new one would certainly be welcomed.

Finally, Glenn proclaimed, "I've found it. Here's a great deal on your new car."

Marylin paused.

Glenn could sense a bit of disappointment in her reaction after looking at the vehicle. "What's wrong?"

"I just don't know if I want to get the same car. I was thinking…" Another long pause followed.

Glenn interrupted the silence. "What are you thinking?"

"You know, my mom always wanted a Cadillac but could never afford one. I think I'd like a Cadillac. My mother would be so jealous," Marylin sheepishly disclosed.

Glenn was quick to action and within minutes had found a few Cadillac SUV that generated a sparkle in his mother's eyes. The very next day, a Cadillac dealer from Denver arrived with the new vehicle in the driveway. While the excitement for Marylin was great, there was also a sense of feeling overwhelmed. Partially, it was guilt for indulging her desire for something so frivolous, and at having spent a large sum of money on something they didn't need. But her greatest cause of concern was from learning the new technologies that came with the vehicle. Simple tasks, like turning windshield wipers on and off, were a challenge. No longer could she reach for the knob and with a twist to engage the heater. Now, touchscreen technology required understanding how to do nearly everything. Even turning the radio volume up and down was less intuitive.

It took two weeks for Marylin to gain the confidence to drive her new car off the property. After a couple of trips to town, she began to enjoy the luxury offered. As for Lyle, getting behind the wheel of the Cadillac was off-limits. The absence of a key alone was enough to keep him from wanting to drive the car, but he also understood this was Marylin's indulgence…and he loved it.

Late in September 2020, Marylin's sister Amy Sue called Glenn. "Jack and I are going to visit your parents. You should bring Michelle and join us. Jack said to bring your golf clubs."

"Oh, that would be great but we were just there a couple of weeks ago," Glenn replied.

"Come on. With the internet, you can work from there. Besides, it's General Conference weekend." General Conference is a bi-annual televised weekend full of talks from church leaders. "You know how much your parents enjoy those meetings. Having you join us would be fun and relaxing."

Glenn didn't need much of a push. He loved spending time in Colorado. He especially loved the fall season in the mountains. Best of all, he loved to be with his parents. Making the eight-hour drive on a beautiful fall Friday evening, Glenn and Michelle entered the dirt road leading to the yellow house.

"I love it here," Glenn said looking at Michelle.

"Me too."

After another of Marylin's dinner feasts, Glenn gathered his parents, Jack, Amy Sue, and Michelle to show them a surprise he'd planned for a Christmas gift. He unfolded a large printout of a bronze plaque he had designed. It described the events surrounding the accident in 1993 that nearly cost Lyle his arm.

"Dad, I never want our family to forget. It will be in bronze and I plan to mount it down by the barn, next to the auger."

"It's beautiful," Marylin replied.

"I'm calling it Rocky Mountain Miracle, Glenn said. "It will be here for Christmas. And I have another surprise." He began unrolling architectural drawings of a planned remodel to the house. He was excited to show his parents the work that was done.

Marylin had heard about Glenn and Michelle's desire to remodel her yellow house. She understood the house needed repairs. She recognized the limits her kitchen had when entertaining large groups. But as her son excitedly began flipping the pages of the drawings, she felt an emotion stirring inside. *My house is perfect.*

Glenn continued enthusiastically describing the expansion of the kitchen, mud room, and garage.

"Just don't start remodeling while we're still around," Marylin said.

"Oh no. This won't begin until I'm ready to retire. At least four or five years from now."

"Good. I like it just the way it is."

Seeing Glenn rolling up the plans, Marylin leaned into her sister Amy Sue and whispered, "I don't plan on being around to witness any of this."

Amy Sue smiled and tried to contain her laughter but a giggle escaped. Marylin had spent a lifetime creating this dream home and for her, a remodel would detract from the heavenly setting.

THE FOLLOWING DAY, Glenn and Michelle were preparing for their return to Utah. It was a magical Sunday morning and ideal for driving. Glenn understood the others would be watching a church service that began at ten, and he wanted to get an early start. After breakfast, Glenn informed his parents they were planning to leave before the church meeting began.

Marylin walked towards her son and hugged him. "You can't leave yet. I have something to show you."

"Mom, we're ready to go. What is it?"

"Not just you, bring Michelle. Oh, and grab a wooden stake and a can of spray paint. I'll meet you in the driveway."

Together, Glenn and Michelle followed Lyle and Marylin down the dirt road leading to the oxbows. It was obvious a lot of work had been completed over the past few months clearing trees and stumps and Glenn was anxious to learn what his mother had in mind. Stopping their vehicle, Marylin jumped out and walked toward Glenn and Michelle, both sitting on an ATV.

"This will be the entrance," she beamed. "I want this park to be a gathering place for our family."

Getting back into the utility vehicle, they ventured farther onto the island. As they drove, Glenn marveled at the amount of work Lyle and Clive had completed. Passing by the freshly cleared ground, they arrived at the southern end of the oxbow. Lyle stopped his vehicle and both he and Marylin got out. Glenn and Michelle followed and walked toward his parents.

"Right here. I want a pavilion built here," Marylin said. She then instructed Glenn to take the stake to mark the area.

He drove the stake into the ground, shook the spray paint, and then applied it. The location was near the south end of the oxbow. Together they discussed the approximate size and agreed this would be the location.

After returning to the house, Marylin made another announcement. "One more thing, before you go. You need to see something."

Glenn and Michelle paused, watching Marylin walk past the candy counter and open an adjacent cabinet drawer.

Marylin retrieved the small piece of paper she'd prepared earlier and unfolded it. "The park and pavilion have a name. Hileman Hide-a-way for the park."

"I like it," Michelle responded.

Marylin handed Michelle the notes she'd written weeks earlier. "And the pavilion will have a name too! Punk's Pavilion."

All agreed. Glenn would begin work on the property the next summer and assist his father in completing the park. He began exploring pavilion ideas, looking for one befitting of his mother's legacy.

Before Glenn and Michelle left, Lyle suggested a family prayer. It took him a while to get to his knees. While the others waited, Glenn thought, *What an example.* At eighty-six, his years of hard work had taken its toll. Lyle gave a prayer offering thanks for their many blessings and then asked God to provide safety for Glenn and Michelle as they drove home. As they rose to their feet, they embraced and said their goodbyes.

Michelle interjected, "Before we leave, I want a picture."

During the prayer, Michelle had been prompted to ask Lyle to show her the scars on his arm. "Dad, I want a picture of your arm. We should have the picture on the bronze plaque."

"Sure thing," Lyle stated.

As he began rolling up his sleeve, Marylin jumped in. "No, that won't do. Take off your shirt."

Standing together in the family room with his dad's shirt removed, Glenn focused in on the scars that covered his father's left arm and shoulder. On Lyle's face, lines of a life well lived were abundant. Glenn walked close and hugged his father for a second time. What an example. What a life. What a man. Turning to his mother, he gave her another hug. "You guys are the best! We'll see you soon."

CHAPTER THIRTY-EIGHT

AFTER THE WAVE of visitors, Marylin was determined to relax and enjoy the few remaining warm days ahead. She knew winter was on the way, but with the sun out and her chaise lounge still occupying space on the deck, she soaked up the afternoon sun. For Lyle, the coming winter reminded him he had a limited number of days to make progress on the park. He and Clive were scrambling to clear as much ground as possible before the first snowfall.

Lyle's body failed to notify his mind of the limitations associated with aging. During the night he was restless, but he didn't mind as to him sleep was a bother. Not that he couldn't ever sleep, but it would be more common to find him sprawled out on the carpet of the family room in a deep nap after pushing himself for hours completing laborious tasks. Before waking, his dreams of work expressed themselves through tossing and turning. Perhaps that is why he slept with a drawer full of yellow mustard packets in his nightstand. Years earlier, he discovered the magic of yellow mustard to quickly relieve muscle cramps. This night would be no exception.   Shortly after four in the morning, in the middle of a dream of driving his blue Ford bi-directional tractor, Lyle's hamstring engaged. It would never be a slight groan, but rather a scream as the cramps would cause him to yell in severe pain. Marylin knew exactly what to do. After all, in sixty-eight years of marriage, it was routine. Quickly she reached for the packets, tore the top, and placed it in her husbands' mouth. Almost instinctively, she would immediately grab a second, as over the years she learned that two packets would get the job done. After a few minutes, Lyle's muscles relaxed and he fell back into the pillow trying to remember where he left off in his plans for the coming morning.

It was now almost five, and Lyle wasn't one to waste a minute of daylight, even if daylight wouldn't appear for another two hours. He dressed and walked downstairs into the kitchen, turned on the electric heater, sat at the kitchen table and began reading his scriptures. Lyle never thought himself to be smart, and having suffered three strokes, his memory wasn't great. He enjoyed reading bible stories in an effort to recall the lessons he'd learned over the years. It was less about learning and more about starting his day in search of the peace he found in personal scripture study. Starting his day in reflection and prayer was a habit he loved.

Looking out the window, he could see it was going to be an amazing day. The sky was clear and though the thermometer outside the kitchen window showed it was only twenty-five degrees, Lyle knew the radiant heat of the sun would quickly warm the air enough that he could re-engage in the project that had occupied his thoughts during the night. While the days were getting shorter, there would still be time to make significant progress on the park.

Marylin was less ambitious and the truth was, caring for Lyle was exhausting. She was awake but longed to fall back asleep for a few more minutes. The warmth of her down comforter was the perfect complement to her pillow and only a few minutes after Lyle left the bed, she was fast asleep. The sound of birds outside her window woke her and her thoughts quickly turned to Lyle. Had he eaten any breakfast? Was he dressed warm enough for the cold morning? With forty-two acres of land, there were many chores to occupy his time but she knew Clive was planning to work again on the park and he'd likely be down by the oxbow. Soon she was alert enough to find the motivation to get up, get dressed, and down to the kitchen.

"Lyle, did you take your pills?" Marylin knew the answer before it was given but liked to make him pause long enough to reflect on all she did to help him. She would take the collection of pills, along with a glass of orange juice, and sit close by while he stopped reading long enough to consume his cocktail of meds. "Do you want some breakfast?" Marylin asked.

"No, not really hungry," was his reply.

"Okay. I'll make you some toast," Marylin said, refusing to register the response of her husband.

Lyle rarely worried about food, in part because Marylin would always ensure he had something to sustain his energy. Food, like sleep, only interfered with his work. Along with the toast and jam, Lyle ate the freshly cut fruit Marylin had lovingly prepared. She sat next to him and watched as he read. *What would become of him if I weren't around?* This was the question that lingered frequently in her mind. Marylin, now eighty-four, felt great. She was enjoying a season of good health and felt at peace. She was confident she'd manage if Lyle were to pass first, but she wouldn't be able to stay alone in her yellow house. Only two years earlier, kidney stones and infections nearly killed her. Concern over Lyle motivated Marylin to regain her health. She enjoyed aging with a man she respected, admired, and genuinely loved for more than sixty-eight years. As Lyle ate, Marylin reflected on how blessed she felt having spent so many years living in a place she considered paradise.

Her reflections were interrupted as Lyle stated, "Clive is already starting. I need to get down there and help."

At his advanced age, "helping" Clive was more like watching the work unfold and wishing he still had the physical capacity to get into the dirt. The temperature had reached thirty-eight degrees and Lyle excitedly announced to Marylin he was heading out.

The sound of Lyle's tractor starting up signaled his day of work had begun. She watched as he drove the big diesel down the road toward the oxbow. She often worried about him on the tractor. Having Lyle drive the tractor made her nervous but she knew it brought him joy and, luckily, nothing too serious had happened so far. As he drove out of sight of the kitchen window, a tug at her heart had her wanting to check on him to ensure he arrived safely. It was too cold for her to walk and driving her new car down the gravel road would be a challenge.

As the disappointment set in, she remembered another indulgence from the summer. A recently purchased ATV was in the garage and made especially for her. She grabbed a jacket and made her way to her new toy. Trying to remember how to get it started, she eventually recalled the steps and was on her way. The ATV brought newfound freedom to Marylin. In truth, she knew it would primarily be used by the kids and grandkids, but at moments like this, she was glad to have the mobility. As she pulled up next to Lyle, his face brightened as he smiled.

"What are you doing down here?" Lyle asked.

Marylin responded, "I need to make sure you guys are doing the job right." Pointing toward the southern end of the oxbow, she added, "Don't let Clive run over the stake where I want the pavilion."

For nearly thirty minutes, they had watched Clive as he drove his giant tractor and with extraordinary skill navigate downed trees and stumps while grading the area to be more accessible. "Okay, I've seen enough," Marylin said before returning to her comfortable home. She longed to get one more nap on her deck before Lyle stored the furniture for winter.

Back at the house, Marylin smiled as she reflected on prior conversations with Lyle on how hard he'd been working. From what she observed, his work at the oxbow was limited to sitting and watching Clive operate the tractor. Not that Lyle couldn't work, he was the hardest worker she'd ever met, but in this case, Clive and his equipment were doing the work.

LARGE PILES OF trees and stumps were strategically organized to ensure they followed guidelines that would allow for burning later. Lyle was directing Clive on where to stack the burn pile when he noticed a truck moving toward him from the barn. It was an old friend, Richard, who had been elk hunting in the area.

"How can I help?" Richard asked.

Lyle responded, "I have no idea. Clive has things under control and I'm trying to figure out how I can be of use."

Without a plan to assist, Richard suggested they return to the house and begin putting away the furniture and trinkets that adorned their patio. Every year, heavy snow would require the removal of everything on the deck. Lyle had done it alone many times, but when Richard would show up in the fall with an offer to help, it was always welcomed. Richard had been visiting Grand Lake for years, and every fall he would make the drive from Kentucky. He loved exploring the Rocky Mountains, and often he would return to his home with a supply of elk meat. Years earlier, he knocked on the door of the yellow house to ask permission to hunt the grounds. Within minutes he felt the warmth of a couple clearly in love and anxious to share their passion for the area with a stranger. Hunting was the initial draw, but as the years passed, spending time with Lyle and Marylin became a significant motivating factor. He loved them and always marveled over the goodness they projected. Hunting was the purpose of his visits, but over the years it was far less important than the overall experience of being on the Hileman property.

It took nearly two hours and multiple trips up and down the stairs to store the patio collection in the basement storage area. Marylin also enjoyed Richard's visits. She knew he loved to hunt but she also sensed a bond that had formed over the years, and with age, having Richard's help was genuinely appreciated.

"Let's eat," Marylin offered.

"Sounds great," Richard responded.

Around four in the afternoon, the three of them enjoyed a classic Marylin-made feast. During the meal, the conversation shifted to accounts of a Colorado fire that had reached the neighboring community of Hot Sulfur Springs. Given that it was twenty-six miles south of Grand Lake, most estimates were that, if it continued north, it would take two weeks to arrive. Both Lyle and Richard were retired firefighters and understood the science behind fires. When Richard asked Lyle what they would do if the fire ever approached, he walked Richard through his plan.

Years earlier, Lyle had strategically placed fire hoses and hydrants around their meadow home. As a young man, Lyle would have dressed and ventured into a fire with his equipment in hand. Now in late October, the pump to the pond and the plumbing to the sprinkling system were winterized and no water would be available. Lyle explained how he intentionally used asphalt shingles and steel siding to protect the home from a fire that many understood was possible due to years of beetle kill that destroyed all the lodgepole pines in the national forest and park. Most residents of the area were diligent in keeping their homes cleared of the dead trees but neither the park nor forest service would allow for controlled burns or even clearing of the dead trees. Scars of the beetle kill were everywhere and what had once been a vibrant forest looked brown and lifeless.

"You know, Richard, we cleared a bunch of trees this summer and the house is nowhere near the tree lines, so we should be fine. If necessary, we'll implement Plan B." Plan B was to retreat to their basement, to an area Lyle referred to as the bunker. Essentially, it was a large closet completely enclosed by concrete with a steel door.

"Lyle, that's a stupid plan," Richard responded. "You couldn't possibly survive a fire hiding out in the basement. The smoke would overtake you should the home ever burn."

Richard understood Lyle had experience in the Denver Fire Department fighting house fires. Rarely would people die from fire. The most common cause of death was smoke inhalation. Richard continued, "Lyle, I hope your home is as safe as you describe because if it caught fire, and you were sheltered in the bunker, it wouldn't end well."

"Maybe," Lyle replied. "But that's our plan."

The conversation shifted to more pleasant topics like the odds of Richard getting his bull elk given the extraordinary drought that had hit the Rocky Mountains.

After their meal, Richard prepared for his drive back to his motel room in Grand Lake Village. "I'll see you in the morning. Hopefully, with an elk to be dressed."

After cleaning up the dishes, Lyle and Marylin sat in their rocking chairs to read. Lyle quickly fell asleep, exhausted from the numerous trips up and down the stairs. Marylin wasn't tired yet but lowered her book as she looked at her husband. We have come a long way. They had come a long way, against all odds, and overcome countless challenges. Marylin felt a sense of peace and calm.

She smiled, then gently reached to touch Lyle on the arm. "Lyle, it's nearly seven. Let's head upstairs and get ready for bed."

CHAPTER THIRTY-NINE

IT HAD BEEN a marvelous day. Now dressed in their pajamas, Lyle and Marylin knelt at their bedside to pray together. This had become a regular close to most days, and they alternated who would offer the prayer.

"It sure is nice to have all the patio furniture stored," Marylin said. "Remember to ask God to bless Richard for being so good to us."

Lyle added, "I will. I don't think I could have done it without his help."

AS RICHARD ARRIVED at his hotel room in Grand Lake Village, he settled into the soft bed and turned on the television. On the screen, a warning sounded with a notification that residents of Grand Lake should evacuate. While the evacuation was not mandatory, the news reported high winds had arrived and if sustained, the community was at risk. It was nearly eight and, as a precaution, Richard called Marylin. "Have you seen the news? The fire is moving north."

"Yes, we just watched it, but it is still nearly twenty-six miles away; we should be fine."

Concerned, Richard pled with Marylin, "I'm on my way. We need to get you guys out of there, just in case."

"Richard, we're nearly ready for bed. We'll be fine."

"Get changed. I'll get us rooms in Granby."

Marylin reluctantly agreed but hated the idea of leaving this late in the evening when reports still suggested they'd be all right.

"If I get there and things have calmed down, we'll just eat some more dessert together before calling it a night," Richard said.

"You know, I made that fresh peach pie special for you," Marylin said.

Earlier that evening, Richard teased Marylin that he was struggling to work with the aroma of peach pie filling the air. A second serving would be a welcomed treat.

Within moments, Richard was on his way back to the Hileman property. Only minutes later, he was stopped by a Grand County sheriff. "What's the problem, sir?" Richard asked.

"Mister, you need to turn around and head south. We are evacuating the area."

"But I thought it was only a recommendation to evacuate?" Richard responded.

"That was thirty minutes ago," the sheriff stated. "We are now in a mandatory evacuation. The winds are over seventy miles per hour and headed our way. We need everyone out."

Richard's heart skipped a beat as he thought about Lyle and Marylin. They felt safe but likely had no idea what was heading their way.

Richard begged, "Sir, please let me go. I just spoke with an elderly couple a few miles up the road. I told them I was on my way."

Concerned, the sheriff agreed, but in a stern and serious voice said, "Okay, but hurry!"

Three miles closer to the Hileman home, Richard encountered a roadblock. It was manned by forest service workers and a park ranger. Richard explained the purpose of his mission. The park ranger was familiar with the Hileman family and agreed to let Richard continue but said he would need to go with him. Richard gladly accepted the proposal and together the two men began the two-mile stretch down County Road 491 toward the property.

As they crossed the Colorado River by the Winding River Campground, the night sky became bright with fire streaking across the horizon. While still a distance away, they could see the fire in the forest to the west.

Richard was startled by the ranger yelling, "Stop the truck!"

Just ahead a tree had been blown down. In the rush to get to the Hilemans, neither had noticed the significant increase in wind and smoke. Ahead, they could see hurricane-force winds blowing trees and debris. Committed to their rescue, they drove around the fallen tree when Richard's phone rang. It was Marylin.

"Richard, turn around. *Do not* come up here. The forest is on fire and there is no way you will make it."

Richard nervously replied, "Marylin, we are at Sun Valley, only a mile away. Get ready."

"We are not leaving," Marylin said with resolve. "We don't want you risking your life, and, even if you got here, we'd likely all be stuck in your truck trying to get out. We are headed to the basement."

The park ranger looked at Richard and his expression spoke loudly what Richard feared. Marylin was right. They were in the middle of a firestorm and unlikely to get in. They would be even less likely to get out.

"Marylin, I'm with the park ranger. We'll notify the Sheriff immediately and let them know where you are." As he turned the truck around he saw what he hadn't noticed while driving north. The entire area was engulfed in flames, and it was moving quickly in their direction.

CHAPTER FORTY

WALKING DOWN THE stairs and into the family room, Lyle and Marylin couldn't believe their eyes. Fire raced across the sky. The fields of dry grass were ablaze. Lyle opened the front door to get a better look at the madness outside. The wind hit the door with a force that pulled the doorknob from Lyle's hand. With the door fully open and smoke blowing into the home, Lyle attempted to step outside but the wind was unlike anything he'd ever felt. He looked to the south and could see a red sky glowing over the fields. Stepping back inside, he quickly grabbed the door and fought to push it closed. "We can't go out there."

"What did you see?" Marylin asked.

"I think the Richmond cabin is on fire."

Together they stood. Watching, waiting, hoping, and praying. Then, they moved to the study to get a different view.

"Look, I think the barn is on fire," Lyle said.

"You can't see that. All I see is smoke down there," Marylin replied. "Even if it is, there's nothing we can do about it."

They then walked to the kitchen to get a different perspective. From that vantage point, they saw what for years they knew was a possibility, but nothing could have prepared them for the images they now observed. The mountain to the west was ablaze. The hillside was glowing and while more than five hundred feet from the house, the grass on both sides of their driveway was burning. To the south, they could see the wooden swing Lyle had installed only a year earlier, ablaze. The Hileman property had been cleared of dead trees but the forest remained full of thousands of tall, dry lodgepole pines, adding fuel to the fast-moving fire. Shocked and in disbelief, Lyle heard his sweetheart whisper.

"Oh, Lyle."

"We need to get downstairs. We'll be safer there," Lyle said.

For years, Marylin kept a backpack in the hallway closet. It contained a supply of food, water, blankets, and other essentials. They grabbed the backpack and headed down the hallway when Marylin took a right turn back into the kitchen.

"Where are you going?" Lyle asked.

"I need my purse."

"You don't need your purse. We need to get downstairs."

"I do need my purse. My phone is in it and we need to call the kids."

Lyle opened the door that led to the basement stairs. He stopped. Looking at Marylin, he said, "I'm scared, Punk."

"Lyle, it will be fine. We've prepared our entire lives for this moment. We'll be fine."

Together they began descending the basement stairs. Before reaching the bottom, power to the house was interrupted and it became dark. Reaching into her backpack, Marylin withdrew a flashlight. With the assistance of light, they walked toward the area they felt would be safe. As they approached the bunker, Lyle moved the weightlifting bench from the adjacent room to create a place to sit.

Marylin took a seat and began searching for her cell phone. "Shut the door. It should keep any smoke from getting in here."

Lyle shut the door and then sat shoulder to shoulder with the love of his life. Marylin was in the process of dialing. "I'm calling Glenn now."

It was nine thirty as Glenn and his family were gathering their children for family prayer. Before beginning they heard the ring of the phone.

"I wonder who that is." Running so he wouldn't miss the call, he saw the name on his phone, *Mom & Dad*

"Hi, Mom. How are you guys?"

"Well, it happened," Marylin said calmly.

"What happened?"

"The big one."

Now on speakerphone and still confused, Glenn pressed, "Mom, what are you talking about?"

Marylin explained that the entire property was on fire. Michelle and her two teenagers, Austin and Marissa gasped with concern.

"Are you safe? What can I do?" Glenn asked.

Marylin calmly explained, "Richard has already offered to get us but we think we're safer here. Even if someone wanted to get here, I don't think they could. I do have a favor to ask. I need to save my cell phone battery life. The electricity is out so we can't use the other phone. Call your brothers and sisters and let them know we are together in the bunker and we're safe."

Michelle and the kids were overcome with worry as a sense of helplessness overcame them.

"I'll call them Mom, but you've got to promise to keep the phone on. Give me a few minutes and I'll call you right back."

"I will, I will but also let them know we love them," Marylin added.

Just as Glenn was about to hang up and begin the task of calling his siblings, Lyle spoke, "The Richmond's cabin is on fire. And our barn is burning."

"You don't know that," Marylin scolded. Her nose took in a few deep breaths. "Lyle, I smell something; it's not smoke."

"Is your house on fire?" Glenn asked.

"No, but something isn't right," she added.

"That's electrical," his father said.

"Glenn, call the others. We'll be fine," Marylin said as she hung up the phone.

Marylin placed the phone back in her purse. She sat next to her husband of sixty-eight years and wrapped her arms around him. There were no tears. It was strange as they knew they were in danger, but they were calm and at peace. "Would you offer a prayer?" Marylin asked.

Falling to their knees, Lyle grabbed Marylin by the hand and offered a prayer of gratitude. He prayed for his family. He asked God for protection and then closed with words that brought Marylin a sense of comfort. "Please Lord, let Thy will be done." He then closed his prayer. Looking at Marylin, he saw tears flowing. Holding her tight, he spoke softly. "You're the best thing that ever happened to me. I love you."

GLENN BEGAN CALLING his siblings. One by one he tried to share the message requested by his mother. It would take fifteen minutes to reach them all, and now nearly ten o'clock, Glenn called his parents back. There was no answer.

CHAPTER FORTY-ONE

THE HILEMAN CHILDREN began scrambling to find any news they could on the internet. They called friends and neighbors but to no avail. Finally, Wayne called the others with news of a live news feed he'd found online. It was the Grand County sheriff and fire chief communications. The family listened intently for anything that might suggest a rescue was underway.

At one o'clock in the morning, the fire chief stated, "I have the dozer. I'm headed to the Hileman property."

Relieved, the family held out hope of rescue. They now understood that people on the ground were aware that their parents were still in the path of fire. Two hours passed with no additional information. However, the chatter was painful to hear as the fireman were making hard decisions as to which homes could be saved and which were too far gone. It became clear as they listened through the early hours of the morning that the East Troublesome Fire was no ordinary fire. Wind gusts of 120 mph were reported, along with balls of fire that flew horizontally more than a half a mile with the wind. Countless homes were consumed. It was also obvious that across the country people were aware that human life was at risk. Several callers pled for rescue workers to save the elderly couple. While inquiries were made, there was no other mention of Lyle or Marylin.

At three in the morning the host of the live feed stated, "It's been quiet for some time. I think I'll sign off for now. Before I go, I should say I just read the fire is now the second largest in Colorado history, and the fastest-moving ever. Our thoughts are with the elderly couple. Let's hope they are rescued."

Glenn and Michelle were exhausted from following the news feed but disappointed the broadcast ended. With no access to additional information, Glenn closed his laptop and they both fell quickly asleep.

At precisely five o'clock, Glenn's sleep was interrupted. "Did you hear that?" he asked Michelle.

"What?" she responded.

"I just heard my mom and her sister, Annetta. They were laughing."

"Were you dreaming?" Michelle asked.

"It wasn't a dream. It was her laugh. She's with her family. It sounded like pure joy!"

EPILOGUE

THE EVENTS SURROUNDING the East Troublesome Fire were devastating. It is estimated that nearly four hundred homes were consumed and that 193,812 acres were burned. Lyle and Marylin were the only casualties.

Twenty-four hours after Glenn's conversation with his parents, he received a call from the county fire chief, Kevin Ratzmann. He explained they were unable to reach the Hileman property because of the severity of the fire. However, he confirmed they were close enough to confirm that survival would have been impossible.

The fire garnered national attention given the size and speed with which it moved. The loss of Lyle and Marylin became the interest of millions around the country. All major networks carried stories that featured the fire in Grand Lake and the loss of life.

On October 23, 2020, the county coroner, Tawnya Bailey, was able to access the property and retrieve the remains of Lyle and Marylin. Their bodies were found in the bunker, and they remained locked arm in arm.

The Grand County mortician, Jordan Ball was with the coroner and also a personal friend to the Hileman family. He offered to personally drive the remains to Ft. Collins to expedite the autopsy which would confirm the cause of death was asphyxiation.

The East Troublesome Fire continued to rage for several days. However, only nine days after the fire, arrangements were made to provide the Hileman family with access to the property. The county sheriff and fire chief coordinated an effort to safely escort the family to the site to bring closure.

On October 30, the entire county was covered in smoke and dense fog. Visibility was poor and the family was escorted to the Hileman property. Along the way, they saw nothing recognizable. The devastation was beyond description. It was also random. After passing the ruins of numerous cabins, a lone cabin stood untouched. It was eerie.

Arriving at the property, the family began to slowly walk around the remains of what had been the yellow house, looking for anything that might have survived. As it was too dangerous to enter the basement area, they were limited to the perimeter of the foundation. For years, the front porch had held a gigantic bell that had once been attached to an old fire truck. In better times, its ring would echo through the mountains indicating a meal was ready.

Wayne notified the others that he found the remains of the bell. Lifting it from the ground and hoisting it above his head it was barely recognizable. The top of it had been broken off and what previously was a beautiful chrome bell was now a round-shaped object of iron.

Cherrie had wandered a bit farther from the foundation and found the face of a porcelain doll, one from Marylin's collections. She gathered it and placed it in her pocket. Wayne searched the garage area and found a toolbox of wrenches and various hand tools. Only the socket set and wrenches were still in one piece. Every other tool had melted.

After thirty minutes of wandering, Lylo noticed something extraordinary. The others had been so focused on looking down for anything of value or memorabilia they hadn't realized that the smoke and fog had completely lifted. The sky was a deep blue and not a cloud could be seen.

The radiant heat of the sun warmed the air, and as the family gathered around the flag pole, there was calm. All stood in reverence as a color guard retrieved the torn and tattered flag. Carefully, the old flag was gathered. Looking around, with nowhere to place the flag, the veteran carefully placed it on the ground. In a matter of seconds, Chief

Ratzmann rushed to gather it from the ground. He stood in his dress whites, at attention, the flag held close to his chest.

A new flag was then carefully raised to the top of the pole and then lowered to half-staff. The color guard then stood at attention as the bugler played Taps. A reverence settled in upon all who were there. The American Legion then presented Lylo with a folded flag. Almost as if on cue, Wayne's wife Terri pointed to the east. All eyes were fixated on a bald eagle flying directly to the north in a straight line. Its flight was only slightly higher than the flagpole and within a few feet of the pond behind the yellow house. The entire party watched as the eagle soared into the distance and finally was out of sight.

After the flag-raising, the family gathered near the two spruce trees that had miraculously survived the fire. The entire area around the trees was burned but a circle surrounding them was left intact. The urns were brought to the site. Glenn dedicated the ground as a final resting place, and then Wayne knelt lovingly next to the two urns. He reached into one retrieving a small handful of ash, then he reached into the other. Holding the remains of his parents, his head was bowed in prayer. While not certain of the words he prayed, his next action was perfectly orchestrated to reflect the thoughts of each family member. Wayne's head lifted. He took both hands and combined the ashes and held them tightly. He then carefully spread them between the two trees, exactly as his mother had wanted.

Lyle and Marylin were gone, but they left a legacy that will never be forgotten.

A LETTER FROM THE AUTHOR

WORDS ARE NOT sufficient to express appreciation for the many individuals who assisted our family. We were overwhelmed with love and support and are forever grateful.

A week after the fire, with arrangements in place to gather our family for a memorial service, deep grief set in. For the first time in days, I had a moment alone. As I sat in my office, I was overcome with emotion. I determined it would be best to find something productive to do that could take my mind off the tragic events. Walking to the garage, I retrieved our lawn mower and began the task of cutting the grass.

Almost immediately, I found myself humming a tune. It was compelling and I couldn't stop repeating the melody. After a few minutes, I returned to my office to grab my guitar, determined to capture the chords of the music. Within a short time, I'd captured the tune and returned to the work of mowing. With the music now resonating in my mind, I was inundated with lyrics, words that told the story of my parents. I finished my task and returned to my office and began to write. In less than an hour, I'd written something that touched my soul. I was determined to share it with my siblings the following day.

I am not considered a musician nor a songwriter; however, I felt inspired to capture something to ease my grief and the sorrow of my family. The lyrics are as follows:

A YELLOW HOUSE IN THE MOUNTAINS

Verse 1
They were young and so in love
He knew she'd be his only one
She was 16, he was more
They couldn't know what was in store

With odds against them, they still knew
Together they could make it through
Trials and challenges would come their way
But deep in love, they'd always stay

Chorus
For most of us, Heaven must wait
But they would never hesitate
They had a dream to build their home
For family, friends, strangers to roam
They lived and loved in bliss
In a yellow house in the mountains

Verse 2
A family was their great desire
Five kids fulfilled their choicest dreams
Kids grew fast, taught to be strong
Each would marry and then move on

Soon they'd retire, their dream took shape
The work was hard but couldn't wait
Created space where dreams came true
The grandkids came, their parents too.

Chorus
For most of us, Heaven must wait
But they would never hesitate
They had a dream and built their home
For family, friends, others to roam
They lived and loved in bliss
In a yellow house in the mountains

Verse 3
Near fatal twist, his sleeve got caught
The auger took his arm, they thought
A miracle happened in that field
And through God's grace, his arm was healed

Two trees were planted as a sign
Their love would grow, just like the pines
A welcome sign was always out
For all to come and play about

Chorus
For most of us, Heaven must wait
But they would never hesitate
They lived their dream, inside their home
Where family, friends, and others roamed
They lived and loved in bliss
In a yellow house in the mountains

Verse 4
The time flew by, the years moved fast
They knew their love would always last
68 years the couple knew
They were blessed, their family too

The evening came, the sky grew bright
A fire raged throughout the night
They huddled close, held each other tight
When morning came, they'd lost their fight

Chorus
For most of us, Heaven must wait
But they would never hesitate
Their dreams fulfilled, their home was gone
Family, friends and others long
To live and love in bliss
In a yellow house in the mountains

Verse 5
Upon the scene, the scars were harsh
Nothing left, only ash and char
Then in the field we saw a sign
Two trees protected, seemed divine

Tears were shed, my chest felt tight
Then I was startled by the sight
Atop a pole their flag still waived
Torn and tattered, but it was saved

Chorus
For most of us, Heaven must wait
But we will never hesitate
We'll take their dream, rebuild their home
Family, friends, others will roam
We'll live and love in peace
The memories never cease
Of our yellow house in the mountains

A video recording, along with photographs that complement the story can be found on the link below:

https://www.youtube.com/watch?v=nPZhSP92i2U

Many have inquired at how our family managed in the days following the fire. We felt a huge loss, and yet, we found comfort in knowing our parents were together in their final moments. When they called me on the night of the fire, they were calm and at peace. A story, based on an Old Testament scripture, may best explain the reason we remain comforted.

THE REFINER'S FIRE

Some time ago, a few ladies met in a certain city to study the scriptures. While reading the third chapter of Malachi, they came upon a remarkable expression in the third verse:

"And He shall sit as a refiner and purifier of silver."
(Malachi 3:3)

One lady proposed to visit a silversmith and report to them what he said about the subject. She went accordingly, and without telling the object of her errand, begged the silversmith to tell her about the process of refining silver.

After he had fully described it to her, she asked, "But sir, do you sit while the work of refining is going on?"

"Oh yes, madam," replied the silversmith. "I must sit with my eye steadily fixed on the furnace, for if the time necessary for refining be exceeded in the slightest degree, the silver will be injured."

The lady at once saw the beauty, and comfort too, of the expression, "He shall sit as a refiner and purifier of silver." God sees it needful to put His children into a furnace; His eye is steadily intent on the work of purifying, and His wisdom and love are both engaged in the best manner for us. Our trials do not come at random, and He will not let us be tested beyond what we can endure.

Before she left, the lady asked one final question, "When do you know the process is complete?"

"Why that is quite simple," replied the silversmith. "When I can see my image in the silver, the refining process is finished."

On my last visit to Grand Lake before the fire, I noticed something in my parents' countenance. They seemed content. They expressed love in words and actions. I couldn't explain to Michelle at the time what I felt, but after the fire, it was clear to me. They were refined. They were Christlike in every way. Truly, they were prepared to meet God. They were complete.

I like to imagine that immediately after my parents passed, their spirits moved from the house to the meadow to protect their two trees. I don't know how a spirit fights a fire, but the scene in my mind is one of Lyle and Marylin facing the East Troublesome Fire during the height of its power. Standing resolute, Marylin raises her fist and yells, "You can take our house, but you'll never get my trees!" The trees were the only sign of life remaining a week after the fire when our family gathered to honor our parents. Their ashes were spread carefully on the ground between the trees. If the two trees survive, I'm grateful. If not, I'm still thankful for the time they remained for us to fulfill my parents' wishes. We remain committed to helping nature in the recovery and look forward to planting many trees around the property.

Adversity often brings out the best in people and our family has been overwhelmed by the outpouring of love and support. We love Grand County and hope to assist in the hard work ahead. We look forward, with others, to once again basking in the beauty of Rocky Mountain National Park, Grand Lake, and the property we consider sacred ground.

On a beautiful Saturday, June 25, 2022, the Hileman family, along with numerous friends met to christen Punk's Pavilion. Ninety-four people drove under the entry and observed the large sign that welcomed all to the Hileman Hide-a-way. As they continued toward the pavilion, a bright yellow sign identified Punk's Pavilion. The pavilion was a perfect place to gather and reminisce. Hot Dogs were flying off the BBQ, but the decision to add a pizza oven was a hit. For more than four hours, the pizza oven was stoked, providing all in attendance a chance to create a custom, personal pizza. Everyone there felt joy in knowing that Marylin's vision for a gathering place was complete. It was perfect! Even better, the park and pavilion were the ideal sites to reflect on the extraordinary lives of Lyle and Marylin. Their hopes for a mountain paradise, now fulfilled, will continue to be the site of many, many more memories to come.

The following day, Sunday, June 26, 2022, was the seventieth wedding anniversary of Lyle and Marylin Hileman. Their dreams live on with their children, grandchildren, and great-grandchildren, who number sixty-one at the time of this writing (July 10, 2023).

ACKNOWLEDGMENTS

I'M GRATEFUL FOR the numerous individuals who assisted me in writing. My wife Michelle was the inspiration to record the stories we'd heard over the months that followed my parents passing. Additionally, she was the first to read and re-read the manuscript and provided helpful suggestions.

Each of my siblings shared their memories that led to the book. My sister, Kim, has been my greatest cheerleader. From the beginning she embraced the project and contributed collections and photographs she had assembled. She was an amazing proof reader and always available to collaborate.

My children each played a role. Alyse and Dallas leveraged their technological skills to help with the images. Lauren and Vanessa provided editing and content suggestions. Austin and Marissa each patiently sat through conversations surrounding the project.

Many of my friends and family participated in reading the advanced readers copy (ARC). Dallas and Marjorie Bradford and Jex Varner provided wonderful insights. Jan Saumweber completed a thorough review and edit. All of the above individuals have shaped the finished product and made countless improvements.

Also of note, I found Reedsy an excellent source for learning. Their professionals were extremely helpful. Hannah Van Vels Ausbury assisted with content editing. Eve Porinchak was an extraordinary editor and provide great direction. Glen Edelstein provided the layout and cover design. Collectively, their work has greatly enhanced the book.

To these individuals and all others who guided me along the way, thank you.